Peace

PEACE

An Idea Whose Time Has Come

ANATOL RAPOPORT

Ann Arbor

THE UNIVERSITY OF MICHIGAN PRESS

Published in the United States of America by
The University of Michigan Press
Manufactured in the United States of America

1995 1994 1993 1992 4 3 2 1

Library of Congress Cataloging-in-Publication Data

Rapoport, Anatol, 1911-
Peace : an idea whose time has come / Anatol Rapoport.
p. cm.
Includes bibliographical references and index.
ISBN 0-472-10315-6 (alk. paper)
1. Peace. 2. Evolution. I. Title.
JX1952.R29 1992 91-46135
327.1'72—dc20 CIP

Contents

A Word to the Reader

It has been said that war begins in the minds of men. If so, then, perhaps so does peace. The metaphor stems from the double meaning of the word *conceive*—in its biological and psychological contexts. In this book, I explore the implications of this metaphor as it applies to peace.

The order of the chapters reflects what I thought to be the proper approach, namely, to start with a background against which the basic ideas could be elaborated. The general reader may not be aware of this intention and so may not immediately see the relevance of some of the material presented. Perhaps he or she should read the Concluding Remarks first. The relevance of the background material may then become clear.

It may also be helpful to explain the interrelationship of the ideas from the start. The thoughts expressed in this book were fed by two sources, namely, a generalized theory of evolution and a general theory of systems. As is generally known, the theory of biological evolution driven by natural selection and adaptation to environments was originally formulated by Charles Darwin ([1859] 1964).[1] In this formulation the "fitness," implied in the phrase "survival of the fittest," appears not as a cause of reproductive advantage but its symptom. That is, the only concrete meaning of "fitness" is in terms of reproductive advantage, not in terms of some preconceived notions of what "fitness" entails. It is this interpretation of "fitness" that has provided a new paradigm underlying the theory of evolution. What is especially relevant to the arguments of this book is that this paradigm can provide foundations for theories of many other kinds of evolution besides the biological, in particular, the evolution of institutions, of attitudes (as in "evolution of cooperation"), etc. Chapters 3 through 6 are devoted to information and explanations

1. Exactly the same conception of evolution, as a process driven by "survival of the fittest," occurred to Alfred Russell Wallace, who communicated it to Darwin in February, 1858. Darwin gave full credit to Wallace in a joint paper presented to the Linnean Society on July 1 of that year.

of how this paradigm illuminates the maturation of ideas about war and peace, and how this maturation is related to the notion that peace is an idea whose time has come.

The other source of ideas developed in this book is general system theory. In its broadest sense, a system is some portion of reality (material or ideational) that can be recognized as something that, in spite of changes, maintains its identity. Physical systems, more precisely models of such, can be defined rigorously in terms of their states at given moments of time and in terms of the time courses of these states. More complex types of systems, for example, living organisms, populations, or institutions, cannot be described in this way. But they can be *recognized,* and this suffices for making them objects of investigations.

Some acquaintance with general system theory induces an appreciation of the circumstance that, in our world, everything is related to everything else, something inadvertently left out of sight when we attempt to understand the world by studying different aspects of it separately (as is done in scientific disciplines). The systemic outlook also directs attention to far-reaching analogies between the structures and forms of behavior of systems of widely different contents and between the ways they evolve. The notion of system is first introduced in chapter 2 in connection with that of irreversible processes, which provides a link between a general theory of systems and the theory of evolution.

In this book, the institution of war is regarded as a system that is, in some ways, analogous to an organism. The evolution of this "organism" and conditions of its viability will be one of my primary concerns. Chapters 8 and 9 supply a background for this approach.

If, after reading this book, dear reader, you feel that it has been worth your while, reread chapter 4 (it is one of the shortest). It presents the principal thesis of the book in compact form.

As I was putting these thoughts down on paper, a revolution occurred in Eastern Europe that everyone agreed had been "unthinkable." One would suppose that when something "unthinkable" occurs, people would be moved to revise their ways of "thinking." Would, then, the men in whose minds war (or, perhaps, peace) was said to begin revise their ways of thinking? Must I do it too, I asked myself.

When the "hard-line" East German and Czechoslovak regimes were overthrown, my book, *The Origins of Violence,* was six months in print. That book was started in 1986, the year of Chernobyl, when the first concrete realization of glasnost became apparent. After two weeks' delay, substantive accounts of the disaster and some indications of its magnitude appeared in the Soviet press, an event without precedent, since even news of airline crashes had been routinely suppressed. Not much later, the dam broke, and the slogan, glasnost (openness), became policy. A political and ideological spectrum emerged in the Soviet Union. Works of dissidents appeared in print. Works of Trotsky, Bukharin, and other erstwhile "enemies of the people" were publicly displayed in libraries. Unpersons resumed their positions in history. In fact, examinations in history courses were canceled because standard answers to standard questions could no longer serve as evidence of acquaintance with the past.

The very foundations of what had been, in effect, a state religion (Marxism-Leninism) and its philosophical underpinning (dialectical materialism) suddenly came under attack with gusto and impunity. Most important, the imperative of the "class struggle"—the cardinal article of faith of Marxism-Leninism—lost its status as the essence of social reality. Instead, a peace offensive was launched, aimed at the foundations of the cold war, not merely by the repeating slogans but making offers that the United States found increasingly difficult to refuse.

In fact, a process analogous to what was called *Vergangenheitsbewältigung* (overcoming the past) in Germany came into the center of public consciousness. During the first timid attempts at de-Stalinization in the first years of Khrushchev's rule, references were made to Stalin's "mistakes" and to the unfortunate effects of the "personality cult." The word *Stalinism* was avoided. Now, in an all-out assault on totalitarianism, not only Stalinism but also a word with much stronger pejorative connotations, *Stalinishchina,* became current.

In *The Origins of Violence* (Rapoport 1989), discussing the dominant ideological orientation of the Soviet leadership, I referred to the Cult of Struggle. The dogma of the class struggle as the prime mover of history was generalized to all aspects of political and social life. The snarling visage became the mark of the Soviet ideologue and, in the early years of the cold war, even of the Soviet diplomat. I remember an article published in the *New Yorker* by a Boston lady who was engaged by the Soviet delegate to the United Nations to coach him in English. She did her best not only in helping her student to speak grammatical and idiomatic English but also in helping him to speak effectively. At one point she suggested, "Mr. Malik, when you speak of peace, don't look and don't sound as if you are about to assault someone. The expression of your face and your voice make it difficult to believe you mean what you are saying." She reported that the delegate was grateful to her for pointing this out.

In *The Origins of Violence,* I developed the idea that this compulsive preoccupation with struggle was an impediment to Soviet efforts to resist the trend toward World War III. (I believed, and still believe, that these efforts were genuine regardless of the nature of the Soviet regime.) In particular, the compulsive preoccupation with retaining, at any costs, a monopoly of power was manifested in the most conspicuous characteristics of the regime, which repelled the very sectors of U.S. society where valuable allies in resising the trend toward war could be found. These were (*a*) pacifically oriented religious groups; (*b*) grass roots movements oriented toward participatory democracy and usually sharply critical of the dominant role of the military and of corporations in U.S. life; and (*c*) liberal or radical intellectuals.

By removing the onus from religious practices and expression, removing restrictions on intellectual freedom, and encouraging free discussion of public issues and the development of autonomous organizations, the new leadership opened the way to collaboration between peace activists in the two societies. Only some passing comments on these developments, added in proof, are included in *The Origins of Violence.* Much more needs to be said about the implications of this truly revolutionary development. Some further thoughts on this matter are expressed in this book.

With 200 years since the end of the French Revolution, it seemed that everyone was happy about the sudden turn of events, at least everybody in Europe and North America, except possibly some who had financial, career, or libidinal stakes in the cold war. However, people of different ideological bents were happy for different reasons. The hawks, particularly in the United States, were happy because they interpreted the "collapse of Communism" as a victory and as a vindication of an aggressive policy—containment, counterinsurgency, saber rattling, and deliberate escalation of the arms race. The doves were happy because the dissolution of the Communist regimes, with the acquiescence of the Soviet Union, removed the basis of rationalization that had made the war machine unassailable. Without this rationalization (so the doves thought), the position of the cold warriors would be untenable.

The enthusiasm of the hawks was somewhat dampened by the prospect of the increasingly vigorous peace offensives and concomitant threats of budget cuts. As it turned out, their apprehensions proved to be groundless. Saddam Hussein obligingly stepped into the role of Enemy Number One, vacated by the Soviet Union, and provided an opportunity for proving that the countless billions spent on high-tech weaponry were well spent. The doves, needless to say, were dismayed to learn that a policy that had lost its moorings might, nevertheless, lose none of its vigor, that institutions, having lost their raison d'être, might remain viable and robust for a long time.

Does all this portend that this book, inspired by the prospect of a united Europe, will become dated by the time it is in print in the way its predecessor became dated, at least in some respects, when cold war issues suddenly became irrelevant? I hope not. If anything can be learned from the events of 1989, it is that predictions about the behavior of systems far from positions of equilibrium are foolhardy. Yet everyone is entitled to hope. In this book, I express the hope that the institution of war, having lost its ideological basis, will wither and eventually die and that the enemies of power worship will be justified in their sense of victory over the cold war and will be energized to carry on the struggle for a just and lasting global peace.

This hope is nurtured by what we know about evolutionary processes I trace the idea of peace from its inception to its maturity. It seems to me that after several centuries of germination, the idea is ready to take off and become a dominating component of the human condition. A desire to share this hope and the ideas that have motivated it prompted me to examine them in the light of what has been learned about us (creatures with ideas) during the century now coming to its end.

1

The Sphere of Knowledge

The planet Earth, our home in space, can be described as a system of layers enveloping each other. At the center is the core, once thought to be molten because of high temperatures there, but now generally assumed to be a solid sphere mostly of iron. Around this sphere is the lithosphere—the crust. Most of it is solid stone (the bedrock), but the outer layer is loose. This is the soil where most of the nutrients of animals and plants living on land are found. The hydrosphere is the watery blanket of seas, rivers, and lakes. Around the surface of the earth is a gaseous layer—the atmosphere.

The core changes hardly at all. The crust changes comparatively slowly, for example, by erosion. The liquid and gaseous layers are in constant flux. Rivers and ocean currents flow, winds blow, vapors rise, condense, and precipitate. All these movements can be explained by the laws of physics. This means that, in principle, they can be predicted. The prediction of weather (events in the atmosphere) is difficult but has been facilitated by sophisticated methods developed in meteorology, a comparatively young science on which computer technology has conferred considerable power.

Besides these inanimate layers, we have the biosphere, comprising the entire living world. The changes going on in this layer are far less predictable than those in the inanimate layers. To a certain extent, the dynamics of the biosphere has been described, for example, in ecology, the science dealing with interactions of animals and plants with each other and with their environment. Ecology is concerned with only comparatively short-term changes in the biosphere. Long-term changes are the concern of the theory of evolution.

Knowledge of physical laws is only of limited value in ecology, in the theory of evolution, and in other branches of biological science. Systematic descriptions of this aspect of reality must resort to concepts not used in the physical sciences, for example, life, death, adaptation, reproduction, parasitism, symbiosis, and so on.

In a figurative sense we can speak of another "sphere" as a constituent of our planet, namely, the noosphere.[1] It comprises the totality of beliefs, concepts, values, and the like, in short, the entire sphere of knowledge and pseudoknowledge, attitudes, and convictions that can be regarded as the content of the mental, emotional, and spiritual life of humans.

Clearly, this noosphere represents a mode of existence different from that ascribed to the lithosphere, the atmosphere, and the biosphere. The elements of these spheres—rocks, air currents, plants, and animals—are directly perceived by the senses. The elements of the noosphere—ideas, superstitions, theories, mythologies—are not directly perceived. They are inferred from our perceptions of how people behave. We hear what they say, see reproductions of their thoughts in print, and so forth. From these directly perceived data, we construct systems of beliefs or attitudes that, we assume, generate the observable data.

The very different level of existence of the noosphere raises questions pertaining to its reality. Such questions, of concern largely to philosophers, have been the subject of lively, at times acrimonious debates, which have by no means been confined to philosophical speculations. Whether the reality of the noosphere and related concepts is accepted or denied has a bearing on what is likely to be included in the realm of scientific research and, therefore, on the directions pursued. Where these directions are determined by political decisions (either by decree, as in totalitarian states, or by allocation of support, as in democratic ones), the implications may be concrete and serious. I will cite two examples showing how what is subsumed under reality determines the content of scientific investigations.

Adherents of the school of psychology called behaviorism maintained that only observable actions of persons or animals should be regarded as data in any psychological investigation and that concepts referring to the inner life of living beings, in the case of a human being, emotions, motivations, compulsions, in short, the content of consciousness, not being subject of direct observation, should be excluded from a psychological theory purporting to be scientific. In the 1920s and 1930s,

---

1. The prefix *noo* refers to "mind" (cf. noology—the study of mental phenomena). The term was first introduced by the Russian geophysicist V. I. Vernadsky (1863–1945), who defined it as the sum total of scientific knowledge. As used here, the term encompasses considerably more.

behaviorism was the most prominent type of psychology in the United States. Although its influence has waned since then, some prejudices about what aspects of the human condition can be studied scientifically have ingrained themselves in psychology. For example, introspection (direct observation of our own inner life), which could be regarded as a way to self-knowledge, is still suspect among "scientific" psychologists as a way of gathering relevant and reliable data in the construction of a theory.

The other example pertains to the damage suffered by many fields of research in the Soviet Union by the proscription of any approach to which the label "idealism" could be applied. The ideological orthodoxy that marked Stalinist repression in the intellectual realm was partly a demagogic weapon in power struggles but partly a quasi-religious faith rooted in the veneration of Lenin, whose thought was incorporated not only in the official political philosophy of the Stalinist era but also in the philosophy of science and of knowledge. Lenin's work that spelled out the tenets of the creed was a book entitled *Materialism and Empiriocriticism* (Lenin [1909] 1964). It portended to be an exposition of the philosophy of science in harmony with dialectical materialism, a system of thought embodied in the writings of Karl Marx and Friedrich Engels. Lenin declared dialectical materialism to be the culmination of progress in the realm of science and philosophy. It was, according to Lenin, to be the ideological weapon of the proletariat, destined to carry out the social revolution and establish a classless society.

Lenin's thesis was an uncompromising attack on all thinking tinged with what he called idealism. In this context, idealism refers not to ideals (as in common usage) but to ascribing primary reality to ideas rather than to matter. The opposite view—materialism—regards matter and laws governing its behavior as the stuff from which reality is made. The mind is, according to the materialistic view, just an emanation of the brain, which is matter.

Clearly, the materialist doctrine was opposed to the teachings of the Christian church, in which the existence of a disembodied deity is assumed to be the source of all being. Marx, in expounding the materialist view of reality, believed that he was combating the teachings of the Church, which throughout the nineteenth century could be said to have been a bulwark against radical ideas. Evidently Lenin, a faithful disciple of Marx, interpreted the ideological struggle between idealism and materialism in the same way.

Ossification of Lenin's teachings had serious repercussions in Soviet science. At the height of Stalinist repression, any thought or methodology in either philosophy or science that departed in any way from the materialist dogma as interpreted by the Party bureaucracy was proscribed. Disciplines such as genetics, psychology, and even statistics were condemned as "reactionary," "bourgeois," or "alien to Soviet society." Institutes and universities were demolished, and their personnel were forced to recant their views in public, often arrested.

In ascribing reality to the noosphere on a par with the other layers enveloping our planet, hence forming a part of our environment, I do not resort to ontological arguments.[2] To me the question of whether something exists is a pragmatic one, not a metaphysical one. In other words, I do not attempt to answer this question by reference to some a priori criteria of existence, but rather to the question of what can be done with the assumption that it exists. It turns out that a great deal can be done with it.

Concepts closely related to the noosphere were advanced by Karl Popper (1982) and Alfred Korzybski (1921). Popper thought of reality as consisting of three "worlds." World 1 is the material universe, both animate and inanimate. It is the universe of observable objects. World 2 comprises human thought processes, ideas, emotions, and attitudes. We have direct access (by introspection) to that part of this world that is within ourselves, and we deem it natural to ascribe similar ideas or feelings to (at least) other human beings and, to some extent, even to some nonhumans. Clearly, the elements of world 2 have only an ephemeral existence. They "happen" rather than persist as material entities do. In contrast, the elements of world 3 are thought of as having a protracted existence.

Popper explains the difference between the modes of existence of world 1 and world 3 as follows. Consider a book. Being a material object, it belongs to world 1. Consider two copies of the same book. They are two different objects. The two books may be similar in their physical appearance; but a tape recording or a microfilm of the book will have an altogether different appearance. Nevertheless, since the ideational content of the different copies, of the tape recording, and of the microfilm is the same, all of them are material representations of the same "object" belonging to world 3.

2. Ontology is a branch of metaphysics concerned with the nature of existence, hence with the nature of "ultimate reality."

Popper insists that world 3 has an "autonomous" existence, which he illustrates by the following example. Consider the (infinite) set of natural numbers: 1, 2, 3, . . . , *n*, . . . This set is an invention of the human mind.[3] We invented it in the process of learning to count. But when we contemplate this "invention," we discover properties of it that we did not invent, properties that are inherent in the set of natural numbers, that are "there" whether we know about them or not. For example, consider the properties of even numbers or the properties of prime numbers. We invented the natural numbers, but we did not invent their properties. We discovered them. In general, we can see that the entire system that we call "mathematics" belongs to Popper's world 3 (and to our noosphere). It represents a compendium of all the thoughts that people had about numbers and other magnitudes, about relations between them, and about abstractions derived from these relations. Unlike the thoughts, which "happen," world 3 "exists" as objects exist, even though it is not material. In particular, its content grows, hence it can evolve, and it is in continual interaction with world 1 and world 2. Being a depository of knowledge, it induces thoughts that can be translated, for instance, into inventions that can be realized as artifacts, objects belonging to world 1. I will mention in passing that belief in the existence of world 3 is entirely consistent with the materialist outlook. All the materialist has to do to justify this belief is to insist that world 1 antedates world 3 and contributes to it via world 2, a reasonable assumption.[4]

Korzybski's point of departure was what he called "time binding," the process of accumulating experience and transmitting it to successive generations.[5] Korzybski declared this process to be the specific survival mechanism of human beings (1921). All other species adapt to their environment in consequence of natural selection acting upon random variations in their genetic material. Essentially, they adapt by modifying their bodies. In this way, practically all the adaptations are hereditary. Few, if any, are transmitted to successive generations through the cultural

---

3. The German mathematician Kronecker quipped, "The good Lord created the whole numbers. Everything else is the work of man." I think all of mathematics was created by the human race.

4. For fuller discussion of the three worlds, see Popper and Eccles 1977, chap. 2; Bunge 1981, 142–48.

5. Korzybski called plants "energy binders," because they are characterized by the ability to bind solar energy to produce sugars from carbon dioxide in the atmosphere. Animals he called "space binders," because most of them are mobile. He called man a "time binder" because of his ability to transmit accumulated experience to future generations.

dimension, which would have permitted the accumulation of experience across generations.

In man, time binding is made possible by symbolic language—a unique human feature. Many animals are able to communicate by signals—sounds, smells, gestures. Human beings communicate by symbolic language. Signals are distinguished from symbols in that their meaning is bound to the situation in which they occur. A signal may be stimulated by the presence of food, by the appearance of danger, by readiness to mate. Its meaning remains constant. For the most part, the emission, reception, and interpretation of signals is innate in the species, that is, genetically determined. A symbol, on the other hand, has no necessary connection to its referents. Whatever the connection a symbol may have to a referent, it must be learned, and it is transmitted culturally, not genetically. Besides, the meaning of a symbol may change. Its range of reference may be broadened by generalization or narrowed by specialization. Also, most important, the meaning of a symbol may depend on the context, that is, on symbols emitted before or after it.

The immense flexibility of human language is a consequence of the fact that its elements are symbols having no fixed connection to particular referents. Specifically, the emission of a symbol need not depend on the occurrence of a particular situation. Humans can speak not only of the here and now but also about events long past, about events that they know about only because they were told about them, about events expected in the future, about events that never occurred but were imagined. In other words, symbolic language makes possible the construction of a world inside the head that is totally unrelated to the real world around one.

It turns out, therefore, that time binding may be a mixed blessing. Not only can experience be accumulated over successive generations, storing more and deeper knowledge of the world at man's disposal, but delusions can also be accumulated, creating an ever-widening chasm between man and his world. Between man and the material world stands the screen of language. In general, man does not have direct contact with the material world. The contact is mediated by language. Man reads what is on the screen. That is, he experiences directly not the world but what he is *told* about the world, both by others and, significantly, by himself.

In his major work, *Science and Sanity* (1933), Korzybski called attention to this double role of language. The title, *Science and Sanity,* refers to the role of science (as Korzybski conceived it) in guarding man's sanity. Korzybski imagined a spectrum of language usage. At one end of the language spectrum is the language of science, characterized by maintaining a connection to reality accessible to the senses and the representation of that reality by symbolic language. This is the "sane" end of the spectrum. In the middle is the language of everyday life. Connections between symbols and their referents in the material world are still maintained in discourse about day-to-day events, about immediate needs and means of satisfying them. However, this language also contains symbols that have been incorporated into it by time binding, that is, transmitted across generations and, in the process, cut off from the world of the senses. On this level we find myths, superstitions, or conventional wisdom that is accepted because it is expounded by accepted authorities. Korzybski called this part of the spectrum the range of "unsane" language—not quite insane but also not quite sane, in the sense of being reality oriented. At the "insane" extreme of the spectrum we find the language characteristic of mental disorders. This language is self-propelled, as it were. Words become stimuli of other words, as in free association. Even the grammatical structure of language dissolves.

These two opposite roles of language suggest a distinction between progress and regress, motion toward mental health and motion toward mental disease. Korzybski put special emphasis on the cumulative process of abstraction. Another screen can be interposed between the screen of language and the world of senses (which Korzybski identified with reality). The second screen reflects what appears on the first screen, and so on. After several such interpositions, nothing may be left on the last screen that has any relation to concrete reality. Nevertheless, human cognitive functions are so constructed that the distinction between reality, verbal descriptions of reality, verbal descriptions of verbal descriptions, and so on (different levels of abstraction, as Korzybski called them) is not generally appreciated.

This blurring of distinctions between images of reality and reality can wreak serious damage on a society. A story is told about a people in the South Pacific who developed a sophisticated boat-building technology. These boats were used for fishing, which provided the people with their livelihood. Their skill in boat building was reflected in the efficiency of their fishing. Because fishing was so important to them, so was boat building. The intricacies of boat building were reflected in rules and traditions handed down from generation to generation. They had to be strictly adhered to in fear of severe retribution for violations. Ultimately, obsessions developed in following the strict rules and rituals.

In consequence, boat building was pervaded with elaborate taboos. Fear of the consequences of breaking the taboos inhibited boat building. Eventually it was abandoned altogether, and the people had to fall back on other ways of making a livelihood that were considerably less lucrative.

I mentioned changes going on in the various layers enveloping the earth, slow ones in the solid envelope, faster ones in the fluid ones. Some of these changes are short term and reversible, for instance, weather and seasonal fluctuations. Others are long term and irreversible. Processes of this sort are called evolutionary. The most conspicuous and intensively studied evolutionary processes are those in the biosphere. One of the reasons for ascribing reality to the noosphere is that it also exhibits evolutionary changes that can be studied as systematically and profitably as the evolutionary changes in the physical biosphere.

The evolution of the noosphere is the evolution of ideas. As we shall see, this evolution has much in common with other manifestations of evolution, both with the "classical" evolution of organisms and the strikingly similar evolutionary processes revealed in the history of artifacts, clothing, and other material products. Belonging to the evolution of the noosphere is the evolution of languages, of religions, of the arts, and, most important, the evolution of institutions. Manifestations of the evolutionary principle in these areas, in particular, the evolution of the institution of war and of the concept of peace, will be a prime concern in this book.

2

Irreversible Processes and the Idea of Progress

I mentioned reversible (short-term) and irreversible (long-term) processes. Cyclic processes are reversible: days alternate with nights, summers with winters, hunger with satiety, sleep with wakefulness. Water can turn into ice, ice into water. Many processes, particularly life processes, are irreversible. A human zygote (fertilized egg) turns into an embryo; the embryo into a baby; the baby into an adult; the adult into a corpse. This process has never been observed going the other way.

The most pervasive irreversible process is the increase of entropy in an isolated system. An isolated system is a portion of the world cut off from its environment, so that neither matter nor energy can go in or out. Although it may be impossible to construct a perfectly isolated system, it is easy to imagine one, for example, a cylindrical container filled with gas and having perfectly insulated and perfectly impenetrable walls, so that neither substance nor heat can get in or out. The walls must also be opaque and soundproof, because both light and sound are carriers of energy, which, by definition, can neither enter nor leave an isolated system.

A precise definition of entropy is technical and will not be given here. A rough definition will suffice. Roughly, "amount of entropy" corresponds to "amount of disorder." An increase of entropy means increased disorder. An increase of disorder can be illustrated by shuffling a deck of cards.

A new deck of cards is ordered by suits and values. The arrangement is statistically not uniform in the sense that a suit, say spades, is not spread more or less uniformly throughout the deck. Instead, it is concentrated in one quarter of the deck. When the deck is shuffled, it becomes increasingly disordered and also increasingly uniform. The four suits will eventually be approximately evenly distributed through the entire deck. Moreover, continued shuffling will not restore the original order. That is, the entropy of the deck will not spontaneously decrease. In this sense, the process appears irreversible.

Imagine now a cylindrical container with one end a moveable piston. Initially, the piston confines a gas in half of the cylinder. Suppose the piston is moved to allow the gas to expand. For an instant the gas will be still concentrated in half of the volume; that is, the density of the gas will not be uniformly distributed in the cylinder. Very soon, however, the gas will expand into the whole space. The density will then become uniformly distributed.

Now when the gas was concentrated in half of the cylinder, there was more order than when the gas became diffused througout the volume. In the former state, we could say something about the position of an arbitrarily selected molecule of gas. We could say that it was located in a particular half of the cylinder. After the gas diffused, we could no longer say this. An arbitrarily selected molecule could be anywhere. The situation with the gas is thus analogous to that with the deck of cards. Before the deck was shuffled, we could say that an arbitrarily selected card was in a specified quarter of the deck. After shuffling, we could not say this. An arbitrarily selected card could be anywhere in the deck. The deck became disordered.

Just as continued shuffling of the deck (i.e., random shifts of the positions of the cards) will not restore the original order, so the chaotic movement of the gas molecules in the cylinder will not restore the original concentration of the gas in half of the cylinder.[1]

The irreversible increase of entropy in isolated systems has been formulated as the second law of thermodynamics. The connection to heat (which is what thermodynamics is about) is established by the fact that heat is a form of energy. Energy appears in different forms—mechanical, as in a coiled spring or in a moving body; electrical, as in a battery; chemical, as in dynamite. These forms of energy can be transformed into one another. For instance, by exploding, dynamite can set rocks in motion. When electric current passes through a wire, the resistance turns electrical energy into heat. Some of these changes are reversible. For instance, work, that is, the expenditure of mechanical energy, can be turned into heat, and, to some extent, heat can be turned

1. Since we assume that the molecules move about randomly, this could theoretically happen by chance, just as the original order of a deck of cards could be theoretically restored by chance. However, the probability of this happening is so small that such an event is, for all practical purposes, impossible.

into work, as in a steam engine. However, the conversion of other forms of energy into heat is only partially reversible. Only a part of the available heat energy can be turned into work energy and that only at the expense of an increase of heat energy elsewhere.[2] Thus, while the cosmic bookkeeping maintains the total supply of energy in the universe as a constant (which is what the first law of thermodynamics asserts), the second law asserts that the total amount of heat energy in the universe must be always increasing at the expense of other forms.

The connection between heat and disorder can be seen when one realizes that heat is essentially the chaotic movement of particles as in, for example, the molecules of a gas. Because this movement is chaotic, it cannot be harnessed to produce mechanical work. Once all the energy of the universe is converted into heat, nothing else can "happen" because, in this supposed final state, the heat will be evenly distributed, just as the density of a gas eventually becomes evenly distributed in an isolated system. In order to convert some heat energy into, say, mechanical energy, some difference in temperature is required. (In a steam engine, this difference is maintained between the boiler and the condenser.) It seems, therefore, to those of us who think that it is events that make life and, by extension, all existence meaningful, this ultimate fate of the universe, sometimes called "heat death," is not an attractive prospect.

This attitude is not shared by everyone. Something like the state of "no happenings" may be envisaged in Nirvana, which, in the Buddhist religion (unless I misunderstand it), is regarded as an ideal state of being (or, perhaps, of nonbeing). Other ideologies may decry this trend, seeking ways of circumventing or refuting the unwelcome conclusion forced by the second law of thermodynamics. For example, in the process of biological evolution, the increasing complexity of organisms can be interpreted as an increase of order, hence a decrease of entropy. At times, this process has been interpreted as a violation of the second law, especially by vitalists (adherents of a theory that life processes are not subjected to the same physical laws as physical or chemical processes). This interpretation, however, is based on a misunderstanding, because the necessary increase of entropy, required by the second law, applies only to systems isolated from their environments, which certainly excludes living systems, since interaction with the environment is a precondition

2. For example, when heat is transformed into work in a locomotive, a portion of the heat must be transferred from the boiler to the condenser (or to the outside). The total amount of heat produced in the process is positive.

of life. Thus, if the universe is assumed to be an isolated system, any decrease of entropy in one part of it must be compensated, in fact overcompensated, by an increase in another, and the prospect of ultimate heat death is inescapable. Whether the universe is, indeed, an isolated system is a philosophical question that cannot be presently answered on the basis of scientific evidence.

Besides the difference in attitudes toward the prospect of everlasting uneventfulness, be it heat death or Nirvana or Paradise, there is a difference in attitudes toward reversible and irreversible changes. Some prefer the former—the steady state, the equilibrium, predictable cycles; others prefer the latter—continual change, at times revolutions. As often happens, attitudes predispose people predominantly to see their preferred mode of existence if they are optimists or, on the contrary, the disliked mode, if they are pessimists. Optimists see change as progress; pessimists see it as degradation. Optimists see the absence of change as stability; pessimists see it as stagnation.

Plato, for example, viewed change as essentially a process of deterioration, a progressive corruption of the state of being that originally was supposedly manifested in "ideals," perfect representations of things and qualities, that we perceive in a modified and, therefore, imperfect state. Plato even believed that newborn babies "know everything" and that they lose this knowledge as they grow up. In short, Plato believed that the universe was regressing.[3]

Aristotle presented the opposite view. He thought of change as striving to realize the "essence" of the changing thing, that is, as a trend toward perfection rather than away from it.[4]

By definition, a conservative worldview induces a negative attitude toward change. This attitude is supported by a concept of the existing state of affairs as reflecting an order, which, by virtue of being ordained by higher authority (e.g., God) or established by some immutable principle (a natural law or "human nature"), is good, right, or just.

One of the most distinguished statesmen of the eighteenth century, Edmund Burke, formulated his theory of the social order in terms of four principles.

---

3. This view is often associated with political conservatism, traditionalism, even reaction, as when the past is pictured as a Golden Age.

4. Here we have the kernel of a teleological (goal-driven) evolutionary process, later developed by Lamarck and Bergson.

1. Social order is part of the natural order that God has created and it exists prior to the individuals who are born into it. . . .
2. Man is a social animal. Therefore, the family, not the individual, is the proper unit of social order. Families are organized into classes that reflect social functions. . . .
3. A nation must have rules of behaviour to bring unity of purpose out of mutual adaptation of conflicting interests.
4. Inequality is inescapable in society. But social leadership is most properly founded on the natural sense of dependence, subordination, and affection, which respond to ability, virtue, age, and graciousness. These qualities of leadership are best institutionalized in a hereditary aristocracy. (Auerbach 1968).

The French Revolution dealt a mortal blow to this ideology. In the nineteenth century, to be liberal, rational, or progressive meant to bank on the future, on progress, hence to believe in and welcome irreversible evolutionary processes.

G. F. Hegel was a hero to young German radicals, among whom was Karl Marx. Here is the way Hegel pictured progress. Underlying all reality was something he called the Idea (presumably a version of a deity). The Idea was engaged in continual contemplation. It came upon the recognition of some principle and formulated it as a thesis. But the formulation induced a recognition of an opposite principle, called the antithesis. The contradiction was resolved by a synthesis of the two principles, a "union of opposites." The synthesis carried the Idea a step forward. Progress consisted in the sequence of such steps.

Fanciful as this formulation may appear to those of us who view the idealistic conception of the world skeptically,[5] it is a rather accurate description of the process of generalization on which all scientific progress depends. To see this, let us examine a trivial agrument between A and B about the location of a house. A maintains that the house is on the right side of the street; B insists that it is on the left side. Obviously, the "conflict" is immediately resolved when the two realize that A was looking north and B south. Now both can agree that the house is on the *east* side of the street.

5. Somewhere, Bertrand Russell quipped, "It seems that the Idea is reading Hegel, rashly realizing what it has been reading."

But east and west are also relative concepts, like right and left. If X maintains that Tokyo is east of London, and Y insists that it is west of London, their conflict evaporates when they realize that the earth is round and that, consequently, Tokyo can be reached from London by traveling either east or west.

The same sort of process is involved in arriving at the generalizations that propel any scientific theory. Such "conflict-resolving" generalizations appear especially clearly in mathematics. In elementary algebra, we learn that the square of any "number" is positive, because the product of two negative numbers as well as of two positive numbers is positive. Thus, we must conclude that the equation $x^2 = -1$ has no solution, since it asserts that the square of a "number" (x) is negative. The contradiction is resolved if we extend the concept of "number," a term that was put in quotation marks because, in the light of the generalization, the old concept appears too restricted.

We can define "number" as a *pair* of what we had thought of as "numbers." We can make the definition consistent with our conception of ordinary numbers (real numbers as they are still called — a carry-over from the time when the generalized numbers were regarded as imaginary) by defining operations of addition and multiplication in a way consistent with these operations on real numbers. These pairs (x,y) are called complex numbers. In particular, the pairs $(x,0)$ behave just like the real numbers x, when subjected to arithmetic operations. It turns out that the pair $(0,1)$ when multiplied by itself under our rules of multiplication, yields $(-1,0)$, which corresponds to the real number -1.[6] Thus, the contradiction between the thesis — the square of every number is positive — and the antithesis — the solution of the equation $x^2 = -1$ exists — is resolved by a synthesis, namely by a generalized definition of "number."

Examples of such generalizations can be multiplied at will. At one time, the action of pumps was explained by the principle "Nature dreads vacuum." Indeed, when a vacuum was formed by moving the piston of a pump, water rushed onto it. Then it was found that water could not

6. The product of the pairs (a,b) and (c,d) is defined as $(a,b)\times(c,d)=(ac-bd,\ ad+bc)$. Note that all pairs $(p,0)$ composed of a real number p and zero "behave" in multiplication like real numbers, because according to the multiplication rule, $(p,0)\times(q,0)=(pq,0)$, just as $p\times q=pq$. Now consider the pair $(0,1)$. We have $(0,1)^2=(0,1)\times(0,1)=(-1,0)$. In other words $(0,1)^2$ corresponds to the real number -1. Thus, in our system composed of pairs of real numbers, called complex numbers, there is a number whose square is -1.

be pumped to more than about 10 meters above its level. Here, then, was an antithesis to the thesis "Nature dreads vacuum" (since the action of the pump produced a vacuum in which water was supposed to rush but did not). A different theory, based on hydrostatic principles, turned out to be in accord with *both* observations. Thus a synthesis was found — a formulation that agreed with both situations, namely, one in which water will fill a vacuum and one in which it will "refuse" to do so.

Another example is provided by the generalizations that led to the formulation of the principle of conservation of energy. Reversible mechanical processes, for example, motions of bodies in a vacuum, are characterized by the conservation of mechanical energy. Potential energy can be converted to kinetic energy and vice versa. Thus, in the absence of friction, a pendulum would swing forever. At each end of the arc, all of its energy would be potential (energy of position); at the halfway point, it would all be kinetic (energy of motion). The sum of the two amounts would always be constant. We thus have a thesis: mechanical energy is preserved. However, if the motion is acted on by friction, mechanical energy is dissipated. The amplitude of the swing keeps decreasing; eventually the pendulum comes to a standstill. Thus the antithesis: mechanical energy dissipates.

In the middle of the nineteenth century, the mechanical equivalent of heat was discovered. That is, the amount of mechanical energy dissipated by friction was accounted for by the amount of heat energy produced. Thus, a more general conservation law was found with which both the preservation of mechanical energy in a vacuum and the dissipation of mechanical energy through friction are consistent: synthesis.

Still later, the energy equivalent of matter was found. The law of conservation of energy and the law of conservation of matter merged into a single law: conservation of matter-energy, expressed by the now famous equation $E=mc^2$.[7]

Note that progress in science is an instance of an irreversible process. Once a theory has been successfully generalized, there is no going back to the more restricted version. As we shall see, progress in science gives a powerful stimulus to the idea of social progress.

---

7. The discovery of this "higher" conservation law was a consequence of another synthesis, namely, of time and space that, in the theory of relativity, were fused into space-time.

The Idea of Progress

Fifty years ago, the idea of progress still dominated the prevailing image of the human condition, at least in the industrialized countries. The idea came to the forefront primarily in England and France in the eighteenth century and spread rapidly during the nineteenth, surely propelled by the rapid pace of technological growth. In this sector of human activity, progress was most conspicuous. It was reinforced by the realization of anticipated developments. Science fiction turned into reality within human life spans. The triumphs of technology inspired romantic dreams of freedom. The most direct feelings of freedom are linked to unimpeded motion. Perhaps for this reason children often dream of flying. It is not surprising that the early science fiction novels dealt largely with new ways of travel. Jules Verne, the most noted science fiction writer of the nineteenth century, wrote about submarine travel (*20,000 Leagues under the Sea*), about heavier-than-air flying machines (*Robur*), and about space travel (*From the Earth to the Moon*).

The dramatic advances in technology induced the notion of social progress in two ways. First, there was a widespread belief that technology alone could provide a foundation for a more just social order. Technology opened the prospect of liberation from demeaning and emaciating drudgery and so could be expected to remove the basis of the invidious distinction between toilers (the poor) and idlers (the rich). Second, science, both the creator and the beneficiary of technology, was recognized as a harbinger of emancipation from superstition, irrational compulsions, and debilitating prejudices.

These ideas are conspicuous in nineteenth-century fiction. Mark Twain's Connecticut Yankee, transported to the Dark Ages, introduces not only firearms and the telegraph into King Arthur's Britain, but also notions about the dignity of the individual and social equality. Edward Bellamy, in his widely read novel *Looking Backward* (1888), depicted a cooperative or semisocialist society projected to the year 2000.

Much faith was placed on the future accomplishments of social science. Auguste Comte ([1830–32] 1877) thought that the mode of cognition characteristic of the natural sciences, namely, regard for observable "facts" and logical deduction, could and should be extended to a social science, which would provide methods of designing a social system based on rational principles, a procedure later to be called "social engineering."

S. Amos (1880) wrote that the process of civilization would make wars ever more "humane" and restricted in space and time. Eventually, they would disappear altogether, simply because the immorality of killing human beings would be universally recognized and the art of statecraft (presumably based on developments in social science) would become sufficiently advanced to provide ways of settling conflicts between states. Colonization was rationalized as a civilizing mission with the goal of turning "savages" and "backward" peoples into facsimiles of Europeans.

Not all nineteenth-century thinkers, however, pictured all progress as a product of the steady advance of rationality and humaneness. Like many others, Karl Marx ascribed a key role to advancing technology — the mode of production, as he called it. However, he saw the industrial revolution not as an emancipation from drudgery, but, on the contrary, as the emergence of a new form of exploitation of human beings by human beings — wage slavery. Under capitalism, a product of the industrial revolution, advanced tools of production (machines) are owned privately. To have access to them, the worker must sell his labor as a commodity in a "free market," that is, in competition with other workers, thus driving the price of this "commodity" down to the lowest level consistent with the worker's ability to work and to reproduce himself.

Nevertheless, Marx was a firm believer in the inevitability of social progress. His point of departure was Hegel's idea of progress by the thesis-antithesis-synthesis spiral. However, he rejected that "idealistic" formulation and interpreted the process in materialistic terms. The prime mover of history, according to Marx, was the class struggle. As long as society was differentiated into classes, one was dominant, the others oppressed. Underlying social changes were changes in the mode of production, which, in turn, changed the relative power positions of the classes. Eventually, the oppressed class becomes more powerful and overthrows the dominant, exploiting class. This was the meaning of the "contradiction" between the thesis and the antithesis. The class struggle culminates in a revolution, in consequence of which a new social order comes into being — the synthesis. The class struggle is then repeated on a "higher level," so to speak. The process represents progress toward a classless society in which exploitation of man by man would no longer define relationships among people.

The Shock

A main effect of the trauma of World War I was the blow to the idea of continual general progress. Most conspicuous was, of course, the double face of technology: progress, in creating abundance and in abolishing demeaning drudgery on the one hand, produced ever-increasing efficiency of destruction on the other. The same ambivalence pervaded social thought. Whereas the nineteenth century, at least in Europe and in North America, was marked by steady democratization and dissipation of ossified privileges, the twentieth gave birth to totalitarian regimes, of which the most tyrannical (Nazism and Stalinist autocracy) seemed like a reversion to the Middle Ages. And, of course, the horrendous outbursts of genocide destroyed whatever remained of the notion of steady, inevitable moral progress.

The twentieth century anti-utopian novel is a clear expression of this disillusionment. In *Brave New World* ([1932] 1964), Aldous Huxley portrays a rigidly regimented civilization, where "security," that is, guaranteed satisfaction of creature comforts and primitive appetites, is achieved at the cost of completely rigid stratification of social classes and complete uniformity within each class. In *Nineteen Eighty-Four* (1949), George Orwell presents a terrifying vision of absolute rule by a brutal power elite and the extinction of individuality, affection, empathy, imagination, and every other trait that continual social progress was supposed to enhance.

Along with the dissipation of faith in general progress, the notion of "advanced" and "backward" cultures came under attack. Cultural anthropologists came to regard their discipline as something akin to natural history. They saw their task as that of describing and, above all, "understanding" cultures alien to their own. Accordingly, they described cultures as the botanist or the zoologist describes species. In these descriptions, adaptation to habitats or milieus plays a central role. No modern biologist regards an insect as a more "backward" creature than, say, a mammal. Thus, the cultural anthropologists abandoned the notion that a native of the Trobriand Islands or a Zulu is more "primitive" than a European or a North American.

Inevitably, the notion of relativity of values rendered the idea of moral progress meaningless. Perhaps the disdain on the part of the cultural anthropologists for the smug attitudes of old-fashioned missionaries toward "natives" served to reinforce the concept of ethical relativity.

Even though the idea of the inevitability of progress suffered a serious setback, one component of it remained intact, namely, the long-term irreversibility of most processes. In particular, biological evolution appears to be irreversible. No case of genuine reversal is known where a species evolves "backward" to assume the form of its ancestors. However, although we can say that there is no going back along an evolutionary path, we cannot say anything about which way is "forward." A superficial examination of evolutionary lines may create an impression that evolution progresses toward "more complex" forms. However, besides the ambiguity of the word *complex,* some evolutionary lines give the impression of leading to simpler forms. Some parasitic organisms, for example, have lost the power of locomotion in the process of evolving. At any rate, whatever direction is taken by an evolutionary line, we cannot call it "progressive" or "regressive" with any degree of assurance. Similarly, we cannot pass unequivocal judgment on historical processes, whether they necessarily lead to "better" or "worse" societies.

The malaise conspicuous in our age stems from a loss of faith in the future. When I say "our," I do not mean the entire, presently living generations but specifically those living in the affluent societies, for the term *malaise* hardly applies to the destitute, hungry, and terrorized people of the Third World. We are spared their misery. Our malaise, at times despair, stems from our habit, developed in the age of faith in progress, of trying to imagine the world to be inhabited by our children. The publicized threatening catastrophes are only the surface. The malaise goes deeper to the nagging and, for the most part, unanswered question, "What can we do?" An answer, however, may be suggested (perhaps a different answer to different people) if we begin by trying to explain just what has happened. In particular, the origin of the most conspicuous threat of all—the threat of sudden demise—must be understood before we can develop ideas of what "we can do."

For the moment, let us abandon our habitual anthropocentric view of life on this planet and regard the extinction of the human race as a commonplace event. (As I write this, several species cease to exist.) From this perspective, if we seriously want to know how to forestall (or postpone) our extinction, it seems advisable to try to understand how life forms become extinct. We can understand extinction better if we also understand how life forms come into being. By "understanding" I mean the sort of insight provided by scientific inquiry since, from the practical point of view, that is, from the point of view of our aim to translate understanding into effective action, this sort of understanding is the most relevant.

3

Pre-Darwinian and Darwinian Theories of Evolution

Understanding how life forms are "born," develop, and die is provided by the modern theory of evolution. By "modern" theory we mean the Darwinian theory. This theory has had precursors, but they are no longer taken seriously as scientific explanations of the diversity of life and of how life forms appear and disappear.

An early account of the life and death of species is found in the biblical stories about the Creation and about the Flood. According to this account, all life forms were differentiated at the Creation just as they are today. Not all the forms, however, survived. Some, which for one reason or another could not take refuge in Noah's Ark, must have perished in the Flood. This explanation is sometimes given by the believers in the biblical account of the fossils of animals no longer among us, such as the dinosaurs. They are sometimes called antediluvian (pre-Flood) forms.

What determined which species survived the Flood and which did not? Were the nonsurvivors unable to reach the Ark? Were they too big to enter it (e.g., the dinosaurs)? Were they marked for extinction by God, whom they somehow displeased? Note that this naive account already contains the germ of modern theory, namely, the concept of selection: some were chosen, some were not.

The other pillar of the Darwinian theory of evolution—adaptation—is the basis of the "providential" explanation of the diversity of life forms. According to this view, it was Providence that supplied animals and plants with mechanisms of survival. The lioness has sharp teeth and claws because she must catch and kill her prey in order to survive and to feed her young. The antelope is fleet and has acute senses and a shy disposition because these qualities help her escape from the lioness.

In neither of these accounts do selection and adaptation appear as *processes*, going on since life began on this planet. These processes form the core of evolutionary theories.

Theories of evolution arose as a consequence of the discovery of fossils of extinct animals. Some of these fossils appeared to be records of species succeeding each other in time, as evidenced by their appearance in geological strata superimposed on each other. Some of these records present a convincing picture of gradual modifications of body build in the same direction. An often cited example is the fossil record of the evolution of the horse.

Early explanations of adaptation as an evolutionary process were teleological. That is, adaptation was conceived as a process directed toward a goal. For example, a theory of evolution advanced by J. B. Lamarck ([1809] 1963) explained the giraffe's long neck by the giraffe's efforts to reach the leaves on trees on which it fed. In doing so, a giraffe stretched its neck and so exercised its neck muscles, causing them to elongate. The increase of neck length of an individual giraffe may have been quite small. But it was transmitted to its offspring. In this way, the increments cumulated over the generations, until the giraffe's neck reached the length it has today.

Two ideas are embodied in this explanation: the notion of goal-directed effort and the assumption that characteristics acquired during an animal's lifetime (say, in consequence of the effort) can be inherited by its offspring.

The idea of goal-directed effort, which underlies teleological explanations, was prevalent in the Middle Ages, when even the behavior of inanimate bodies was explained by their "strivings." Stones were said to fall because Earth was the predominant element in them. Consequently, their "natural" position was on the earth. In contrast, smoke rose from the chimney because, being a product of Fire (another basic "element"), it sought its "natural position" in the region of eternal fire beyond the stars. Birds could fly because their "natural" position was in their nests, which were in the trees.[1]

1. We read in Moses Maimonides' (1135–1204) *The Guide for the Perplexed:*

> Each of the four elements occupies a certain position of its own assigned by nature: it is not found in another place, so long as no other but its own natural force acts upon it. . . . When moved from its place by some external force, it returns towards its natural place as soon as that force ceases to operate. . . . The rectilinear motion of the four elements when returning to their original place are of two kinds, either centrifugal [i.e., away from the earth], viz. the motion of the air and the fire; or centripetal [i.e., toward the earth], viz., the motion of the earth and the water; and when the elements have reached their original place, they remain at rest. (Maimonides 1919, 114)

With the advent of physical science, teleological explanations of physical phenomena, such as motions of inanimate bodies, were excluded. However, teleological explanations of phenomena involving living organisms persisted considerably longer. As we have seen, Lamarck based his theory of evolution on explanations of this sort.

Darwin's theory of evolution, based on the concept of natural selection, made teleological explanations of the evolutionary process superfluous. I recall how the possibility of refuting "purposefulness" in nature was brought home to me. Traveling by train in the western United States, I saw a peculiar miniature landscape at the foot of a bluff close to the tracks. The area was covered by conical columns resembling stalagmites seen in some caves. On top of each column was a pebble. It is quite natural to imagine that someone placed a pebble on each "stalagmite." But, of course, on reflection this conclusion must be dismissed as absurd. It seems more reasonable to assume that, originally, the pebbles were strewn about on a level surface. As water flowed over the surface, it eroded the ground. Since, however, water had to flow around each pebble, it left the ground underneath the pebble in place. As a result, stalagmitelike columns were carved out. The pebbles remained on top of the carved-out columns.

We turn to the notion of inheriting characteristics acquired by the parents during their lifetimes. There is no evidence that this can occur. On the contrary, there is evidence that transmission of acquired characteristics does not occur. Consider the bees. They are of three kinds: males (drones), females (queens), and workers. The latter are undeveloped females. They are, in effect, sexless, because they have no functional reproductive apparatus. Therefore the workers have no progeny. Only the drones and the queens have progeny to which they can transmit inherited characteristics. But the life styles of the three kinds of bees are widely different. The worker bees do everything that we, humans, customarily call work. They gather food, nurse the young, build the containers for storing honey, and so forth. The queen does nothing of the kind. Her only job is to lay eggs. The drones do nothing but compete for access to the queen and, if successful, fertilize her. Therefore, if the worker bees have "learned" anything in the course of their activity (e.g., more efficient food gathering or their "dance language"), these skills cannot possibly be passed on to the next generation, since neither the queen nor the drones could have learned them.

Actually, the far-reaching discoveries of genetics, by identifying the carriers of inherited characteristics (the genes), have shown conclusively that genetic transmission of acquired characteristics is impossible. Darwin, who wrote before these discoveries, apparently hypothesized transmission of acquired characteristics, but this hypothesis is not necessary to support his theory of evolution, which rests on two fundamental concepts: random variation and natural selection.

According to Darwin's own account (Darwin. [1859] 1964, 63) the impetus to the development of his version of evolution came from Malthus's essay on population ([1798] 1966). It was Malthus who first warned of the impending dangers of overpopulation. He assumed that human populations grow exponentially, that is, increase by a multiplicative factor in equal intervals of time. Thus, if it takes, say, fifty years for a population to double, then it will double again in the next fifty years, and so on. Consequently, in five centuries, a population growing at this rate would increase more than a thousandfold. Further, Malthus assumed that the area of arable land can increase (at most) linearly, that is, by arithmetic progression, whereby equal areas are added to the existing area in equal intervals of time.

From these hypotheses, Malthus deduced that, regardless of the rate of increase per capita of the population and the rate of increase per unit time of arable land, the population must eventually outgrow the available food supply. Therefore, if no measures are taken to limit population growth, the growth will eventually be checked by mass starvation. To avoid this painful result, Malthus advised sexual abstention, which may have been the only form of birth control known to him.

To Darwin, the most important implication of Malthus's theory was that organisms tend to produce more progeny than can survive to reproductive age. This leads to the conclusion that those that do survive to reproductive age must somehow be more "fit" than the nonsurvivors. We have thus effectively a sort of competition for survival, suggesting the principle of "struggle for existence, survival of the fittest." Below we will discuss the role that this formulation may have played in facilitating the acceptance of Darwin's theory and in shaping the ideational climate of the nineteenth century. For the moment, let us examine the implications of Darwin's theory, which not only removed teleological explanations from the foundations of biological science but also provided a fertile soil for far-reaching generalizations.

Random Variation

Although offspring generally resemble their parents ("Like begets like," says the adage), not all individuals of a species are alike. Variations can be seen with the naked eye. These variations stem from two sources. Some result from influences of the environment: some individuals get to eat more than others and consequently grow bigger; animals capable of learning from experience have different experiences and learn different habits; some have accidents; others get diseases. All these events induce variations of individual appearance and behavior patterns, which remain the characteristics of the individuals. These variations are not inherited by descendants.

Other variations stem from different genetic makeups of individuals. The genetic makeup is the set of genes carried by every cell of the organism. A "program" is inscribed on each gene, and it is the combinations of the programs that determine the characteristics of the individual that are passed on to its offspring. As far as can be determined, the changes affecting individual genes, called mutations, and the various recombinations of genes occurring in sexual reproduction (the particular combinations inherited from the father and the mother) occur by chance. The *rate* of mutations can be affected by external factors such as radiation, but their *direction*, as far as we know, is not. It is this independence of specific genetic changes from environmental influence that is subsumed under the phrase "random variation."

Differential Reproduction Rate

The observable features of an individual organism define its phenotype. These features define the relative fitness of the individual to its environment. The phenotype is determined partly by environmental influences, partly by the genetic makeup. What is called "fitness" is reflected in differential reproduction rates. That is, different proportions of the various phenotypes survive to reproductive age and/or have different numbers of progeny. Since it is the genetically determined characteristics that are inherited, different reproductive rates of phenotypes result in different proportions of genotypes (carriers of different sets of genes) in the population. Under different environmental conditions, different genotypes will have a different degree of reproductive success. However, in order for a genotype to "succeed," that is, eventually to become dominant in the population, it must be initially present in the population. Or, more precisely, the genes that determine this "successful" genotype in combination must all be present for natural selection to work upon. To be sure, individual genes may appear by mutation. But this is to say that they appear in the genetic makeup of the population at some time. Only when they are present can they be acted on by natural selection.

The circumstances that confer a reproductive advantage on this or that genotype may change. Thus, we can have a gene present in the population that does not yet have a reproductive advantage—"its time has not yet come." Eventually, however, "its time may come," that is, the environment may change in a way that gives it a reproductive advantage, and it "takes off" on the way to evolutionary success. We must assume, however, that during its dormancy, this gene does not have a reproductive *disadvantage* that would eliminate it from the population. As we shall see, the notion of the dormant gene can be generalized to the notion of a dormant idea.

Evolution by Accretion

The complexity of some survival mechanisms of living organisms make the hypothesis of random variation and accidental combination difficult to accept. To this day, the so-called creationists, who, apparently for ideological reasons, refuse to accept the theory of evolution, advance arguments against it that are based on a misunderstanding of the randomness hypothesis. They call attention to the immense complexity of some organisms and refuse to believe that these organisms could have been formed "by accident." The existence of a watch, they argue, should be sufficient evidence for the existence of a watchmaker. A watch could never "happen" by accidental combination of parts in just the right way.

The argument carries some force if random combination refers to all the parts combining simultaneously. Of course, the number of ways they can combine is superastronomical, and so the probability of the "right" combination occurring by chance is infinitesimal. However, if we suppose the random events to be random modifications of *already* existing combinations that enjoy a reproductive advantage, a different picture emerges.

To see this, let a "population" consist of results of tosses of fair coins. Each toss results in either heads or tails with equal probabilities. After all the coins have been tossed once, approximately half of them show heads, half tails. Assume now that only the coins that show heads reproduce themselves, while those that show tails do not and eventually die. Then one half of the next generation will consist of coins that have shown heads on the first toss and heads on the second, and one half of coins that have shown heads on the first toss and tails on the second. Again we assume that only the former reproduce and the latter die. So the next generation consists of coins that have shown three heads in succession and coins that have shown two heads and one tails. Continuing in this way, we see that the coins of the twentieth generation, when they reach "reproductive age," will consist only of coins that have shown twenty successive heads.

Now the chance of getting twenty successive heads is less than one in a million. The objection of the creationists to the assumption that a complex organism resulted in consequence of random variations rests on the tacit assumption that the complexity appeared all at once. In our hypothetical example, however, complexity arises by accretion, as it were. The selective process works only on the "organisms" that have already achieved a certain degree of complexity and produced additional complexity by favoring these organisms. Note that we have retained the assumption that the probability of heads on each toss is one half.

We have exaggerated the differential reproductive success of heads and tails. Note, however, that even if the reproductive advantage of a particular genotype is quite small, after several generations the relative proportion of that variant in the population can become very large. This is because the excess of progeny grows according to the law of compound interest. Observe that $1 invested at 2 percent per annum interest compounded annually will increase to almost $21,000 in 500 years.

The explanation of how most improbable complex features arise by random variation has a number of important implications. To begin with, it is clear that, for selection to produce an evolutionary process, there must be genetic diversity in the evolving population. If all the individuals comprising a population were strictly alike, none would have a reproductive advantage and the population would stay homogeneous and unchanging forever. Second, in order for some feature to become predominant in the process of evolution, it must already exist, potentially, in the population. We say potentially because it may come into existence by a mutation. But in order to be "selected for," it must be there. To borrow G. G. Simpson's (1950) picturesque expression, evolution is "opportunistic," that is, it works on what is at hand. We will subsequently draw an analogy between such "dormant" genes and "dormant" ideas, waiting for their "time to come" in order to take off and change the composition of the noosphere.

In the 1930s, T. D. Lysenko, a Soviet plant breeder, succeeded in developing varieties of wheat that could be grown farther north than the usual varieties. He did this by sowing successive crops farther and farther north. He explained his success by invoking the Lamarckian principle of evolution. He insisted that the plants were "trained" to withstand cold, each generation becoming "tougher" and transmitting its acquired tolerance to cold to the next generation. This explanation contradicts the principle that characteristics acquired during the lifetime of an organism cannot be transmitted by inheritance. Since, however, Lysenko was a protégé of Stalin, he succeeded in getting genetics condemned as a "bourgeois pseudoscience" with horrendous consequences for an entire generation of biologists.

The notion of the dormant gene provides an explanation of Lysenko's breeding success, based on natural selection. There was genetic diversity in Lysenko's wheat "population." In particular, some genes made the plants more resistant to cold than others. When the crops were sown farther north, these acquired a reproductive advantage over the others and consequently became more numerous in the next generation. After several generations, they became predominant.

The obverse of the dormant gene is the vestigial gene, one that once was manifested in some prominent feature but is no longer, because the feature was suppressed in the course of natural selection. We all have a vermiform appendix. A feature from which it was descended may have been functional in some remote ancestors of ours. Vestigial gills appear early in the development of a human embryo, a throwback to our fishlike ancestors. The scientific homily, "Ontogeny recapitulates philogeny," refers to the observation that the development of an individual organism appears to go through phases that the forms along its evolutionary line of descent had gone through.

What Is Fitness?

We have spoken interchangeably about "fitness" and "reproductive success," justifiably so, because fitness and reproductive success are synonymous. There is no way of defining fitness a priori, that is, by indicating such and such properties that contribute to fitness. Fitness can be defined only in retrospect. Those variants are the most fit that have exhibited the greatest reproductive success. This is because fitness has a meaning only in relation to a particular environment. For those animals that live in water, gills are an effective apparatus for imbibing oxygen from the environment. Gills are useless to land-dwelling animals. These must use lungs. Sharp teeth and claws are of no use to a grass-eating animal. The ability to digest grass is of no use to a flesh-eating animal.

Not only the external environment but also the "internal" one determines the fitness of a feature. Our versatile hand, which can perform intricate manipulations, could not function if our brain had not developed the ability to control these delicate operations. The fierceness (as it appears to us) of predators is an advantage if physical strength goes with it but not otherwise.

We will subsequently note that the dominant world outlook in Europe in the second half of the nineteenth century was especially receptive to the idea of evolution driven by natural selection. A simplified notion of a "struggle for existence" emerged expressed in an image of nature "red in tooth and claw," a picture that ignores the vast range of the meaning of fitness. In some environments, the big and strong are fit; in others, the small and inconspicuous; in some the swift; in some the sluggish. Some animals ensure the continuity of their species by producing thousands of young, of whom only a few survive; others produce only a few but take good care of them. Thus, fitness depends not only on the external and internal environments but also on the lifestyle of the organism in question, which, in turn, is determined by what has developed as the basis of fitness.

Coevolution

Consider a population of predators. In the process of evolution, they developed features that made them adapted to their environment. The environment comprises not only the climate, the landscape, and other physical features. It also comprises other populations, among them the prey that the predators feed on. Thus, part of the adaptation process of the predators includes adaptation to the prey, for example, the development of sharp teeth, claws, springing and sprinting prowess, and so forth.

The prey also evolve and adapt to their environment, which includes the predators. Their survival mechanism includes an ability to become aware of the predators, even at considerable distance. It involves swiftness, some techniques of collective defense, and so forth. There is, thus, a reciprocal relation between a population and at least a part of its environment. The part can be another population, so that each population can be regarded as part of the environment of the other.

Consider next a population of hosts and a population of parasites that infests them. The hosts may evolve by developing a resistance potential against the parasites, say ways of eliminating them from the body. If the parasites cannot survive outside that body, they may evolve by developing resistance against the host's resistance mechanisms. The two populations coevolve, the one developing a more effective defense, the other a more effective offense. This coevolution resembles, in some ways, the coevolution of naval artillery and naval armor. As artillery becomes more efficient in piercing the armor of a battleship, the battleship develops thicker armor. We will subsequently return to nonbiological evolutionary processes.

The coevolution of a parasite with a host may resemble mutual accommodation instead of an arms race. As a rule, being infested with a parasite harms the host. When the host dies, the parasite usually dies with it. Then it may happen that becoming less lethal benefits the parasite. Accordingly, the parasite may evolve in this direction. On the other hand, it may be to the host's advantage to develop a tolerance for the parasite. This coevolutionary process may resemble the development of "peaceful coexistence." It may even happen that the parasite may benefit the host by taking over some of the latter's physiological functions. In that case, one can speak of symbiosis instead of parasitism. We are in a symbiotic relationship with bacteria that live in our digestive tract. We nourish them; they help us digest our food. In this way, evolution can be conducive to cooperation as well as to conflict.

The phenomenon of coevolution explains the evolution of entities incapable of reproduction. A striking example of evolution of this sort was described by A. E. Emerson (1939). Termites, like ants, build elaborate structures in which they, being social insects, live in tightly knit communities. When the termites of such a colony die, the "termite city" remains an empty shell. Examining a large number of these shells, Emerson established an evolutionary series manifest in a system of gradual modifications. Thus, it could be said that this "artifact" evolved together with its builders. What was most striking about the discovery was that the evolution of the shell exhibited "vestigial parts" in the form of galleries sealed off from both ends and, therefore, inaccessible. In earlier fossils, these galleries were accessible, hence presumably functional.

If we assume that the termite city is built according to a plan that is essentially a program inscribed on the termites' genes, we can imagine an evolution of the program. Originally it contained instructions to build a particular gallery. Then a mutation occurred in the form of an instruction to seal one end of the gallery. For some reason, this gene had a reproductive advantage over the original one and displaced it. Why this was so we do not know. Perhaps the gene did something else that was an advantage to the colony or perhaps the gene did something in conjunction with other genes that was advantageous. But now the termite city contained a dead-end gallery. In conjunction with other conditions, this may have become a handicap. For instance, running in and out of the gallery resulted in loss of time. Thus, when another mutation occurred generating an instruction to seal off the other end and so to eliminate the dead-end passage, it conferred a reproductive advantage and was fixated. The useless gallery became a "vestigial part" of the evolving termite city.

Note that in this example, reproduction takes place only in the sexual form of the termites. The working termites, like the worker ants and worker bees, do not reproduce. This circumstance adds force to the argument that characteristics acquired during the lifetime of an organism are not inherited, since the reproducing individuals of social insects do not acquire the characteristics that the nonreproducing individuals may have acquired by learning. Actually, insects learn very little (if at all) during their lifetime. Whatever learning, in the sense of a modification of behavior, occurs comes as a result of genetic changes. Thus, the behavior of an insect is very largely "built-in." To put it in another way, the behavior of insects is determined, to a very large extent, by instincts. This explanation of instincts in genetic terms frees it from the aura of mystery with which it was surrounded before the advent of genetics. It also makes the providential interpretation of adaptation superfluous.

Another idea suggested by the coevolution of the termites and their inanimate abode is that the definition of an "organism" is not sharp. We tend to think of individual termites as organisms and of their colonies as populations of organisms. But we can also regard the entire colony as an organism, especially since only the sexual forms of termites reproduce. These sexual forms can be regarded as the sex "cells" of the "organism" and the sexless forms as the other (somatic) cells. Even the shell can be regarded as part of the organism analogous to, say, a sort of external skeleton, like the shell of an oyster. Thus, there is nothing unusual in the fact that this structure, being an anatomical feature of the superorganism, evolves. Its reproduction is the result of the reproduction of the sexual forms, but so are the working termites.

Actually, the evolution of any organism possessing specialized sex cells can be regarded as coevolution. Not even the sex cells are the ultimate reproducing units. These are the genes. They are the carriers of heredity. Their evolution induces the evolution of all the cells of the body (soma) in which they are embedded. We can, therefore, speak of coevolution of the genes and the soma. The soma is the "environment" of the gene. The gene produces the specific shape of the soma. The soma confers greater or lesser reproductive success on the gene, since it is the soma that is better or worse adapted to its environment, namely, the outside world. And even the external environment may coevolve with the populations it supports. Forests turn into grasslands, grasslands into deserts. For the most part, this "evolution" is a consequence of climactic changes. But sometimes the evolution of a portion of the biosphere plays an important part. We are increasingly aware of the interdependence of an environment and the human population that inhabits it. Therefore, we can speak of coevolution in that context also. This kind of coevolution may depend only distantly on genetic factors. Nevertheless, it is a form of coevolution and can be examined in the light of a generalized evolutionary theory.

Sociobiology

The discovery of the gene as the "atom of life" put the Darwinian theory of evolution on a solid scientific basis. Of course the speculative aspects could not be eliminated because even the "hardest" theories, such as those of physical science, for example, must include speculative components. But the spectacular advances in genetics that laid the foundation of a new branch of biological science—molecular biology—brought biology much nearer to the exact sciences. In particular, the study of social insects developed into a border area between the biological and the social sciences—sociobiology.

A principal task of sociobiology is that of bringing genetics to bear on the study of the social behavior of animals. The behavior of social insects is, at times, especially enlightening in this respect, since there is good reason to believe that their behavior patterns are practically all genetically determined. The extreme rigidity of their behavior patterns lends support to this conjecture.

The behavior of the digger wasp is a vivid example. This insect lays its eggs on the body of a tarantula that has been stunned but not killed by the wasp. The wasp performs a sequence of complicated acts. First it must find a tarantula, which is to become the source of food for its young. Only a certain kind of tarantula will do for the particular kind of wasp. Having found the right kind of tarantula, the wasp stings it and drags the paralyzed victim to a previously dug "cave." The wasp then deposits the tarantula near the entrance of the cave and enters it presumably to "inspect" it. (Slipping into anthropomorphic interpretation is often unavoidable.) The inspection is necessary because, at times, the cave can be appropriated by another wasp—another form of behavior that may have been selected for because it saves effort. If the result of the inspection is satisfactory, the wasp comes out of the cave, drags the tarantula inside, and lays its eggs upon the body. When the larvae are hatched, they will feed on the tarantula.

The extreme inflexibility of this instinctive behavior can be experimentally demonstrated. While the wasp is inspecting the cave, the tarantula is moved a few centimeters away from the entrance. Then the wasp, upon emerging from the cave, will "look" for the tarantula and, having found it, will drag it to the entrance and will again enter the cave "to inspect it," although this operation had been performed only a few seconds before. If, during the second inspection, the tarantula is again moved a few centimeters, the sequence will be repeated. Evidently the chain must always be performed in a fixed order: dig cave, find tarantula, drag to entrance, inspect, emerge, drag tarantula in, lay eggs, leave. If the chain is broken, it must be reconstituted exactly. No part may be omitted.

It seems incredible that a behavior pattern of such complexity could have arisen simultaneously "by chance." However, it does not make it much easier to understand as something that developed by accretion, since any incomplete part of the pattern seems to be useless, and it is not clear what sort of fitness it could confer on the wasp while it is "waiting" to be completed. In some cases, however, sociobiologists succeeded in providing an explanation. Of course, they could not study the successive evolutionary stages of the pattern because behavior patterns leave no fossils. However, sometimes coexistent species reveal variations of a behavior pattern that could have been successive stages.

The courtship of empidid flies provides an interesting example. "In some species of this family, the male initiates courtship by presenting the female with an elaborate balloon of his own making. Why?" (Barash 1982, 37–38).

The secret is unraveled by comparing the courtship procedures in related species. It turns out that the males of some species do nothing elaborate. They simply approach the female with unmistakable intent. Unfortunately for these males (from our anthropocentric point of view), the females are much larger, are predatory, and apparently do not distinguish very well between lovers and other small insects. The suitor often ends up as a meal instead of a mate. Males of other species bring a gift, some edible morsel. They accomplish their task while the female is busy eating. This variation in courting behavior can be reasonably explained as a result of natural selection, since it confers a reproductive advantage on the male's progeny (gives him a better chance of having progeny at all). Males of still other species are observed to present their gift adorned with silk; still others surround it with a silk balloon. Actually, all these variants exist side by side, but we can imagine that the elaborate ones are later versions, having evolved by accretion from the simpler ones. The survival value for the male is in the prolongation of the time during which the female is engaged in unwrapping and consuming the gift. By the time she turns her attention to the small insect (possible prey), he has successfully inseminated her. There remains the final step: omission of the edible morsel, which saves labor without significantly shortening the time during which the female is preoccupied. By the time the female realizes that she has been had, it is too late.

The impressive successes attained by sociobiologists in providing at least reasonable explanations of the elaborate, genetically transmitted behavior patterns could have stimulated them to extend their methods to explanations of some forms of human behavior by Darwinian principles of evolution. In fact, deriving the evolution of cultures as results of reproductive advantage conferred by certain behavior patterns (customs, taboos, etc.) became a research program pursued by many sociobiologists.

E. O. Wilson, author of the path-blazing treatise on sociobiology, wrote as follows on the presumed origins of war.

> Throughout history the conduct of war has been common among tribes and nearly universal among chiefdoms and states. The spread of genes has always been of paramount importance. For example, after the conquest of the Midianites, Moses gave instructions identical in result to the aggression and genetic occupation by male langur monkeys.[2] Combinations of genes able to confer superior fitness in contention with genocidal aggression would be those that produce either a more effective genocidal aggression or else the capacity to prevent genocide by some form of pacific maneuvering. (Wilson 1975, 572–73)

The facile conclusion that war is rooted in human nature can be easily drawn from this interpretation of human aggressiveness and can serve as a rationalization of "peace through strength" and similar hawkish policies. The same applies to "social Darwinism," an interpretation of progress as a result of ruthless competition, justifying gross social inequalities.

Related to such justification is the sociobiological explanation of altruism as a variant of selfishness, which advances selfishness to a universal principle—a justification of complete economic individualism now usually associated with political conservatism. I will return to this theme in chapter 6.

---

2. Langur monkeys live in troupes. Occasionally a troupe attacks another, killing all the males and appropriating the females. This is what Wilson calls genetic occupation.

4

Dormant Ideas

Like dormant genes, ideas "take off" when their environment, that is, the state of the noosphere, becomes favorable for their germination and development.

Hero of Alexandria demonstrated a steam engine in 130 B.C. In the eighteenth century, the steam engine was the centerpiece of the Industrial Revolution, which radically changed the mode of production, first in England, then in all Europe, and finally everywhere. Why did it take almost two thousand years for the steam engine to "take off"?

The basic idea of the atomic theory of matter was formulated by Democritus in the fifth century B.C., according to some accounts even earlier by Leucippus. But it was not until 1803 that the theory became the foundation of chemistry. What was happening in the meantime?

It was also in the fifth century B.C. that Empedocles had an idea that contains the kernel of an evolutionary theory based on chance combinations and natural selection. Empedocles supposed that, at one time, parts of bodies were strewn about: heads without torsos, torsos without heads, solitary limbs, and so on. As one could expect, these fragments were not viable. Occasionally, however, they combined in just the right way to make a viable organism able to reproduce its kind. And that is the way the earth became populated. This idea also "slept" for over two thousand years until Darwin and Wallace "wakened" it. As the atomic theory became the basis of the science of matter, so the theory of evolution driven by random variations and natural selection became the basis of the science of life. Why did the original ideas need so long to blossom?

In the case of the steam engine, a need for it had to arise before it occurred to any one to develop it. A need arises with an awareness of a discrepancy between how things are and how they ought to be. In societies where practically all work is done by slaves or serfs, an awareness of a discrepancy of this sort does not arise. The masters regard their status as natural, and the slaves or serfs are resigned to theirs as inevitable. A discrepancy becomes apparent when attention is turned to the productivity of labor. Productivity is not important if almost everything that is produced is consumed locally. The nonworkers consume more than the workers, but this discrepancy is regarded as part of the natural order of things. Productivity becomes of paramount importance if most of what is produced becomes the wherewithal of trade and trade becomes a means of enrichment. Such was the case in England when she became the world's weaver. English cloth was in demand. The more cloth was produced, the more could be sold, and the richer those who sold it became. They were not the actual producers. They were the organizers of production. Factories appeared in which scores of weavers worked in close proximity. It became practical to attach the looms to a flywheel, and a job was found for the steam engine to drive the flywheel. Once the steam engine was seen as a source of enrichment (through increasing the productivity of labor), inventors appeared who thought up improvements and more jobs for the steam engine to do—to pump water out of mines, to drive ships, eventually to pull strings of cars on tracks carrying people and goods. The idea of the steam engine "took off."

The idea of the atomic structure of matter bore fruit when chemists turned to quantitative methods of investigation. Such investigations were introduced into physics long before they were adopted in chemistry. In the seventeenth century, Galileo studied the motion of bodies rolling down inclined planes. His attention was turned away from the question of why bodies move (the central question of medieval physics) to the question of how they move. In particular, he measured the distances passed by a cannonball rolling down an inclined plane at various angles of inclination to see how these distances varied with the time elapsed and with the angle. In short, he measured and reasoned about the results of measurements.

At that time, the alchemists, the predecessors of the chemists, were still speculating about "affinities" and "antiaffinities" governing the behavior of substances. Their attention was still fixed on "why" rather than on "how." Two hundred years passed before measurement was introduced into experiments designed to study combinations and recombinations of substances. It was such measurements that led to the replacement of the phlogiston theory of combustion by the oxidation theory. According to the older theory, "phlogiston," a substance thought responsible for combustion, left the burning body. It was for this reason, so the argument went, that the body, after having burned, lost weight: the ashes were lighter than the body before it burned. A. L. Lavoisier (1743–94) showed that, after burning, magnesium became heavier. This was ascribed to the combination of the burning substance with some external substance. That external substance turned out to be oxygen.

As measurement became routine in chemical experiments, a curious fact was discovered. As a rule, substances combined with each other in quantities that were simple multiples of each other (the law of multiple proportions). This phenomenon could be explained if matter could be assumed to consist of minute indivisible particles, which, in remembrance of Democritus, were called "atoms." If varieties of matter were due to different combinations of different kinds of atoms, it would follow that quantities entering different combinations of the same substances should be multiples of each other. Thus, if it took one atom of oxygen combining with one atom of carbon to produce one molecule of carbon monoxide (CO) and two atoms of oxygen combining with an atom of carbon to produce a molecule of carbon dioxide (CO_2), it would take twice as much oxygen per unit of carbon dioxide as per unit of carbon monoxide. And this was observed.

In 1865, Georg Mendel, a monk from Brunn (now Brno, Czechoslovakia) pursued his hobby of breeding varieties of sweet pea plants. As he crossed different strains, his attention was called to certain quantitative regularities of the results. Of special interest were the following observations. When he crossed pure breeding strains of plants producing respectively red and white flowers, he got plants with only red blossoms. When, however, he crossed these "first filial generation" plants among themselves, he got a "second filial generation" in which some plants had red blossoms and some white, whereby the proportions of reds to whites was very nearly 3:1. Crossing peas from plants with smooth yellow seeds and those with wrinkled green seeds produced only plants with smooth yellow seeds in the first filial generation. But when these were inbred, they produced four types: smooth yellow, smooth green, wrinkled yellow, and wrinkled green.

These results have a striking resemblance to those governed by the law of multiple proportions. However, the idea of an "atomic theory of inheritance" lay dormant until Mendel's discoveries were rediscovered thirty-five years later. Then the idea "took off" and became genetics, which, coupled with the theory of evolution, is now the backbone of biology.

Bizarre as Empedocles' ideas about the origin of life are, they contain the core of the Darwinian theory of evolution, namely, random combinations and survival of combinations that "fit."

It is interesting to note that Darwin's theory of evolution at first met with strong opposition, particularly by church authorities, since it cast doubt on the uniqueness of man as the sole possessor of a soul, by suggesting that man evolved from "lower animals." But the very intensity of the polemics about evolution attests to its enthusiastic acceptance in some segments of society, namely, those where competition, the struggle for power, represented the true meaning of life.

To be sure, this fixation came to the forefront long before the theory of evolution appeared on the intellectual horizon. It was generated by the triumph of materialism and individualism over otherwordly concerns: the triumph of the ideology of the Renaissance over that of the Middle Ages. Thomas Hobbes's mechanical materialism was expressed in his conception of freedom (which he extended to inanimate objects) as unimpeded movement and the consequent conception of everything and everyone that stands in the way of such movement as an obstacle to be removed or destroyed. Coupled with individualism in its starkest guise, this conception generated the idea of "man in the state of nature" engaged in a war of everyone against everyone.

In a milder form, absolute individualism and the dominance of competition as a basic determinant of human motivation, hence the essence of social life, pervades Adam Smith's model of a market economy. As in Hobbes's model, the fundamental unit is again the human individual, this time in the role of a trader. Human needs are satisfied by commodities produced by human beings. As human beings increasingly aggregated into large communities, a system of the division of labor developed, making for more efficiency in production. An individual specializing in producing a particular commodity, for example, potatoes or nails, could produce quantities far in excess of his needs. He could then come in contact with producers of other commodities and trade his surpluses for theirs to the benefit of all.

In this situation, an individual, far from regarding others as his enemies, like Hobbes's "man in the state of nature," depends on them as potential trading partners. Still, the interests of the traders, although they converge in some respects, diverge in others, since it is in the interest of each to surrender as little as possible and to acquire as much as possible. The traders compete for trading partners. Further, those who can unload their goods for less have a competitive advantage. Consequently, it is in the interest of each to increase the efficiency of production. "Survival of the fittest" in this context means that the most efficient producers remain in the market. The others are eliminated. Thus, in this model, competition benefits the economic system as a whole and so, presumably, everyone in the system.

The "free market" can be clearly seen as the rationale of an economic system based on unrestricted free enterprise, a rationale still frequently invoked for the economic system based on it. A profound idea is embodied in Smith's model. Namely, every member of a society may be motivated in his actions only by his individual self-interest; yet the result of all these strivings to promote one's own self-interest is a benefit to all. In this way, "selfishness" need not be the polar opposite of altruism. Competition and cooperation are not necessarily incompatible. In competing, individuals tacitly cooperate by increasing the efficiency of the productive process, by stimulating creative inventions, and so on. The following passage from *The Wealth of Nations* (Smith [1776] 1910) is especially revealing.

> It is not from the benevolence of the butcher, the brewer, and the baker that we expect our dinner, but from their regard to their own interest. We address ourselves not to their humanity but to their self-love and never talk to them of our own necessities but of their advantages. Nobody but a beggar chooses to depend chiefly on the benevolence of his fellow citizens. (1:13)

By the time Darwin's *Origin of Species* was published (1859), the free market had evolved into mature industrial capitalism. Along with it, ideals of democracy, at first in harmony with emerging free enterprise, appeared incompatible with the gross social inequalities generated by the concentration of wealth in the hands of entrepreneurs, contrasting with miserable living conditions of urban working masses. Here the "struggle for existence, survival of the fittest" paradigm provided a most convincing rationale (convincing to the rich, that is). An example of the affirmation of social inequality as both natural and good can be seen in the following passage by a leading social Darwinist of a century ago.

> The class distinctions simply result from the different degrees of success with which men have availed themselves of the chances

> which were presented to them. Instead of endeavoring to redistribute the acquisitions which have been made between the existing classes, our aim should be to increase, multiply, and extend the chances. . . . Such expansion is no guarantee of equality. On the contrary, if there be liberty, some will profit by the chances eagerly and some will neglect them altogether. Therefore, the greater the chances the more unequal will be the fortune of these two sets of men. So it ought to be, in all justice and right reason. . . . If we can expand the chances, we can count on a general and steady growth of civilization and advancement of society by and through the best numbers. (Sumner [1883] 1952, 144–45)

In the nineteenth century in England and the United States, the predominant preoccupation of the most active was with pursuit of wealth. In nineteenth-century Germany, preoccupation with war was much more conspicuous. Among German nationalists, a sort of vulgar Darwinism stands out as a rationalization of war. F. von Bernhardi, in his *Germany and the Next War,* wrote:

> The struggle for existence is the life of Nature, the basis of all healthy development. All existing things show themselves to be the result of contending forces. So it is in the life of man. The struggle is not merely the destructive but the life-giving principle. (Bernhardi 1914, 18)

Bernhardi goes on to cite Claus Wagner, author of a book entitled *Der Krieg als schaffendes Weltprinzip* (War as a Creative Universal Principle).

> The natural law to which all laws of Nature can be reduced is the law of struggle. All intrasocial property, all thoughts, inventions and institutions, as indeed in the social system itself, are a result of the intrasocial struggle, in which one survives and another is cast out. The extra-social, the supersocial struggle which guides the existence and development of societies, nations, and races is war. The internal development of the intrasocial struggle is man's daily work—the struggle of thought, wishes, sciences, activities. The outward development, the supersocial struggle is the sanguinary struggle of nations—war. In what does the creative power of the struggle consist? In growth and decay, in the victory of the one factor and

> the defeat of the other. The struggle is the creator because it eliminates. (Bernhardi 1914, 19)

I have suggested that dormant ideas sprout when the "soil" in which they were planted becomes nourishing. The metaphor uses terms referring to the geosphere. Actually, however, we are speaking of the noosphere. We have discussed two contexts. In one, the soil was the scientific component of the noosphere. It is in this soil that the atomic theory sprouted, grew, and blossomed. In the other context, we had in mind the social climate, also that of the noosphere. It became especially favorable to technological innovation, which accounts for the "awakening" of the steam engine, and to enthusiastic acceptance of an evolutionary theory based on a "struggle for existence and survival of the fittest."

One final example of how something dormant can turn into something prominent or dominant when the social milieu favors it will shed some light on the chronic (and for the most part futile) controversy about the nature of human nature.

"You can't change human nature," says the homily. Usually, this verdict is a signal that the speaker is ready to dismiss any view of human behavior potentiality different from his or her own. Belief in the immutability of human nature reflects a conviction that things are what they are because that is the way they are. Kenneth E. Boulding has advanced another principle, to our way of thinking one with greater explanatory power: "Things are as they are, because they got that way." Unless one believes in absolute determinism, one can interpret Boulding's principle to imply that things could have been otherwise than what they are. If so, there is some point in trying to guide processes into some directions rather than in others, in other words, to avoid a defeatist attitude suggested by the belief that "you can't change human nature."

On some reflection, it appears that almost anything one can say about human nature in the sense of ascribing moral qualities to it can be shown to be true. There is plenty of "evidence" for assertions like "people are cruel," "people are kind," "people are brave," "people are cowardly," "people are altruistic," "people are selfish," "people are covetous," or "people are generous." All of these statements could be regarded as "proven" if a "for instance" could be admitted as proof. But, of course, the citation of instances cannot be accepted as proofs of general statements unless one is willing to believe assertions that contradict each other.

To say that any statement about human nature can be justified (that is, supported by some evidence) is simply to say that there are many kinds of people. However, one is often particularly concerned with certain kinds of people, specifically those who cause a great deal of grief and misfortune. The defeatist attitude about the immutability of human nature leads to the conviction that acts of cruelty, destructiveness, ruthlessness, and the like reflect the "true" human nature. What is more likely is that, under certain conditions, people with certain properties are *selected* one way or another to positions of power. Being in positions of power, their actions are far-reaching and conspicuous. It is, then, natural to conclude that these people represent a dominant type. For example, from 1933 to 1945, Germans were responsible for horrible atrocities. Nothing can be inferred from these actions about the "bestiality" of human beings, nor about the bestiality of Germans. It is not even justifiable to conclude that certain conditions made Germans bestial during that time. A more reasonable assumption is that the German population (like any other population) contained at that time (and still contains) both cruel and gentle people and many other kinds of people. Because of certain special circumstances, it is the sadists and the power addicts who were selected into positions of power. In those positions they were able to perpetrate mass atrocities. To put it in another way, bestiality may be dormant in a population and may be awakened, not necessarily in the sense that people become brutal under certain conditions but in consequence of the fact that bestial people are "selected for" (under some circumstances) to become prominent and powerful. In this way, it seems as if they are representatives of the population.

In suggesting that peace is an idea whose time has come, I conceive peace as an idea that has been dormant for at least twenty-eight centuries. There are some indications that the noosphere now contains sufficient nutrients for this idea to permit it to sprout and grow. In its development, it will enter a struggle for existence with the institution of war. The outcome of the struggle will depend on whether the political climate will enable more people possessed by the idea to come into positions of political power. If so, the world will become more peaceful, not necessarily because "people became more peaceful" (we need not invoke a change of human nature), but because the relative political weight of people concerned with power struggles and people attuned to cooperation has changed. The outcome of the struggle will have a bearing on the longevity of the human race.

5

Evolution by Selection: A Generalized Theory

Can something be said about all forms of evolution? That is, are there general principles underlying all of them? In particular, is selection one such principle? If it is, we should be able to identify three things: (1) the units on which the selection principles work; (2) the reproductive process; and (3) the way the units are more adapted or less adapted to their environment, that is, the basis of the differences in reproductive success.

As our first example of evolution that is not biological evolution, we will examine the evolution of languages. The languages spoken by humans can be represented as branches of a tree, which in many ways resembles the tree representing the evolution of biological species. The tree of biological species shows branchings of phyla into classes, of classes into orders, of orders into families, of families into genera, of genera into species. Languages can also be so represented. Going from the special to the general entities, we can see dialects grouped into languages, languages into families, and so forth. Thus, English, German, and Swedish belong to the Germanic branch; the Germanic, Italic, and Balto-Slavic families belong to the more general "phylum" of Indo-European languages. Moreover, common ancestors of related languages have been identified. Latin was the common ancestor of the languages of the Romance group. Proto-Indo-European has been reconstructed as the common ancestor of all the languages of the Indo-European group, and so on. Some of the branches terminate, showing the extinction of languages, just as some branches of the "tree of life" terminate showing the extinction of species, genera, or larger units.

How does language evolution take place? First we must recognize that if selection is a mechanism by which the evolution of languages is driven, then the languages cannot be the units on which selection works. There are not enough of them. A biological species contains millions or billions of phenotypes, differing (usually minutely) in their degree of adaptation, hence in their reproductive success. Here, the action of selection is clear. But the number of languages that have ever existed probably does not exceed some thousands. Moreoever, except for the branching that may separate geographically separated dialects into languages, we cannot identify the "reproduction" of languages, in terms of which differences in reproductive success could be defined. If selection is a factor in the evolution of languages, it must act on units considerably smaller than languages.

We will assume that these units are utterances, say specific sounds (which linguists call phones) of which speech is composed. We can also identify the reproduction of these units. We know that a child acquires language through imitation. We observe also that, before a child begins to speak, it babbles, that is, produces more or less random sounds. Some of these sounds may accidentally resemble some of the sounds comprising words of adult speech in the child's environment. As the child stumbles on them, the production of these sounds will be reinforced by the responses of the adults. Others will not, and, as a consequence, their production will be inhibited and finally extinguished. In this way, the child's learning to speak, that is, the "evolution" of the child's language, can be said to be determined by a selective process.

The evolution of a language may be a similar process. Again we take the phone for our unit. Reproduction will be identified as the production of the phone by others. Sometimes the reproduction will be more or less exact; sometimes it will be a slightly modified version of the phone. Such modification corresponds to a mutation of a gene. The modified form may be imitated by others or it may not. The probability of its being imitated may depend on how "acceptable" it is to the members of the speech community. For instance, the modified form may require less effort without a loss of the information carried by the phone.[1] The dropping of phones once pronounced and now represented by silent letters in written language may have been due to a process of this sort. In short, the modified form may be "better adapted" to its "environment,"

1. The amount of information carried by a signal is inversely related to the probability of receiving the signal. For example, in written English, the probability that *u* follows *q* is very nearly 1.00. Therefore the *u* following a *q* carries little information; it may well be omitted without impairing intelligibility. Instead of "quantity" or "queen" we could write "qantity" or "qeen" and still be understood. In contrast, *w* following *ma-* (a three-letter word) carries considerably more information, because, without knowing the context, we could not guess whether the word is *mad, man, map, maw,* or *may.*

where the environment in this context comprises the members of the speech community.

The readiness of others to reproduce the modified phone (by imitation) defines the reproductive success of the phone, which we can now regard as an analogue of the gene. In this way, the proportion of phones in a language undergoes long-term, for the most part irreversible, changes; its phonetic structure evolves.

A similar process may govern the evolution of a grammar. Certain grammatical forms may disappear because they are redundant—unnecessary for clarity of meaning. On the whole, we typically observe tendencies to simplification in the grammatical evolution of languages. Changes in the semantic aspects of a language (relations between words and what they stand for) may reflect different experiences of successive generations. This is particularly evident in words with several meanings. In the twelfth century, if people were asked what they expected to find under a hood, they would probably say "a monk." Today the answer is more likely to be "a motor." To our parents, a "program" was likely to be associated with a theater. Today we are more likely to think of a computer. All these changes can be reasonably explained by an operation of a process that, in many ways, resembles natural selection, except that the word *natural* no longer applies to it. The selection is done by human beings, not by nature.

The analogy between biological evolution and the evolution of languages appears even more convincing when we note some genuine "vestigial parts" in written language, particularly conspicuous in English spelling. Examples are silent letters left over from earlier forms of the language when they were functional. Thus, the English word *night* is clearly a cognate of the German word *Nacht.* The *ch* in *Nacht* is pronounced, while the *gh* in *night* is not. However, it remains in written form, a vestige from the past like the rudimentary wings of penguins, no longer used for flying, like our coccyx bone, the puny remains of a tail that our arboreal ancestors may have been proud of. The regularity of occurrence of the spelling vestiges provides additional evidence. Compare the English word *through* with German *durch,* the English *know* with Greek *gnosis.* Note, further, that in some words derived from *gnosis,* the gutteral consonant is pronounced, for example in *acknowledge* or *agnostic.* We may have here a clue of why the initial *g* and *k* become silent. The sequence *kn* or *gn* is more difficult to pronounce in the initial position than when it follows a vowel, as in *acknowledge* or *agnostic.*

This conjecture is consistent with our guess that "mutations" in spoken language have a reproductive advantage when they reduce effort without the loss of information.

Evolution of Artifacts

Another evolutionary process that bears a striking resemblance to biological evolution driven by natural selection is the evolution of artifacts. A complete "fossil record" of technological devices, such as automobiles, telephones, or weapons, can be seen in any museum featuring such exhibits. The first automobiles, called horseless carriages in those days, were almost exact copies of horse-drawn carriages. Some of them even had stands for whips. As they evolved, they lost height and changed shape, becoming more streamlined, evidently in order to minimize air resistance as their speed increased. (Note the slip. I still say "in order that," even though I have called attention to the expulsion of teleology from evolutionary theory.) In the 1920s and 1930s automobiles still had running boards. These finally disappeared, but before they disappeared completely, a "vestige" was still visible in the form of a narrow, completely useless strip below the doors.

Note that, in the process of evolution, automobiles became more and more uniform—an instance of convergent evolution. Here we can identify changes of state as mutations and reproductive success—adaptation to the preferences of the buying public. Reproduction takes place literally on the assembly lines.[2]

Learning as a Selection Process

In drawing a parallel between the evolution of languages and that of a population, we assumed that imitation is a form of reproduction. If we draw this parallel in the context of learning, we can see that certain kinds of learning can also be regarded as analogues of evolution driven by selection.

By learning in this context we mean routine learning, the sort that occurs in operant conditioning, as when an animal is trained to behave

2. The following item appeared in the *Toronto Globe and Mail* (January 28, 1991). "Teddybears evolve as toy stores observe which models sell best, say British biologists. The original teddy had a low forehead and a long snout; the trend, except for the Pooh Bear model, is toward bears with larger foreheads and smaller noses."

in a certain way in response to stimuli. For example, an earthworm can learn which way to turn in a tube in the shape of a T. At the end of the stem, the worm has a "choice" of turning either left or right. If it turns left, it reaches a warm, moist chamber, which, we assume, it "likes," as is evidenced by the way its behavior is modified over a long sequence of trials. If it turns right, it has to crawl over sandpaper, which, we assume, it "dislikes." At first, the worm's choices are random. It turns left or right with approximately equal frequencies. Gradually, however, after hundreds of trials, the left turns become more frequent until the worm no longer turns to the right.

Certain kinds of human behavior are also learned in this way, which behavioral psychologists call operant conditioning. Examples are muscular skills, as in learning to skate or to play a musical instrument. Such skills are learned not by reasoning or by associating ideas, but by going through motions. Initially, one uses one's muscles in a more or less haphazard manner. Some of the movements produce acceptable results, others unacceptable ones. Accordingly, the neural and muscular actions that lead to the former are reinforced (facilitated), while those that lead to the latter are inhibited (blocked). Eventually, the former will replace the latter. We clearly see here the operation of a selection process. Moreover, the selected movements are those better adapted to their "environment." The environment in this case is the learner. The well-adapted movements are those that meet with his or her (usually unconscious) approval.

Having interpreted learning as a selective process, we can now see how the evolution of an institution can be subsumed under such processes, even though the institution itself does not reproduce the way organisms reproduce. To be sure, a bank may establish branches; a university may spread to several campuses. Such proliferation, however, does not apply to institutions in the broad sense, for example, the banking system or the system of higher education. How, then, do institutions evolve?

The "cells" of an institution are its personnel. They are continually replaced. Employees, managers, and officers come and go. In this process, they are selected according to the perceived "needs" of the institution. These perceived needs are determined by the interaction of the institution with its environment, primarily the social environment. As the environment changes, the perceived needs change, and the characteristics of the personnel change. In this way the institution evolves. Namely, the personnel is recruited (i.e., selected) out of the general population in accordance with the changing needs of the institution.

If the institution is a business, for example, this relation is reflected in the relation between the assets and the liabilities of the business. If liabilities exceed assets, the business usually dies. The viability of a political party depends on the relative number of voters that support it. If that number dwindles, the political party dies. Some institutions can adapt to a changing environment. A business that can no longer sell the product it was making may switch to another product. A party that no longer gets support from its program may change that program. The Catholic Church is a very different institution today than what it was in the thirteenth century. It adapted effectively to a changing social and political environment. Another vivid example of institutional evolution is the evolution of monarchy in Europe. At the time the system of sovereign states was firmly established by the Treaty of Westphalia in 1648, the predominant form of rule was absolute monarchy. This form of monarchy was overthrown in England in 1649, briefly restored in somewhat modified form in 1660, and finally replaced by a constitutional monarchy in which the political power of the monarch was explicitly and substantially limited. Thereupon, some monarchies developed in the same direction; others did not.

All four states in which the monarchs stubbornly resisted curtailment of their power, namely Germany, Austria-Hungary, Russia, and Turkey, were defeated in World War I and were overthrown as a consequence of the defeat. The institution survived in Britain, the Low Countries, and in Scandinavia and is now apparently in no danger of extinction. Viability has been conferred on it by adaptation to political democracy, which meant abandonment of all political functions and retention of purely ceremonial ones. Note, however, the vestigial marks of power, such as the title of "head of state," guards in the gaudy attire of past centuries, and so forth.

All of these examples illustrate cultural evolution. This process has all the essentials of biological evolution. It is driven by principles that are in many ways analogous to those driving biological evolution but are also fundamentally different in two ways. We have mentioned one, namely, a different form of reproduction. In the case of language evolution, for example, imitation performs the role of reproduction. In the case of artifacts, imitation was still practiced by individual artisans but, in the industrial age, became replaced by mass duplication in mass production. Note the parallel between the reproduction of artifacts and the reproduction of written material. Manuscript copying corresponds to imitation; printing to mass production.

The most fundamental difference between biological and cultural evolution, however, is in the dependence of the latter on the transmission of acquired characteristics, a process excluded on compelling theoretical grounds from biological evolution. It is the possibility of this sort of "inheritance," rooted in the ability to communicate by symbolic language instead of relying on signals, that has made possible the transmission of acquired characteristics to successive human generations.

Many animals can learn. In the case of learning by conditioning, some animals can learn as quickly as, or more quickly than, humans. But the ability to transmit what they have learned to progeny is extremely limited. Kittens may be able to learn some forms of behavior from their mothers. But knowledge acquired in this way cannot be accumulated. The successive generations of cats are not more "experienced" than their ancestors.

A vital characteristic of human learning is that it does not depend on gradual conditioning. Recall the earthworm taking hundreds of trials and errors to turn left and not right in a T-tube. Compare this type of learning with the way a human learns which of two distinguishable keys opens a door. No more than one trial is required. If a key opens the door, this is it; if it does not, it must be the other one. Note the meaning of "must." It expresses an abbreviated syllogism. "One of these keys opens the door. This one does not. Therefore, the other must." Even if the keys are not distinguishable, they can be made so by marking one key in some way. Learning by deduction is, as far as we know, confined to human beings and depends on the acquisition of a symbolic language.

Not only does deduction drastically reduce the time required for learning, but it also makes possible the transmission of what has been learned to others, in particular to progeny. A young lioness can, perhaps, learn to hunt by imitating her mother. But the lioness cannot say to its offspring, "Always place yourself upwind; otherwise the prey will smell your presence. Zebras run in herds. Therefore, in tracking a zebra, always wait until one who may be weak or ill falls behind. . . . With an antelope, you have a different problem. . . ."

The most significant difference between human and nonhuman languages is that only the former can express *conditionality.* Initiating a young warrior, an old warrior of the May Enge tribe instructs him as follows.

> Never waste arrows on a difficult target, such as your enemy's head; always aim at his body.
>
> Do not start to dodge until your adversary has drawn his bow to the point of release, for then he will have difficulty in aiming anew. . . .
>
> If you can see the pale shaft of your enemy's arrow in flight, remain still, for that arrow will miss you, but if you see the point approaching you like a black insect, duck or dodge. (Meggitt 1977, 62)

It is the ability to express conditionality that enables humans to imagine situations without actually experiencing them. It enables them to go through a process of trial and error in their heads, thus drastically shortening the time of learning and avoiding situations where an error may result in injury or death. Above all, transmission of knowledge by language makes accumulation of knowledge in successive generations possible.

These three faculties, learning by reasoning, learning by imitation, and transmitting what has been learned to future generations (what Korzybski called time binding), provide a basis for a mode of evolution fundamentally different from biological evolution, namely, cultural evolution. As far as we know, this evolutionary process uniquely distinguishes the human species. Other species have these three faculties in elementary form. Learning by reasoning (rather than by conditioning) has been observed in apes.[3] Some animals, primarily carnivores, appear to learn behavioral patterns from their parents. Imitation is not uncommon among primates and birds. Some birds, for instance, learn to "speak," aping remarkably accurately the accent and intonation of a human speaker. All of these processes, however, are quite limited in time and space. In contrast, in humans, a behavior pattern can spread rapidly and widely like a pandemic and may become permanently incorporated in the behavioral repertoire and passed on to future generations.

3. After unsuccessfully trying to reach a banana by jumping at a bunch hung high, a chimpanzee was observed carrying a crate from the corner of the cage, placing it under the bunch, and then getting a banana by jumping from the crate.

A faculty that is unquestionably unique in human beings is the preservation of what has been learned by means of more or less permanent records. At present, a large variety of modes of preservation exists: print, microfilm, recordings, and so forth. These records have enormously increased human memory capacity, where by memory capacity in this context we mean that of the entire human race rather than of individuals. Spatial compression of records, for example, microfilm and electronic storage, has made this capacity practically unlimited. The contents of a large volume can now be "inscribed" on a head of a pin.

A fundamental difference between biological and social evolution is in the circumstance that an evolving feature of cultural evolution does not depend on the biological reproductive success of its carrier as does an evolving biological trait. To see this, consider the evolution of some clearly discernible cultural trait, say a particular musical form. In Western musical tradition, compositions are preserved in written form and constitute a sector of the noosphere accessible to musicians. Much of the musical education of composers consists of becoming familiarized with this fund. In learning to compose, imitation plays an important part. Of course, every composition should be different, and this requirement provides the basis of variation. Selection depends on musical taste, which, in turn, is developed through interactions between composers and the listening public. Here, then, are the makings of an evolutionary process that can be traced as clearly as the evolution of a species recorded in fossils.

As an example, it is instructive to examine the evolution of an important form developed in occidental instrumental music called the sonata. Originally a composition for a single instrument, this form spread to chamber music (combinations of few instruments) and to orchestral music in the form of a symphony. All the basic features of the form were preserved in this development: predominance of three or four movements (self-contained parts); a typical structure, at least of the first movement, built around the juxtaposition of two themes, one usually energetic, the other more tranquil; and an alternation of quick and slow tempos of the movements. Among these features is the form of the third of four movements, namely, the form of the minuet. This movement underwent an evolution of its own particularly conspicuous in Beethoven's sonatas and symphonies. In some of these compositions, its tempo was increased, transforming a smooth, gracious piece with mildly marked rhythm into an extremely rapid one with a driving, strongly accented, staccato rhythm. The movement was now called a scherzo, which means joke in Italian. The liveliness of the piece may have suggested humor. However, in the treatment of the romantic composers (Beethoven among them), the mood of the movement also underwent a "mutation." It became sardonic, at times demonic. Many music lovers will agree with this interpretation of Beethoven's scherzos, particularly those of the Third and Ninth symphonies.

Aside from the inadmissibility of ascribing all these changes to mutations or recombinations of composers' genes, it seems futile to see a biological reproductive advantage accruing to composers adapting innovative features.

In general, the irrelevance of biological reproductive advantage to directions of cultural evolution is quite apparent, especially in cultures influenced by Western civilization. For one thing, the dramatic reduction of infant mortality in these milieus has reduced the effectiveness of natural selection to practically zero except in the case of gross congenital deficiencies. What is even more important is the spread of birth control techniques that enable practically everyone to choose the rate of reproduction. Finally, an important determinant of reproductive success in nonhuman species, namely, the opportunity to inseminate more females, repeatedly cited as the origin of the "agressive instinct" in males, cannot be expected to operate in humans. The promiscuous male may have contacts with more women than the monogamous one, but this does not mean that he is likely to have more children, who, according to the natural selection hypothesis, are supposed to inherit his inclination to promiscuity. In short, psychological traits often ascribed to "human nature" (by which genetically determined characteristics are presumably meant) are more reasonably ascribed to the driving forces of cultural evolution, which depend on mechanisms not operating in the evolution of nonhumans. Possibly aggressiveness, commonly attributed to males, also belongs to this category of traits.

The persistent efforts of sociobiologists intent on tracing strands of cultural evolution to genetic variation and natural selection seem to be misguided. Yet they are understandable on three grounds. First, rigorously defensible demonstrations of the genetic basis of some cultural traits would yield a high payoff in the currency of academic prestige, because the a priori likelihood of such a confirmation is, in the minds of skeptics, small. Second, once a path has been beaten in some field of science, it tends to be followed, especially if marked successes have been achieved along it. Sociobiologists have, indeed, scored important successes in explaining complex behavior patterns of animals by classical mechanisms of variation and natural selection. Sociobiology has become an important subdiscipline of biological science. Persons active in this subdiscipline are familiar with its methods, its language, and its problems. They are "at home" in this field. It is not surprising that they continue to think along the lines of their teachers and transmit these ways of thinking to their students. In seeking new territories into which to extend their successful techniques, they have undertaken to bring cultural evolution into the realm of sociobiology.

Finally, in discussing the philosophical underpinnings of sociobiology, the ideological issue cannot be avoided, not because this and related issues are necessarily incorporated in the sociobiological approach but because they have repeatedly been raised. On occasions, sociobiologists have been accused of racism. There may be a hint of guilt through association in this accusation, since racists, too, emphasize what they believe to be genetic factors in characteristics of identifiable human groups, in particular "visible minorities." For a while, acrimonious polemics raged around the views of J. P. Rushton (1988), who concluded, on the basis of sociobiological data, that Orientals were morally superior to whites and whites to blacks. It is possible that sociobiologists who find the accusation of racism leveled against Rushton and others groundless would be motivated to persist stubbornly in pursuing research of this sort as an act of defiance.

In my view, the discovery of genetically determined differences between human groups can be a valuable contribution to knowledge, provided politically motivated conclusions are exposed for what they are. Moreover, in all likelihood, such differences will be shown to be confined to features that, in an enlightened social mileu, would carry no trace of opprobrium. If, contrary to expectations, some differences in traits that are associated with morally sensitive characteristics are traced to genetic factors, criticism should be directed at defects in the social milieu that ascribes such opprobrium to such traits. Few would object to research that might disclose genetically determined differential predispositions to certain organic diseases. Research on probable genetic bases of behavioral or temperamental predispositions could make equally valuable contributions to knowledge.

Ironically, the ideological overtones of favorable and unfavorable attitudes toward sociobiological theories of human behavior are the opposite of what they were toward the antecedents of sociobiology in Darwin's time. Then it was the opponents of the theory of evolution, deriving their views from religious orthodoxy, who insisted that man, as the possessor of a soul, was unique, while the political left, to which most atheists and agnostics adhered, insisted that man was part of nature. Now, the sociobiologists who emphasize man's prehuman origins are thought to lean toward the political right, while their opponents emphasize man's uniqueness based on the uniquely human mechanisms of cultural evolution. It is worth noting that the idea of man's uniqueness and the view of man as an integral part of the biosphere (instead of its self-appointed master) are by no means incompatible.[4]

---

4. D. P. Barash, defending sociology against accusations of racism, sexism, and defense of the status quo, writes: "We are indeed unusual in our extreme development of social learning and cultural traditions, but it seems unlikely that culture has completely freed Homo sapiens from biology" (1982, 161–62).

6

The Evolution of Cooperation

As we have seen, sociobiologists attempt to reestablish the dominant role of heredity as a determinant of human behavior. In particular, they seek to develop a genetic theory of cultural evolution. In the minds of many, these attempts are associated with the ideology of the political right. We mentioned the controversy around the ideas of J. P. Rushton (1988), a proponent of sociobiological theories of cultural evolution, who was accused of racism for suggesting, on the basis of behavioral differences observed in people of different ancestry, that Orientals were morally superior to whites and whites to blacks. Analysis of this controversy and of the evidence marshaled by Professor Rushton in support of his theory are beyond the scope of this book. We will, however, lend some credence to the idea that the ideational framework of sociobiology has some affinity for the ideological framework of the contemporary political right.

The human traits of altruism and selfishness are seen by the adherents of the two political camps (the Left and the Right) in different ways with regard to their genesis and their implications for the social order. In our day, the Right is characterized by an affinity for individualism; the Left by an affinity for collectivism. These affinities reflect attitudes toward an economic system based on free enterprise and one based on cooperative enterprise or nationalized means of production, respectively. A clear expression of individualism is found in our previous citation from Adam Smith's *Wealth of Nations* (chap. 4). It is interesting to note the attempt of P. H. Wicksteed (1933), writing a century-and-a-half later, to remove the stigma of selfishness from individualism. He calls the principle underlying the free enterprise system "non-tuism," an ethically neutral synonym of egoism. Somewhat later, Buchanan and Tullock, in writing about the U.S. political system, called their approach "methodological individualism" (1962). Here, too, the qualification, methodological, was meant to remove the association with egoism. It was meant to convey the idea that individualism was used in constructing a descriptive, not necessarily a normative (value-oriented) theory of political behavior.

Methodological individualism is a reductionist approach. It represents an attempt to reduce the behavior of a collective to the behavior of the individuals who comprise it, whereby each pursues his own interests. It is in this way that each individual is pictured as selfish regardless whether his behavior hurts or benefits others.

Now, in the context of the theory of evolution by natural selection, individualist and collectivist outlooks are reflected in the attitude to the theory of group selection. From the collectivist perspective (as well as from the perspective of an organismic system theory to be discussed subsequently), a collective can be regarded as a (generalized) organism and, therefore, can evolve like any other type of organism. We have seen how the evolution of such generalized organisms can be explained within the paradigm of natural selection (chap. 5). However, from the individualist perspective, a reduction of the evolution of collectives to the evolution of individuals comprising them is more attractive.

The sociobiologists have succeeded in carrying reductionism to its extreme. A seminal work representing the reductionist point of view in the theory of evolution is *The Selfish Gene* (Dawkins 1976). The discovery of the gene as a physical entity was a milestone in biology, particularly in the theory of evolution, just as the discovery of the atom as a physical entity was a milestone in the physical sciences. The Darwinian idea of diversity in a population as the basis of its evolutionary potential was given concrete meaning. Diversity meant diversity in the gene pool. The idea of fitness was endowed with strictly operational meaning; fitness means reproductive advantage and nothing else. Organisms do not possess reproductive advantage because they are "fit." Organisms are seen to be fit because they are observed to have reproductive advantage. Finally, reproductive advantage is the exclusive possession of the gene, for it is the gene that is the carrier of inherited traits; if these become predominant in the population, it is because copies of the genes that carry them have been reproduced in greater numbers.

Now the gene is regarded as the carrier of a "program" (a term borrowed from computer science) that directs the development of some trait in an organism as it develops from the zygote (the fertilized egg). Genes are thought of as specializing in particular traits. These may be anatomical (say the size of an organ) or physiological (say the ability to produce a particular enzyme) or psychological (say some predisposition). It is not clear just how much of a trait, which we recognize holistically, a gene can determine, but this is not important. Important is the assumption that predispositions to particular forms of behavior can be determined by genes or, perhaps, by combinations of genes.

Assume now that a certain gene produces a tendency in the organism in which it is embedded to behave altruistically toward individuals that are closely related to it. Altruistic behavior in this context can be easily defined. It is the sort of behavior that enhances the reproductive success of the individual at whom it is directed at the expense of the reproductive success of the altruistically behaving organism. To make sense of this assumption, we must somehow specify how the altruistic organism recognizes close kin. This is easy in the case of birds and mammals. The young of these species depend for some time on parental care. Consequently, they stay in close proximity of the parent(s) and to each other, that is, the siblings. Now in the sense of genetic endowment, siblings (litter mates) and offspring are the closest kin. Therefore, at least during the period of dependence, the problem of recognizing close kin does not arise.

In conferring reproductive advantage on closely related individuals, the altruistically behaving organism automatically confers a reproductive advantage on the beneficiary's genes. But if the recipients of altruistic behavior are close relatives, they are carriers of many genes that also belong to the altruist. Therefore, in behaving altruistically, the altruist confers reproductive advantage on its own genes. Recognition of this phenomenon justifies the expression "selfish gene." Namely, in producing a soma inclined to behave altruistically, a gene enhances its own reproductive advantage (realized in the reproductive advantage of closely related individuals.) Moreover, the gene has no other "interests" except to reproduce as many copies of itself as possible. Of course, we speak of interests figuratively. It is a habit carried over from the days when teleological causation was taken seriously in biology. Purging our language of teleology, we say those genes are fit that enjoy reproductive success. And those genes enjoy reproductive success that produce somas that are predisposed to altruistic behavior.

If ascribing Right political bias to sociobiologists is justified, this explanation of altruism as a manifestation of a predisposition that, in the final analysis, turns out to be selfishness strengthens the case. It must be admitted, however, that this reduction of altruism to selfishness is considerably more sophisticated than what, following the cue of D. S. Wilson (1989), we would call "cheap selfishness." By cheap, Wilson meant not something reprehensible but something trivial. Thus, many argue that altruistic behavior is "really" selfish behavior, because the altruist derives satisfaction from behaving altruistically, hence, in the final analysis, behaves "selfishly." If everyone is selfish, however, there is no point in distinguishing between selfishness and altruism. In other words, the word *selfishness* carries no semantic load (distinguishing potential) and could therefore be dropped from the vocabulary.

What the "selfish gene" theory shows is that altruistic behavior on the part of the *whole organism* can be reduced to selfish behavior on the part of the *gene.* In this context, selfish and altruistic are distinguished. The altruist enhances reproductive success of others at the expense of his or her own reproductive success. The selfish gene does nothing but enhance its own reproductive success, possibly at the expense of the reproductive success of other genes.

A dramatic manifestation of altruism induced in an individual by his selfish genes is seen in the sex act of some organisms. The sex act can be regarded as the most fundamental cooperative act in the biosphere. In some organisms, the sex act is also an instance of the most extreme altruism. After performing it, the male ant usually soon dies: he is of no further use to the species. The drones are usually killed by the worker bees after they have done their duty. Among some spiders, the female devours the male immediately after copulation. We might, in our anthropocentric naïveté, suppose that the male "knows" what awaits him, for he apparently tries to hit and run. But the actual danger is not sufficient to prevent him from doing what he must do to ensure the perpetuation of the species.

How Important Is Kinship in Humans?

As we have seen, the most direct way of explaining altruistic or cooperative behavior as an instance of selfishness is to relate the altruistic behavior of the whole organism to the way the organism has been "programmed" by his selfish genes. This explanation is convincing if altruistic behavior is directed exclusively at kin. Indeed, the preferential treatment of kin in preindustrial societies lends support to the theory that cultural as well as biological evolution of humans is driven by Darwinian natural selection. For instance, a stranger coming into an

Australian aboriginal village is likely to be questioned by a village elder (versed in genealogical complexities) to ascertain whether the newcomer is related to anyone in the village. If such a relationship can be established, he is admitted; otherwise he is killed.

It is equally noteworthy, however, that since contacts were made with enforceable prejudices against killing strangers, ways were devised to circumvent this rule. For instance, an anthropologist coming to study the aborigines in their habitat is customarily assigned a fictitious kin relationship to someone in the village; on this basis he is allowed to stay.

The old custom lends support to the theory relating the evolution of altruism (or empathy or cooperation) to natural selection. But the circumvention of the custom demonstrates that, among humans, the genetic imperative can be overridden. In fact, the very concept of kinship has undergone a "retrograde" evolution in industrial urban societies. It has been impoverished rather than enriched. Vocabularies of some languages still contain a plethora of kinship terms that have become inessential in modern society. In Russian, for example, fathers-in-law and mothers-in-law are designated by different terms depending on whether they are parents of the husband or the wife. Brothers-in-law and sisters-in-law are also distinguished in this way. In many cultures, sharp distinctions are made between parallel and cross cousins with regard to permitted or prohibited intermarriage. Presumably, these distinctions are carryovers from a time when the degree of kinship played a much more prominent role in relations among people.

In modern urban societies, practically the only family relations that "count" (i.e., carry certain obligations) are those in the nuclear family. Extended families are likely to be scattered far and wide. Hardly anyone keeps track of cousins. On the other hand, the practice of adoption establishes parent-child relationship between genetically unrelated individuals. Frequently, persons closest to us are our associates, persons who have a similar outlook or similar tastes or similar politics, rather than kin.

The evolution of cooperation can be explained without reference to the preferential treatment of kin, namely, by the effects of reciprocity. Reciprocity is manifested in "mirror image" behavior patterns. Here, no more than in the case of altruism toward kin, ethical considerations need not be invoked. All that is required is the ability to recognize some behavior pattern characterizing another individual and to reciprocate it.

Individuals reciprocating each other's behavior need not be genetically close. They need only to share the propensity to reciprocate. In fact, reciprocity can be generalized to include complementary instead of identical behavior patterns, frequently observed in symbiotic relationships. This form of cooperation may involve individuals of different species or even phyla.

A seminal paper exploring the reproductive advantage conferred by reciprocity was published by Maynard Smith and Price (1973). Observations that directed the attention of these biologists to this question were of restraint in combat characteristic of animals that resort to fighting, usually for possession of females or territory. These combats seldom end in fatalities. And this seems to be due to the circumstance that the weapons available to these animals are usually not lethal. Observe the swept-back horns on some mountain goats. If we believed in providential explanations of adaption, we would say that these horns were designed this way so that they would not do serious injury in fighting. However, we have already rejected providential explanations in favor of explanations consistent with the theory of natural selection.

Maynard Smith and Price subjected explanations of this sort to experimental testing. They simulated repeated encounters between pairs of animals of different types. A type was defined by the sort of strategy an animal used in fighting. Specifically, it could do three things. It could fight fiercely. This type of fighting was designated as *D* (for dangerous). It could fight with restraint (*C* for conventional fighting). Or it could retreat (*R*). Each encounter consisted of a series of "moves" used alternatively by the "players."

The following were five types of players, each characterized by a particular strategy of fighting, that is, by the choice of the mode of fighting in response to the mode chosen by the opponent, that Maynard Smith and Price identified.

> *The "Mouse."* This type of player never uses *D*. If the opponent plays *D*, the Mouse immediately retreats. Otherwise, it uses *C* until the combat has lasted a fixed number of moves.
>
> *The "Hawk."* This type always starts the combat with *D*. It continues to use *D* until it is seriously injured or until the opponent retreats.
>
> *The "Bully."* Starts the combat with *D*. Uses *D* in response to *C* (i.e., bullies the opponent who fights with restraint). Uses *C* when

the opponent resorts to *D*. Retreats when the opponent uses *D* the second time.

The "Retaliator." If making the first move, uses *C*. Thereafter uses *C* in response to the opponent's *C*, *D* in response to the opponent's *D*. Retreats if the combat has lasted a preassigned number of moves.

The "Prober-Retaliator." If making the first move, plays *C*; likewise in response to the opponent's *C* with high probability. "Probes," that is, plays *D* (with low probability) to the opponent's C, provided the contest has not ended. After "probing," reverts to *C* if the opponent retaliates with *D*. However, if the opponent continues to play *C*, takes advantage of this by continuing to play *D*. After receiving a probe, plays *D* with high probability.

It remains to specify the probabilities of the various events. Maynard Smith and Price used the following in their simulation. Serious injury on any move was received with probability 0.10 if the opponent used *D*. The Prober-Retaliator probed on the first move or after the opponent played *C* with probability 0.05. The Retaliator and the Prober-Retaliator always retaliated with *D* against *D*.

Finally, the following payoffs were assigned to the outcomes. The payoff for "winning" the encounter (i.e., if the opponent retreats or is incapacitated by serious injury) was 60. The payoff for receiving serious injury was −100. The payoff for each *D* received if not seriously injured was −2. The payoff for saving time and energy (retreating without being seriously injured) varied from 0 (if the combat lasted a preassigned maximum number of moves) to 20 for very short combats. The results of the simulation are shown in table 1.

The entries in each row of table 1 represent the average payoffs to each type of fighter represented by that row when it was paired with the type of player represented by the column. For example, the Bully received an average payoff of 80 per encounter when paired with the Mouse and an average of 11.9 when paired with the Retaliator. The payoffs can be interpreted as reproduction rates. It remains to deduce the ultimate fate of this population resulting from the differential reproduction rates.

The ultimate fate of a population acted upon by natural selection under constant environmental conditions is characterized by the distribution of genotypes in the population after natural selection has acted

TABLE 1. Average Payoffs in Simulated Intraspecific Contests for Five Different Strategies

Contestant Receiving Payoff	Contestant from Whom Payoff Is Received				
	Mouse	Hawk	Bully	Retaliator	Prober
Mouse	29.0	19.5	19.5	29.0	17.2
Hawk	80.0	−19.5	74.6	−18.1	−18.9
Bully	80.0	4.9	41.5	11.9	11.2
Retaliator	29.0	−22.3	57.1	29.0	23.1
Prober	56.7	−20.1	59.4	26.9	21.9

Source: Data from Maynard Smith and Price 1973.

on it for a long time. In our example, the genotypes are represented by the fighting types. Ultimately, the overwhelming majority of the population will be of a single type if the corresponding strategy is a so-called evolutionary stable strategy (ESS). This means that a population consisting of such individuals cannot be "invaded" by individuals using any other strategy. If such "alien" individuals are produced by mutations, they will be eliminated by natural selection.

The precise definition of an evolutionary stable strategy is given by the following conditions. Let I and J be two strategies. Let $E_I(I)$ be the reproduction rate of a strategy when it is used against itself (i.e., the corresponding type confronts one like itself), and let $E_I(J)$ be the reproduction rate of J, when it is used against I. Then I is an ESS if either $E_I(I) > E_I(J)$ for all $J \neq J$ or $E_I(I) = E_I(J)$ and $E_J(I) > E_J(J)$. In words, either I must be "best" against every other strategy used against it, or, if I and J are equally good against I, then I is better against J than J is against itself.

From table 1 we can see which, if any, of the strategies used in the simulation appear to be evolutionary stable strategies. For instance, Hawk, when used against itself, receives a payoff of −19.5. Retaliator and Prober-Retaliator do worse, getting −22.3 and −20.1, respectively. But Mouse and Bully do better. Therefore, Hawk is not an ESS. Similarly, examining other columns, we see that neither Mouse nor Bully are evolutionary stable strategies. Only Retaliator is an ESS and Prober-Retaliator is almost an ESS. What can we expect to be the ultimate fate of this population? Maynard Smith and Price write:

> It will come to consist mainly of Retaliators and Prober-Retaliators, with the other strategies maintained at a low frequency by mutation. The balance between the two main types will depend

> on the frequency of Mouse, since the habit of probing is only an advantage against Mouse. For the particular values in Table 1, it can be shown that if the frequency of Mouse if greater than 7%, Prober-Retaliator will replace Retaliator as the predominant type. It is worth noting that a real population would contain young, senile, diseased and injured individuals adopting strategy Mouse for non-genetic reasons. (1973, 16)

Interpreting the encounters as intraspecific combats for possession of females, Maynard Smith and Price discuss this result as follows.

> Briefly, the reason that conflict limitation increases individual fitness is that retaliation decreases the fitness of Hawks, while the existence of possible future mating opportunities reduces the loss from retreating uninjured. (16)

Interpreting the encounters as confrontations between states that could result in war, compromise, or victory for one side intimidating the other, we can examine the results of changing the parameters. For example, Maynard Smith and Price point out that changing the probability of serious injury from a single *D* from 0.10 to 0.90 would give an advantage to a "preemptive strike" (unprovoked *D*) and would make Hawk an ESS. Another way of making selection favor aggression would be by giving the same penalty for retreating uninjured (give in to the aggressor immediately) as for receiving a serious injury.

Social Traps

Models of conflict of this type have shed considerable light on the possible ways cooperation could have evolved in a population composed of selfish individuals. However, long before this question was raised in a biological context, experimental games were used to illustrate a type of situation frequently occurring in human conflicts. In these situations, it is quite clear what a "rational" individual should do in order to maximize the expected payoff of the outcome, where the outcome depends not only on his choice among available alternative courses of action (strategies) but also on everyone else's choices. It turns out, however, that if every participant in the situation of this sort acts "rationally," that is, with the view of maximizing his own payoff, everyone, including himself, is worse off than if they had acted with the view of maximizing everyone's payoff, that is, in accord with collective rationality. It is for this reason that I put "rational" in quotation marks—to point out that in situations of this sort, the term *rationality* does not have an unambiguous meaning. Specifically, individual rationality must be distinguished from collective rationality. Situations of this sort have been called social traps.

Consider the simplest social trap. It is represented by a game that has been widely used in social psychological experiments. In this game, each of two players chooses between two strategies, a "cooperative" one (labeled *C*) and a "noncooperative" or "defecting" one (labeled *D*). The choices of strategies are made independently. The payoffs accruing to the players after each play of the game depend on their choices of strategy. If both choose *C*, each gets a moderate win. If both choose *D*, each gets a moderate loss. If one chooses *C* while the other chooses *D*, the former suffers a large loss, while the latter gets a large win. The game has been named Prisoner's Dilemma.

In Prisoner's Dilemma, the choice of *D* is individually rational. It turns out that choosing *D* while the coplayer chooses *C* results in a larger win than choosing *C*. Also, choosing *D* while the coplayer chooses *D* results in a smaller loss than choosing *C*. Since *D* brings a better payoff than *C* regardless of the coplayer's choice, it follows that *D* is unconditionally the better choice. Nevertheless, if both players choose *C*, both are better off (get a modest win) than if both choose *D* (suffering a moderate loss). Therein lies the social trap.

During the last thirty years or so a great number of experiments have been performed where human subjects were asked to choose *C* or *D* under various conditions. The results are complex and, at times, richly instructive. For example, it is by no means the case that human subjects invariably choose *D* (the individually "rational" strategy), which may be due to a number of reasons, including preference for cooperation under certain conditions, even when noncooperation appears to be more advantageous.

Especially instructive are experiments with Prisoner's Dilemma where subjects are asked to play the game several times in succession, with the results of each play being announced. Some very long sequences of plays of this sort have been observed. The protocols of response show distinct learning effects. In the early phases of the sequence, the frequency of *C* choices decreases, as if the subjects learned the relative disadvantage of choosing *C* (since it results in a worse outcome regardless of whether the coplayer chooses *C* or *D*). However, if the sequence is long enough, the initial decline in cooperation is followed by a recovery. The subjects seem to learn that it "pays" to cooperate. This learning may well take place unconsciously, as it were. A choice of *D* is likely to elicit a choice of *D* by the coplayer on the next play and so may become inhibited in the long run. The simultaneous choice of *C* is rewarding for both; eventually the cooperative response may become "fixated." However, the defecting response may also become fixated, because once the players get into the *D* "trap" (simultaneous choice of *D*), attempts to get out of it unilaterally (by switching to *C*) are immediately punishing. In fact, long sequences of plays eventually exhibit both "lock-ins"—on *CC* and on *DD*—while the asymmetric responses *CD* and *DC* are extinguished. Thus, two types of player pairs emerge—cooperating pairs and defecting pairs.

Let us now analyze the iterated Prisoner's Dilemma game with the view of identifying a rational strategy. "Strategy" in this context means a plan of action that specifies the choice between *C* and *D* on each play, which may depend on the outcomes of all the preceding plays. Examples of strategies of this sort may be among the following:

> "I shall choose *C* on the first play. Thereafter, I shall choose *C* if the coplayer chose more *C*'s than *D*'s on the previous plays; otherwise *D*."
>
> "I shall choose *D* on the first play. Thereafter, I shall choose *C* only if the coplayer chose *C* on three consecutive plays."
>
> "On each play, I shall choose *C* only if the coplayer chose *C* on the preceding play. (On the first play I shall toss a fair coin to decide between *C* and *D*.)"
>
> "I shall choose *D* unconditionally on every play."
>
> "I shall choose *C* unconditionally on every play."

Note that, whereas in a single play of Prisoner's Dilemma individual rationality dictates *D*, this choice does not seem as compelling in iterated play. A choice of *D* is likely to elicit a retaliatory *D* on the next play, and if one continues to play *D*, *DD* will result to the disadvantage of both. In fact, it may be reasoning of this sort that leads to the "lock-ins" on *CC* frequently observed in iterated play of Prisoner's Dilemma. Nevertheless, it is easy to show that if the number of iterations is known to both players, and if the players carry out the strategic analysis to the end, the only rational strategy appears to be an unconditional choice of *D* from the beginning to the end.

To see this, observe that the rational choice on the last play of the iteration must be *D*, since "deterrence" is not effective on that play (no retaliation can follow). The rational choice on the last play having been determined, the question arises what the rational choice is on the penultimate play. But if the outcome of the last play is a foregone conclusion, the penultimate play becomes the "last" play, and the same reasoning applies to it. Continuing the reasoning, we see that *D* becomes the rational choice on every play. We must conclude that two "rational" players playing iterated Prisoner's Dilemma for 100, 1,000, or 1,000,000 iterations of the game must play *D* unconditionally throughout, incurring a loss at every play instead of a win, which they would have gotten, had they both played *C* throughout.

The question now arises of what is the "optimal" strategy for playing iterated Prisoner's Dilemma, if such exists. An attempt to answer this question empirically was made by Axelrod (1984). He announced an iterated Prisoner's Dilemma tournament. Interested persons were invited to submit strategies for playing the iterated game 200 times. As noted, a strategy must be a prescription for choosing either *C* or *D* on every play of the game, the choice being possibly determined by the outcomes of all (or some) of the preceding plays.

Every strategy submitted would be matched with every other submitted strategy (and also with itself). Since a strategy is a complete set of instructions about how to choose the response on each play, given all previous responses, two strategies matched with each other would completely determine the protocol of the iterated game and, with it, the "score" obtained by each strategy, that is, the total number of points accumulated in the 200 plays, where the points represent the payoffs associated with each combination of choices. In this tournament, each player received 3 points if both played *C*, 1 point if each played *D*. If one played *C* while the other chose *D*, the former would receive zero points, the latter 5 points. It is easy to verify that these payoffs satisfy the definition of Prisoner's Dilemma.

In all, fourteen strategies were submitted in this tournament. Each was matched with each, including itself. Besides the submitted strategies, a "random" strategy participated in the tournament, namely, one where each play was either *C* or *D* with equal probabilities.

The total score of each strategy was the number of points accumulated in all the encounters. The highest total score was obtained by a strategy named Tit-for-Tat. This strategy prescribes *C* on the first play and thereafter the choice that imitates the coplayer's preceding choice (hence the name). In this tournament, Tit-for-Tat got the highest score.

The results of this tournament were publicized, together with the strategies submitted and the total score obtained by each. A second tournament was then announced. This time, sixty-three strategies were submitted. The contestants varied in background. Among them were psychologists, economists, mathematicians, and political scientists. Six countries were represented. Tit-for-Tat was again submitted, in fact, by the same contestant, who was again the only one submitting it. It again obtained the highest total score.

The result is paradoxical, because it is clear, after a moment's reflection, that Tit-for-Tat can never obtain a higher score than any program with which it is matched. The only way one program can obtain a higher score than its coplayer in an iterated Prisoner's Dilemma is by choosing *D* more frequently than the latter. Observe that every time both programs choose *C*, they both get the same number of points (3); every time they both choose *D* they again get the same number of points (1). Only when a program chooses *D*, while the coplayer program chooses *C*, does the former get more points (5) than the latter (zero). But Tit-for-Tat can never choose more *D*'s than the program with which it is matched, for the only time it can choose *D* is following the coplayer's choice of *D*. Consequently, it cannot possibly obtain a higher score than the coplayer. How, then, was it possible for Tit-for-Tat to get the highest score in the tournament? This happened because other programs, playing against each other and, incidentally, against themselves, reduced each other's scores.

To see this result clearly, imagine a tournament in which just three programs participate. One, All *D*, plays *D* unconditionally; one, All *C*, plays *C* unconditionally; one plays Tit-for-Tat. Each is matched with the other two and with itself, and each encounter consists of 200 plays. The payoffs are the same as in Axelrod's tournament.

All *D* matched against All *C* gets a score of $5 \times 200 = 1000$—the highest possible score. Matched against itself, it will get 200, since all the outcomes in this encounter will be *DD*. Matched against Tit-for-Tat, All *D* will get 204 points, since it will get 5 points on the first play (having played

D against Tit-for-Tat's *C*) and 1 point on each of the 199 plays thereafter, since Tit-for-Tat will also play *D* in response to each *D* by All *D*. Accordingly, All *D*'s total score will be $1,000+204+200=1,404$ points.

All *C* matched against All *D* will get 0 points; matched against All *C*, it will get 600 points; matched against Tit-for-Tat, it will also get 600 points, since that sequence, like the one with All *C*, will also consist of all *C*'s. Thus, All *C* will get a total of 1,200 points.

Tit-for-Tat matched against itself will get 600 points, the same when matched against all *C*. Matched against All *D*, it will get 199 points—0 on the first play and 1 on each play thereafter. Its total score will be $600+600+199=1,399$ points.

So far, the result corresponds to the intuitive conclusion: All *D*, which got the higher score than the coplayer when matched with All *C* and when matched with Tit-for-Tat, also got the highest total score. It was clearly the "strongest" program. All *C*, the "pacifistic" program, was the "weakest."

Suppose, then, the "weakest" program is eliminated, and the contest is repeated. All *D* matched against itself will get 200 points as before; matched against Tit-for-Tat, it will get 204 points, as before, that is, 404 points in all. Tit-for-Tat, on the other hand, will get 600 points when matched against itself and 199 points when matched against All *D*, or 799 points in all. It will be the winner of the tournament.

In general, the success of Tit-for-Tat in a tournament of this sort will be assured if the number of Tit-for-Tat programs participating is sufficiently large compared with the numbers of All *D* and All *C* programs. In general, suppose these numbers are given by t, d, and c, respectively. The Tit-for-Tat's total score will be $600t+199d+600c$. All *D*'s score will be $204t+200d+1000c$. All *C*'s score will be $600c+600t$. Hence, All *C*'s score will be larger than All *D*'s if $396t>200d+400c$. This inequality can always be satisfied if t is sufficiently larger than d and c. Since Tit-for-Tat's score will always be larger than All *C*'s, it will be the winner of the tournament.

The most aggressive program, All *D*, will do well in any environment in which "nonretaliating programs" such as All *C* are sufficiently numerous. However, the facile conclusion that success in a tournament of this sort results primarily from readiness to retaliate alone is not warranted. To be sure, Tit-for-Tat is certain to retaliate. But it is also certain to "forgive," that is, to respond immediately with *C* to the coplayer's *C* regardless of how many times the coplayer chose *D*.

In fact, an analysis of the programs submitted to the two tournaments arranged by Axelrod revealed that those that got the highest scores all resembled Tit-for-Tat in four ways. All of them were "nice" in the sense that they were never the first to "defect" (resort to *D*). They were all "provokable": they always responded with *D* to the coplayer's *D*, thus punishing defection. They were also "forgiving." That is, they always reverted to *C* after the coplayer reverted to *C* after having played *D* any number of times. Finally, they were all simple. For example, Tit-for-Tat required only 4 lines of FORTRAN to be programmed. Some of the programs submitted to the two tournaments required over 100 lines. On the whole, they did not do very well.

Following the analysis of the results of the tournament, Axelrod resorted to "experimental evolution," a simulation of the sort performed by Maynard Smith and Price. His "genotypes" were selected programs from the tournaments. Several of these constituted the initial population, that is, a population consisting of different "genotypes." Natural selection was simulated in the following way. After each encounter (i.e., play against another program or itself), each program "reproduced" in the sense that copies of it were introduced into the "population." The reproduction rates were directly related to the scores achieved by the programs in each round of the tournament. Thus, the scores reflected the different reproduction rates: after repeated encounters, the genetic composition of the population underwent a change, as expected. Ultimately, the relative frequency of Tit-for-Tat became by far the largest. The genotype represented by Tit-for-Tat became the predominant one in the population. In this way, a "mini-evolution" was demonstrated in the laboratory, whereby "cooperation" emerged as a consequence of "natural selection," that is, independently of ethical or ideological factors.

From these exercises, we see how game-theoretic analysis can be incorporated in a theory of evolution. It seems strange to speak of strategies adopted by organisms that cannot be supposed to engage in analysis. However, in this context, a strategy means simply a way of relating to the environment. For instance, a plant can be said to "choose" between two strategies to procure water. It may grow long roots so as to reach water lying deep below the surface, or it may grow short roots for reaching water near the surface. Alternately, it may develop long roots growing only in horizontal directions "in search" of water near the surface. This figurative language should not lead us to believe that the plant is guided by purposes or anticipates the consequences of its "choices." The different strategies represent only different genotypes that result from mutations or recombinations of genes.

This model reveals the dependence of the "success" of a strategy on how many others are using the same strategy. If, in a population of plants, only a few utilize surface water, then there may be enough surface water for all, and the strategy may be a successful one. But the success of the strategy is reflected in the reproductive advantage of the genotype using it. Thus, the population of the short-root variety may increase, and with it the intensity of the competition for surface water. Under these circumstances, the long-root strategy may become more advantageous.

We observe similar situations in human affairs. Persons driving to work listen to radio broadcasts that inform them of traffic conditions. Some streets are crowded, others relatively free. The immediate impulse is to go to the less crowded streets. But if many motorists do the same thing, the streets with sparse traffic will become crowded, and the apparently "rational" strategy will be frustrated.

If among states vying for military superiority only one acquired the "ultimate" weapon, it seems to have acquired a decisive advantage. But if the possession of the "ultimate weapon" confers an advantage, all the states may seek to acquire it, and if they do, the advantage of possessing this "ultimate weapon" will have disappeared.

Conversely, if all the states comprising the international system are armed, unilateral disarmament seems to be an invitation to aggression. If, nevertheless, a state disarms and survives, and if one or more other states follow suit, the prospect of a disarmed world becomes more realistic. As it becomes more realistic, disarmament becomes more attractive. Eventually a threshhold may be reached after which the momentum of disarmament carries the process to its conclusion. "Snowball" effects of this sort have been observed in real life. The evolution of cooperation on a global scale could be the result of a similar snowball effect.

7

Conflict and Cooperation: Two Sides of a Coin

A few years ago, while seaching for historical material on cooperation among nations, I found an interesting document dated 1464. It attests to an attempt by King George of Bohemia to form a confederation of European states devoted to the preservation of peace. For example, in article 5 of the proposed covenant, we read:

> In order to facilitate the suppression of dissidence and wars, the very thought of which pains those who have to experience them, and in order to strengthen peace also among others . . . who are not parties to the present covenant, we hereby provide and order that if discord should occur between other Christian princes and magnates who are not included in our fraternity, our below described assembly shall dispatch in our name and at our mutual expense envoys whose task will be to restore concern between the parties to dispute. (Czechoslovak Academy of Sciences 1964, 84)

There follow detailed provisions describing the structure of a body strikingly similar to its modern versions, the League of Nations and the United Nations.

In 1964, the 500th anniversary of the proposal, the Czechoslovak Academy of Sciences presented the document to UNESCO. Doubtless national pride played a part in the gesture, displaying evidence that progressive, humane ideals flourished in the fifteenth century in a country that was to become socialist Czechoslovakia.

The following commentary of the Academy on the proposed treaty is noteworthy.

> Mankind of the fifteenth century was shown the prospect of a world without wars in which even the apparently insurmountable antagonism between the Christians and Muslims appeared to be replaceable by a situation for which we can hardly find a more fitting,

> modern-day term than *peaceful coexistence.* This is clearly indicated by the final part of article 13, which expressly envisages the possibility of peace between Christians and the Turks. (30)

This interpretation, however, was not accurate. In the very same article of the covenant, we read:

> . . . we . . . pledge and swear to our Lord Jesus Christ, to his most glorious mother, the Virgin Mary, and to the Holy Roman Catholic Church that we shall defend and protect the Christian religion and all the oppressed faithful against the vilest prince of the Turks . . . and we shall not cease to pursue the enemy, if our assembly deems it expedient, until he is driven out of Christian territory. . . . (86)

To be sure, the idea of peaceful coexistence is envisaged, but under rather stringent conditions. The statement continues:

> . . . or until it is jointly resolved to conclude peace, which may be done only if the security of neighbouring Christians is deemed insured. (86)

What is foreshadowed here is not so much the idea of peaceful coexistence as the idea of "rollback and containment," which was to dominate the thinking of U.S. cold warriors half a millenium later.

It occurred to me that cooperation is a two-sided coin. Its obverse side is conflict. Indeed, the most conspicuous instances of cooperation are often accompanied by the intensification of conflict. Or, to put it another way, conflict proves motivation for cooperation. Military alliances are obvious examples of this sort of complementarity. It is noteworthy that the covenant on keeping peace in Europe was proposed by King George just eleven years after the Eastern Roman Empire was given a coup de grace by the Turks, who captured Constantinople in 1453. It is further noteworthy that the most far-reaching forms of cooperation, to the extent of people sacrificing their lives for a common goal, are found on the battlefield. It seems that something like a fusion of individual psyches takes place, resulting in the dissolution of the individual in a collective such as is found among social insects. Thus, it appears that "love" as much as (perhaps more than) "hatred" provides the fuel of violent conflict, in particular of wars, at least of a certain type.

It seems that we humans perceive the world in terms of juxtaposed opposites: good and evil, salvation and damnation, dominance and submission, freedom and necessity. In view of the first discoveries of modern science, we might even suppose that this juxtaposition of polarities is the very essence of reality. Philosophers have built their systems on this idea. I mentioned Hegel and his idea of progress as repeated confrontations of opposites and their resolutions: thesis, antithesis, and synthesis. We have seen how Marx adapted this idea to his materialist view of history as successive confrontations between classes. Whether the confrontation of opposites is a fundamental principle of being or becoming, I will not venture to say. It seems, however, clearly to be a principle of perception. To perceive anything at all, we must separate what we perceive from its background. That is to say, to perceive means to be aware of a contrast. We become aware of the presence (or existence) of something only by comparing it with its absence. We tend to appreciate something fully only when we are deprived of it: sleep, freedom, health. It is only natural to project the ubiquitousness of contrast as the indispensable component of perception to the "nature of reality," as Mephistopheles explains himself to Faust:

> I am part of that Power, not understood
> which always wills the Bad, and always works the Good . . .
> . . . .
> Part of the Part am I, once All, in primal Night,
> Part of the Darkness which brought forth the Light.

Conflict (or competition) and cooperation are among these opposite pairs. Each stimulates the other, justifies itself by the existence of the other. Each is a cardinal principle of life. It has become a truism to say that the fate of our species depends on how these two principles will mesh in our collective existence.

We have mentioned the primal cooperative act: the sex act, the union of two cells that initiates reproduction. The attendant exchange of hereditary substance increased formidably the potential for variations and thus accelerated the rate of evolution by orders of magnitude. In the theory of evolution, as it crystallized with the advent of the idea of natural selection, competition (a form of conflict) played the more conspicuous role. We have conjectured that the social milieu in which the theory was formulated was especially favorable to this emphasis. The idea appeared in economics several decades before it attained its prominence in biology. In the work of Adam Smith, the dialectic union of opposites gave the idea its power. The pursuit of individual interests seemed to result in the common good. Everyone seemed to act selfishly, but the result of all these selfish acts seemed to benefit all, as if through the operation of a benevolent, invisible hand.

We have also seen how, in Germany, militarists and their ideological allies purported to see war as a creative principle, a prime mover of progress. Aside from driving progress, war (which to most of us seems an orgy of destruction) appeared to the state worshippers of the last century as a fountainhead of social virtue. Toward the end of the last century, Heinrich von Treischke, a noted German historian, wrote:

> It is war which fosters the political idealism which the materialists reject. What a disaster for civilization it would be if mankind blotted its heroes from memory! The heroes of a nation are the fighters which rejoice and inspire the spirit of its youth, and the writers, whose words ring like trumpet blasts, become the idols of our boyhood and of our early manhood. (Treischke [1897–98] 1916, 1:87)

It is common to attribute the presistence of wars in human history to an aggressive drive. Freud regarded an addiction to destruction as something given, an irremovable component of human nature. In juxtaposing the "death instinct" (thanatos) to the creative urge (eros), Freud thought in the language of metaphysics. However, to some extent, the idea of innate human aggressiveness can be supported on scientific grounds. Konrad Lorenz, in his extensive studies of animal behavior (1966), has noted that, at least among the vertebrates, combats for possession of females is extremely widespread. He has also shown that aggressive behavior in males need not be stimulated by the presence of a rival male (i.e., one of the same species). Among the cichlids (a species of tropical fish), for example, if no rival males are present, males will attack individuals of other species and, if none are available, even females of their own species. Evidently aggressiveness can become a "drive" (like hunger or sex) that manifests itself even in the absence of appropriate external stimuli.

We have also seen how E. O. Wilson attempted to explain war as a way of conferring reproductive advantage on an organism's own genes (chap. 3). Note that, in supporting the idea that aggression has become rooted in human nature in consequence of natural selection, Wilson does not succumb to "vulgar Darwinism." He concedes the possibility that "nonaggressiveness" (in the form of some kind of pacific maneuvering) as well as aggressiveness may be selected for. If that is the case, it is possible that aggressiveness has ceased to be a dominant feature in human nature. This conjecture may seem surprising, but an attentive examination of procedures that characterize modern war make it credible. Direct contact with the enemy has become ever less frequent in the conduct of war. Weapons that kill at a distance make such contact unnecessary. Nor is it necessary to harbor aggressive feelings in order to kill people one does not see. A nuclear war would probably dispense with the battlefield altogether. The modern warrior need not possess any of the characteristics ordinarily associated with a warrior. He need not be strong, since he is no longer required to wield heavy weapons. He need not be brave, because he need not see the enemy and his choice is not between facing danger and seeking safety. And he need not be fierce in order to go through the motions that activate the engines of total destruction. In short, it is not readiness to fight that underlies the conduct of the modern war but, on the contrary, the readiness and the ability to cooperate, to become a link in a vast system of interlocking, precisely functioning parts.

The idea of hatred and aggressiveness as concomitants of war is of comparatively recent origin. The professional soldier of European standing armies in the eighteenth century was brainwashed to become an automaton, responding with jerky but precise movements to barked commands. "Patriotism" was largely a product of the French Revolution and of the Napoleonic Wars, when it spread from France to other nations. The consequent change in the nature of war, entailing the use of citizen armies (*leveé en masse*) promoted "morale" to an important component of victory. Morale did involve hatred of the enemy; but, in equal measure, it involved loyalty (a feeling akin to love) to one's country and even more to the comrades fighting alongside.

For this reason, the efforts of religiously oriented pacifists, who hope to prevent future wars by making people less aggressive, more tolerant, more loving, may miss the mark. Altruism or dedication to cooperation may be sentiments more responsible for the persistence of the threat of war and the robustness of its supporting institutions than hatred or destructiveness.

Conflict and cooperation are complementary. The most conspicuous examples of international cooperation are military alliances. And, in general, the surest way of stimulating cooperation is by calling attention to a common enemy. Interpersonal, intergroup, and international relations often seem to be guided by the following elementary principles.

The friend of my friend is my friend.
The enemy of my friend is my enemy.
The friend of my enemy is my enemy.
The enemy of my enemy is my friend.

If these principles were applied without exception, all of humankind would be split into two camps within each of which everyone would be everyone's friend and any two from different camps would be enemies. Of course, this is not the case. But tendencies toward establishing what social psychologists call attitudinal balance are observed. Here, the duality of conflict and cooperation is seen most clearly.

The duality of competition and cooperation is also seen in the process of evolution. At times it is difficult to distinguish one from the other. Consider the explanation of "aggression" in the animal world on the basis of natural selection. As has been repeatedly pointed out, aggressiveness, especially in males competing for females, contributes to the vigor of the species if the most aggressive and, therefore presumably, the most vigorous males have a reproductive advantage. Thus, this sort of competition has a cooperative component: as if by competing the contenders for females "cooperate" in the task of promoting or preserving the vigor of the species. The same can be said of territoriality. Possession of a breeding territory from which rivals are excluded has survival value if overcrowding is detrimental. So in fighting for territory, individuals also "cooperate" by ensuring adequate territory to breed in. Where does competition become cooperation?

Innumerable instances of conflict for mates or territory have been observed, where there is no bodily contact between the "combatants." The "combat" is confined to gestures. We tend to interpret these gestures as threatening, but perhaps we are anthropomorphizing in doing so. We cannot experience what birds or fishes experience and thus have no way of knowing whether they are expressing or experiencing hostility or threat. A case in point is the "conflict" for territory between certain spiders, where the "combatants," as a rule, do not even see each other.

The female spider of this species spins a web that then becomes her domicile and a snare for insects on which she feeds. At times, a spider that did not bother to spin a web of her own will try to "take over" another's web. As she enters the web, she makes her presence known by causing vibrations. The possessor of the web replies with vibrations of her own. The amplitude and the frequency of the vibrations apparently give information about the weight of the vibrator. It turns out that if the weights of the two spiders differ by at least 10 percent or so, the outcome of the "combat" is decided right then. The lighter spider loses and leaves the web. But if the weights differ by less than about 10 percent, the web remains in the possession of the owner (Riechert 1978).

Is this exchange an instance of "combat" or is it not, rather, evidence of adhering to certain rules that, in the final analysis, promote the vigor of the species by giving reproductive advantage to heavier (presumably more vigorous) individuals? When my wife vacates the seat next to mine in the waiting room at the airport and someone intends to occupy it, I say, "Sorry, this seat is taken." Is this "territoriality" stimulted by aggressive instinct; or is it a reminder to the newcomer that we both subscribe to certain rules of conduct that serve to make social life more amenable and harmonious?

It is this beneficial, progress-promoting aspect of competition (a form of conflict) that was brought out in Adam Smith's model of the free market: competition on the level of individuals adds up to cooperation (albeit unconscious) on the level of the society. The argument was convincing against its historical background. Consider what the free market replaced: the mercantile conception with its fixation on possession of precious metals, on stubborn defense of a "favorable" balance of trade, and of government monopolies. But when the iniquities of unfettered free enterprise invited an attack on capitalism, the defense of unrestricted competition by the social Darwinists became compulsive, as can be seen in Sumner's defense of inequality cited previously (chap. 4). Similarly, when voices started to be raised in Europe against institutionalized warfare, the defense of war became compulsive, as can be seen in the previously quoted passages by Wagner and Treischke.

Hardly anyone dares to defend war on its own merits any more. But the adaptability of war to its social milieu is evidenced by the fact that the crass defense of war (as we still remember it in the last spasms of unabashed militarism of a Hitler or a Mussolini) is no longer necessary.

The war system survives because it offers unprecedented opportunities for cooperation, a sense of participation, outlets for feelings of collegiality, of sharing enthusiasms. Nowhere is this aspect of the war system more conspicuous than in the United States. No doubt the ideational climate of the United States has been especially favorable for creating an attractive image of the war system, because Americans did not experience modern war on their own soil. In fact, they emerged as unscathed victors in both world wars and these victories were attributed (in the public mind) to the righteousness of the cause and even more to U.S. technological genius. The nature of the climate during the Vietnam War was vividly described by Charles W. Tait.

> The air of technical efficiency and objectivity which surrounds decisions made by computers; the impressive apparatus of intelligence agencies with their networks of agents and almost instantaneous transmission of top-secret, evaluated intelligence to policy makers; the jet transports, aircraft carriers, helicopters, radio communications from the Pentagon, to forward command posts—all these give an illusion of purposeful action. Is it any wonder that they impress men who worship technical gadgetry and pride themselves on their ability to make speedy executive decisions? (1965, 138).

No less important in projecting this attractive image of war is its portrayal as a vast cooperative enterprise. Robert Kennedy described his brother's feelings during the Cuban missile crisis of 1962:

> President Kennedy was impressed with the effort and dedicated manner in which the military responded—the Navy deploying its vessels into the Caribbean; the Air Force going on continuous alert; the Army and the Marines moving their soldiers and equipment into the southeastern part of the U.S.; all of them alert and ready for combat. (Kennedy 1968, 118)

In his book, *Star Warriors,* William J. Broad describes the tight community of young, brilliant scientists working on problems of putting ultrasophisticated weapons into outer space.

> The young scientists of the group were close friends. They were smart and sassy and could play pranks like nobody else. Being with them was fun. . . .

> The fabric of friendship extended even to the language they spoke. Classified projects led to classified jokes. After a while, the young scientists began to be cut off from the spontaneity of the outside world. A visitor could engage them in polite conversation . . . but free-ranging discussions could occur only with other "Q-cleared" people. It was like the Gulag. Stalin's concentration camps were the only place in Russia where people could really criticize the state. Freedom came only in captivity. (Broad 1985, 116)

Again the "union of opposites." Feelings of collegial solidarity, perhaps even of affection, bound these young people into a genuine community of shared enthusiasms, at the same time insulating them from the rest of humanity, producing the ultimate alienation.

Perception of a Common Enemy

Political history can be seen as successive integration of human groups into ever-larger political units. In this process, comparative peace is established within these units, largely as a consequence of the monopolization of physical power by some central body. At the same time, this concentration of power increases the potential for violence directed at other political units. The integrative process has now transcended national boundaries. Internal peace can now be observed throughout most of the European continent and throughout North America. Concurrently, the entire industrialized world became polarized after World War II. The two blocs, East and West, have faced each other for over four decades, each threatening the other and being threatened by it. The integration and the polarization have been in constant, supportive interaction. Before the disintegration of the Communist bloc in 1989, massive destructive violence within each bloc seemed unthinkable. With the break-up of the Eastern bloc, militant nationalism, at times bursting out in violence, surfaced in the Soviet Union.

Is there a way of enhancing integration of human groups without aggravating intergroup enmity at the same time? There is. The role of the perception of a common enemy can be utilized in promoting cooperation without, at the same time, nurturing hostility against outsiders if the "common enemy" is perceived as a condition adversely affecting both groups rather than a group of outsiders. An experiment performed by Sherif et al (1961) provided a dramatic demonstration of the principle of diverting conflict into channels without human enemies as an effective means of conflict resolution.

Two groups of preadolescent boys were taken to a summer camp and initially kept in ignorance of each other's existence. A strong esprit de corps developed in each group. Each adapted a romantic name, "Rattlers" and "Eagles" respectively. Thereupon, as if by accident, the groups became aware of each other. Contacts were arranged. As expected, feelings of rivalry developed rapidly into strong intergroup hostility. Various efforts to allay the hostility failed. There were attempts to arrange "people-to-people" contacts between the groups that resulted in no discernible improvement of relations. Attempts by the leaders to arrange a modus vivendi were interpreted as "treason" by the rank and file. Competitive games only fed mutual aversions.

Then the one sure remedy was applied. A breakdown of the water supply was arranged and members of the two groups were obliged to work side by side to repair the facility. There was a marked improvement of relations, further reinforced by a joint financing of a film that both groups wanted to see. Finally, the camp truck "broke down" (again by arrangement), and the two groups had to cooperate (push the truck uphill) to restore the service. Hostility gave way to solidarity. At the end, everyone insisted on going home in the same bus. An objective index of the change of attitudes is given in table 2.

Perception of Other as Extension of Self

At times, when a conflict is resolved, the resolution generates a strong and lasting bond between the erstwhile antagonists. The process is somewhat similar to the thesis-antithesis-synthesis sequence that produces a steady advance in understanding the world. For the resolution of a conflict often depends on the ability of the antagonists to put themselves into each other's shoes and to realize that they have a common problem.

An incident from the film *M*A*S*H* illustrates a situation of this sort. The setting is a U.S. field hospital during the Korean War. For the first time in history, the U.S. armed forces have been desegregated. News gets around that a black surgeon is about to join the staff. A southerner is profoundly shocked, but realizes that nothing can be done about it. After much soul-searching, he takes the new colleague aside and says to him, "Captain, you and me got to have a talk—just the two of us, because them damnyankees won't know what we are talking about."

TABLE 2. Percentage of all Ratings by Eagles of Rattlers and by Rattlers of Eagles

	Favorable	Neutral	Unfavorable
Initial	27	10	63
Final	78	9	13

Source: Data from Sherif et al 1961.

Here, chronic racial strife is suddenly seen as a *common* problem of *southerners,* black and white. By implying that northerners "won't know what they are talking about," the white man establishes a bond with the black man—"us southerners know what we are up against."

In their book on productive negotiation, Fisher and Ury (1981) emphasize the necessity of steering the conflict away from a confrontation of "positions" to a realization, by the contenders, of each other's *interests.* Positions are like points in space. They have no common ground. Negotiations centering on attempts to yield as little as possible (i.e., to remain as closely as possible to one's defended position) can, at best, result in a compromise, which in general leaves both sides dissatisfied because both have yielded. Concessions are regarded by both sides as losses. In addition, the tone of negotiations focusing on positions is often antagonistic. A gain by one side is a loss by the other. In contrast, interests are like regions rather than points. They may well have a nonempty intersection that a negotiation concentrating on interests may reveal. Then the conflict of interests may become a common problem of the conflicting parties. The central question then becomes not "How can I get the best deal?" but "How can we enhance our common interests?" Obviously, if there is no common interest, negotiations are a waste of time. It goes without saying that some antagonistic relations are devoid of common interests. There is nothing that a dog and his fleas can negotiate about. We have seen, however, how even the relation between a parasite and a host can evolve into a symbiotic relationship as a consequence of natural selection acting on both the parasite and the host.

Among humans, as we have seen, learning, time binding, and cultural evolution are incomparably more important agents of change than natural selection. They, too, can transform certain kinds of conflict into cooperation. This happens if, as a result of conflict, antagonists are able to imagine themselves in each other's situations. Developmental psychology has shed some light on this process. Piaget, who has conducted extensive investigations of the intellectual and moral development of children, describes the following simple experiment (1928, chap. 2). The subject is a small boy who has one brother. The experimenter asks him,

"Have you a brother?" The answer is usually, "Yes." The next question is "Has your brother a brother?" Up to a certain age, the answer is usually "No." The very young child still does not understand that the word "brother" refers not to a person but a relationship between persons. Consequently, he does not see that he himself is his brother's brother. To put it in another way, the very young child is still unable to assume the point of view of another.

Further evidence is provided by an experiment in which very young children are asked to make a choice between two alternatives. The result of the choice depends on the simultaneous choice between two other alternatives by the experimenter. The child's preferences for the four possible outcomes (say amounts of candy accruing to the child) have been previously established. The preferences of the experimenter, which are diametrically opposite to those of the child (say he gets the rest of the candy after the child gets what it has won) are also known to the child. The experimenter's better choice does not depend on the child's choice and is, therefore, obvious. The child's better choice, however, depends on the experimenter's choice. If the child could see the game from the experimenter's point of view, its better choice would also be obvious. Up to a certain age, however, the child cannot deduce the experimenter's better choice. Consequently, the child makes a choice that results in a worse outcome for it than the outcome that could have been effected.

In its most generalized sense, conflict is a perception of a contradiction; cooperation is the perception of identity. But contradiction and identity are complementary. Emperor Charles V of the Holy Roman Empire is said to have remarked with grim humor: "I desire what my brother desires; the city of Milan."

In conflict situations where the participants have a common interest, resolution can sometimes be achieved by negotiation. Among negotiators, advantages and disadvantages of a "hard" approach and of a "soft" approach are often discussed. Fisher and Ury (1981) reject both the "hard" approach, aimed at forcing maximum concessions from the other side, and the "soft" approach, a policy of yielding in the interest of preserving a "valued relationship." Both approaches are likely to induce a hard approach in the other side. A confrontation between two hard-liners is likely to lead to an outcome bad for both. In a confrontation between a soft bargainer and a hard one, the former is likely to lose most without preserving or improving a "valued relationship." All too often, readiness to yield induces contempt instead of friendship or respect. Instead of demonstrating readiness to yield, Fisher and Ury recommend demonstrating readiness to understand the opponent.

The recognition of the opponent as a mirror image of Self is a step toward integration. In the aftermath of the East European revolution of 1989, meetings were arranged between military personnel of East and West, at which some awareness of a common problem—that of preventing the outbreak of a war—was discernible. It was the protracted conflict of the cold war that created this common problem to begin with. In a way, therefore, the conflict could be regarded as a precursor of cooperation. Clearly, the duality emerges only if the conflicting parties recognize the fundamental similarities that suggest the productivity of conflict resolution. If this happens, the resolution leaves both parties better off than they were before the conflict started.

To sum up: conflict can, under some circumstance, contribute to the awareness of the Other as someone like oneself and may generate feelings akin to empathy, preparing the way to cooperation and integration.

8

The Idea of System

System is a typical example of a heavy-duty word—one with many meanings in many different contexts. We speak of social, political, and economic systems, of systems of classification and of bookkeeping, of the solar system and a nervous system, of mechanical, electrical, and chemical systems. All of these instances barely skim the surface of the world of meaning that subsumes the term. As is usually the case with the various meanings of heavy-duty words, the meanings of system have a common denominator. The notion of organization is embodied in almost all meanings of system. Organization, in turn, refers to the possibility of constructing a comprehensible description of a whole in terms of the interrelatedness of its parts. Thus, a piece of machinery is organized in the sense that its parts are in definite spatial and functional relations to each other. The spatial arrangement of the parts constitute the "anatomy" of the system; the functional relations constitute its "physiology." The same can be said of a living organism. In fact, the terms *anatomy* and *physiology* are borrowed from descriptions of living organisms.

In the more or less exact sciences, for example, physics, astronomy, or chemistry, system has a somewhat different meaning. It refers to any portion of the world that is delineated for the purpose of differentiating it from its environment so as to study it "from the inside" and "from the outside," as it were. Thus, a gas in a container or a number of substances interacting chemically in a tank can be regarded as systems. So can the solar system, thought to consist of the sun, the planets, their satellites, and comets with periodic orbits, all immersed in empty space.

These two ways of viewing systems can be distinguished by the different underlying definitions of system. We can distinguish an *analytic* theory of systems, whose "habitat" is essentially in the physical sciences and in technology, and a *holistic* or *organismic* theory, characteristic of biological and social sciences. The distinction between the two approaches becomes clear in light of their points of departure, namely, the definitions of system.

From the analytic point of view, a system is defined essentially as a set of numbers, usually changing in time. Because they are constantly changing, they are called variables. The clearest example of a system defined in this way is the solar system. At a given moment, each planet has a position in space, which can be defined by three numbers, say, the coordinates in three-dimensional space, where the sun is taken to be at the origin of the coordinate system. Besides, each planet or satellite can be assigned three other numbers, representing the components of its velocity. Thus, if the solar system contains (besides the sun, assumed to be at the origin and stationary) n other objects, $6n$ numbers can be ascribed to the system at a given moment of time, $3n$ to define the positions of the n bodies and $3n$ to define their velocities at that moment. This set of numbers is called the *state* of the system at a given moment. Since the positions and the velocities are constantly changing, so is the state of the system. A description of the courses of the variables in time is called the *trajectory* of the system. The task of a theory of the solar system can be viewed as predicting its trajectory beginning with any initial state.

Knowledge of laws governing the interactions among the variables enables us to predict the trajectory of a system defined in this way. In the case of the solar system, these laws are Newton's laws of motion and the law of gravity. Specifically, the law of gravity determines the force with which any two bodies attract each other, namely, in terms of the masses of the bodies and the distance separating them. The laws of motion translate forces into accelerations. These are rates of change of velocities, which, in turn, are rates of change of positions.

Equations that relate rates of change of variables to the variables themselves are called *differential equations.* Thus, the solar system is described by a system (a set) of differential equations. These constitute a mathematical model of the system. From the point of view of analytic system theory, the system is defined by its mathematical model. Indeed, the classification of systems from this point of view corresponds to a classification of mathematical models, in this instance by the types of differential equations that represent them.

The power (or "theoretical leverage") of the analytic system theory is that it suggests rigorously established analogies. If two systems are described by the same set of differential equations, for example, they are identical from the point of view of analytic system theory. Any theoretically derived statement pertaining to one pertains equally to the other.

An elementary analogy of this type is between a mechanical system called a *harmonic oscillator* and an electrical system comprising a source of electric potential generating an alternating current, an inductor, a resistor, and a condenser. Both are described by the same type of second-order differential equation. The variables describing the mechanical system comprise the position of a weight suspended by a spring and oscillating up and down about its position of equilibrium, the velocity of its motion, and the acceleration (rate of change of velocity). These variables enter a differential equation that also contains *parameters*, that is, quantities that remain constant in this situation. The parameters in this case comprise the mass of the weight, the resistance of the medium through which it moves (friction), and the elasticity of the spring. The variables of the electrical system comprise the electric potential, the magnitude and direction of the current, and the charge in the condenser. The parameters comprise the inductance, the resistance, and the capacitance of the condenser.

The analogy is expressed by the correspondences between the respective variables and between the respective parameters. For instance, the electric potential corresponds to position, the current to velocity, and the inductance corresponds to the mass. The physical meanings of these variables and parameters are quite different; but the roles the correspondents play in the mathematical model are identical. In this way, different contents are described by a single theory.

In common parlance, analogies are often dismissed as superficial or inconsequential, as "mere" analogies. Mathematical analogies (called isomorphisms) are taken seriously. They point to genuine "unity in diversity," which is at the core of any rigorously developed scientific theory.

The power of analytic system theory is bounded by the range of its application. If a mathematical model is to be taken as a reasonable representation of a portion of reality, the variables in it must represent the most essential features of the process described. Moreover, the laws governing the interactions between the variables must be known sufficiently well to be stated in precise mathematical language. Once we go beyond these situations, we encounter difficulties that are well nigh insurmountable. To take an example, suppose we undertake to construct an analytic model of a behaving living system. Events of this sort are not, in general, representable by moving points in the way, say, the solar system is describable. We may attempt to describe behavior in terms of contracting muscles. However, aside from the tremendous complexity of such a description, we are at a loss how to classify these motions.

To fix ideas, consider the description of a most elementary action. A psychologist, describing the behavior of a rat may state, "The rat pressed the lever" or "The rat ate the pellet delivered in consequence of the lever being pressed." Now the part of the statement beginning with "delivered" can conceivably be described in terms of specified motions—the movement of the lever, the way the movement of the lever triggers the delivering mechanism, the fall of the pellet, and so forth. However, the events comprising the behavior of the rat cannot be so described. Specifically, the rat may perform those acts (pushing the lever and eating) in entirely different ways, for example, by using different sets of muscles in different sequences. Yet for the purpose of describing the observed events, all these actions are described in the same way: the rat pushed the lever; the rat ate the pellet. We have, therefore, an indication of how to classify all these different muscle movements, so that they correspond to our classification of acts.

The events that constitute the units of analysis in, say, a psychological experiment are not defined in terms of minute component events (e.g., muscle contractions). They are simply *recognized.*

Organismic System Theory

Organismic or holistic system theory is based on the assumption that systems can be recognized as wholes and that such acts of recognition are valid. For instance, the experimenter recognizes the rat's action (pushing the lever). In spite of the fact that each occurrence of the action may be composed of entirely different events, the experimenter lumps all these component events into a single event. Thus, all lever pushings are regarded as instances of the "same" event; in spite of the fact that they are all different, the identification is valid in the sense that verifiable predictions can be made on the basis of a record of such events.

Acts of recognition are so common that we take them for granted without giving them a second thought. Moreover, babies are already capable of performing these acts, for instance, recognizing mother's face or voice.

From the standpoint of organismic system theory, a system is defined as something that can be recognized as "itself" and something that maintains its "identity" in spite of changes going on inside it. This maintenance of identity is revealed in the act of recognition. From this point of view, an organism is a system par excellence. The material composition of a person or an animal keeps changing because of metabolism or replacement of parts. Every molecule in the human body may be replaced by another in the course of a few months. Yet persons and animals retain their identity. We know this not only from our ability to recognize and identify individuals, but also introspectively. We are aware of our memories, and it is the continuity of our memories that assures us that we have kept our identity.

There are other examples. A city, an organization, an institution are all systems defined from the standpoint of organismic system theory by their ability to preserve their identities despite internal changes. Rome is still Rome despite the fact that no inhabitant of Rome in Caesar's time is alive today. Similar statements can be made about long-lived firms, about army regiments, and about many other types of organized aggregates.

The key word in the preceding sentence is *organized*. It is the organization of a system that enables it to preserve its identity. Among the well understood organizational devices are the so-called homeostatic devices. They are well understood because they have been incorporated in modern technology. I mentioned the steam engine as an invention that "took off" when "its time came." A crucial event in the development of a steam engine was the invention (by James Watt) of the governor, a primitive homeostatic device.

A major problem in using the steam engine as a constant source of energy in continual mechanical work is keeping the speed of a flywheel constant. The governor makes this possible. Its basic feature is a pair of balls at the end of rods rotating around a column to which they are hinged. The rods form an angle with the column that depends on the speed of rotation. When the speed increases, so does the angle because of the action of centrifugal force. As the angle is increased, a jacket around the column is moved upward, which decreases the aperture through which steam is supplied to the engine. Consequently, the speed of rotation tends to decrease. As the speed decreases, so does the angle between the rods and the column, which causes the aperture to increase. In this way, any deviation of the speed of rotation from a preset constant speed is "corrected."

Homeostatic mechanisms of this sort are found in living systems. When our skin becomes warmer than it should be, sweat glands are activated and we perspire. As the secreted moisture evaporates, the surface of the skin is cooled. When we are cold, we shiver. Shivering generates heat. After physical exertion, we pant, that is, breathe more rapidly and more deeply and so restore the concentration of blood oxygen that was depleted during the exertion. Thus, homeostatic mechanisms of a system serve to maintain certain variables (temperature, concentrations of substances in the blood, etc.) within certain limits, the transgression of which disturbs the functioning of the system and may lead to its destruction.

More generally, we can define a homeostatic mechanism as any arrangement that tends to restore some state of the system after it has been disturbed. Consider hunger. We feel it when the concentration of sugar in the blood falls below a certain level. If food is available, we eat. If food is not immediately available, we seek it. We observe similar behavior in animals. Since eating serves to restore the level of blood sugar, we may extend the notion of homeostasis to everything that helps the organism restore the concentration of sugar. In this sense, a homeostatic mechanism can be said to exist by definition—that which helps restore a steady state. The definition raises the problem of identifying the homeostatic mechanism in each case. In complex organisms such as mammals or, in particular, humans, these mechanisms may be exceedingly complex, including not only identifiable physiological processes (e.g., perspiration or shivering) but also, at least in humans, culturally conditioned purposeful actions. I said we "seek" food when we are hungry and do not find food in our field of vision. For a human being, seeking may be a quite elaborate process, involving culturally conditioned mental states and culturally transmitted knowledge, for instance knowledge of where food is available, say in stores or restaurants, and knowledge that, in order to obtain it, one must be in possession of certain objects (money, credit cards, whatnot). Moreover, we do not confine food-seeking behavior to times when we are hungry. In urban life, food is obtained by shopping, usually in designated places at designated times, not necessarily related to the depletion of sugar in the bloodstream.

Analogies

A principal task of organismic system theory is that of identifying mechanisms, structures, processes, and the like, existing and operating in different kinds of systems, so as to explore the extent to which these mechanisms, structures, or processes are analogous and permit inferences across the special theories pertaining to special systems. At times these analogies are clear. A motor vehicle "consumes" fuel in a way clearly analogous to the way an animal consumes food. Oxidation of the fuel releases energy which the car "uses" to propel itself. Food is also oxidized in the process of digestion and absorption into the bloodstream. And the energy so released is used up in moving about, performing the various life functions, and doing all kinds of work. The brain controls a tremendous complex of neural processes by transforming received signals into outgoing signals to appropriate muscles or glands. The command post of an army unit performs analogous functions. So much is clear. The important question is how far such analogies can be pursued. In the Middle Ages, naive analogies were drawn between the human body and the state. The head was regarded as the analogue of the king, the arms of the army, the heart of the Church, the back of the peasantry, and so on. The comparisons may have been suggestive of the functions supposedly performed by the various parts of the body and of the state but also may have been misleading. For instance, if the king is identified with the head of a human being, a state without a king might appear as unthinkable.

Analogies suggested by organismic system theory are more than metaphors. They are regarded as hypotheses, not as conclusions. If an organism protects itself against invasions by pathogenic and parasitic organisms by "recognizing" them as such, the question arises whether a society does something analogous. And, if analogous mechanisms are suggested, this is not the "answer" to the question posed but rather a stimulus for further questions and further investigations. For example, the mobilization of an organism against "invaders" suggests that such reactions may be observed in societies, regarded as analogues of organisms. We are motivated to look for historical examples. I will cite two.

A System "Defends" Itself

About the middle of the seventeenth century, Japan isolated itself from foreign influences by closing its borders to foreigners. This state of affairs lasted until 1853, when a U.S. admiral threatened the Japanese with reprisals if they did not permit access. The Japanese gave in, and their history was from then on marked by events that would have been unthinkable before the dismantling of the barriers.

Let us look at a particular subsystem of the system comprising the Japanese culture of the time to see how the isolation helped to preserve the subsystem. We are referring to the Samurai, a caste of warriors whose business it was to fight for the lord to whom they owed allegiance in the perpetual warfare among the lords. The fighting was developed into a fine art. The combat weapon was a large sword, wielded by both hands. Success in one-to-one encounters, which took place in battles, depended on the skill in wielding the sword. The Samurai aspired to victory not merely for the resulting benefits but also, perhaps mainly, as evidence of personal superiority. The feeling of self-esteem included, in large measure, faithfulness to a certain code of conduct. The notion of honor was developed to the extent that guilt resulting from violations of the code (or failure to punish incursions against it) led to mandatory suicide.

At one time, before the total exclusion of foreigners, firearms were introduced into Japan. These weapons were regarded as a horrendous menace by the Samurai, since they threatened the entire ideational edifice built on the basis of the fighting cult, at the center of which was sword worship. The sword was, of course, no match for the gun. It would make a mockery of swordsmanship and, with it, a mockery of victory and so would put an end to the libidinal involvement with personal success in battle. Thus, the exclusion of firearms was in a very real sense an act of self-defense, where Self includes also a definition of oneself, selfhood, if you will.

Another example, still in living memory, is the attempted isolation of the Soviet Union against foreign influences during the last years of Stalin's rule. Originally, the intellectuals who led the Bolshevik Revolution of 1917 regarded themselves as Marxists. In Russia, this meant that they belonged to the pro-Western or internationalist wing of the intelligentsia, that is, were emphatic opponents of the so-called Slavophile wing, who looked to traditional Russian values (as they understood them) as the basis for the postrevolutionary society. One would think, therefore, that after a victorious Bolshevik-led revolution, contact with the West would be eagerly sought. Things, however, turned out differently.

After Lenin's death, Stalin succeeded in consolidating absolute power to himself. He was able to do so because of his strategic position in the bureaucracy of the Communist party, namely, as general secretary, a post mistakenly regarded as a minor one by the ideological leaders little concerned with practical politics. After Lenin's death there was a massive influx into the Party, mostly by young workers and peasants of limited education. Admission to membership was in the hands of the general secretary. Those admitted owed Stalin the opportunities opened to them in their upward mobility. Thus, Stalin was able to command majorities in the internal political struggles during the 1920s. As he became more powerful, he could afford to become increasingly more ruthless, until the struggle was decided by expulsion and, ultimately, execution of all of Stalin's potential rivals regardless of whether they opposed or supported him in the struggles.

Stalin's autocracy was protected by a cult built around his person, which, except for the terminology in the liturgy, was indistinguishable from the deity- and potentate-worshiping cults of antiquity. It is unlikely that the cult could have been kept intact if the country were not virtually hermetically sealed from outside influences. The isolation of the Soviet Union during Stalin's reign was comparable to that of Japan in the age of the Shoguns.

Like any fundamentalist religion, Stalinism was nurtured by a mythology. Its core was the belief that the Soviet Union was the most advanced society in the world and that its citizens were the most prosperous and the happiest, that its leadership, that is, Stalin and his henchmen, were the wisest and the most humane. The myth was viable because travel abroad by ordinary Soviet citizens was virtually nonexistent and, even in the Soviet Union, contact with foreigners except under the scrutiny of the secret police was prohibited, characteristically not by law but by effective intimidation. This isolation was threatened when, at the close of World War II, Soviet soldiers saw some parts of Europe. Damaged as it was, it must have produced a culture shock.

Another source of doubt about prescribed dogmas may have been the change in tone in the propaganda about the West during the war. Something positive had to be said about Britain and the United States—allies in the struggle against a common enemy. At any rate, it was difficult to reestablish the myth about absolute Soviet superiority in all aspects of life and all fields of endeavor. However, a determined attempt to do so marked the years following the end of World War II. A vicious anti-Western campaign was launched in all areas—in literature, the sciences, the arts, and entertainment. It was in those years (1948–53) that legends were invented ascribing practically all important inventions to Russians. Raids were organized against scientific institutions where theories were developed (e.g., genetics) that might be construed as a challenge to the dogmatic verbiage of official philosophy. Campaigns of villification were launched against "cosmopolitans," a euphemism for Jews, who could always be cast in the role of scapegoat.

Here, then, was a vivid instance of a system defending itself against the incursion of alien elements. The system in this instance was the apparatus of entrenched power concentrated in an autocrat and protected by a police state. The alien elements were heretical ideas, where any form of doubt, let alone deviance, was persecuted as heresy. This included deviance not only in content but also in form. Thus, it was mandatory not only to sing paeans about the regime and the autocrat but also to cant these paeans in a certain completely stereotyped language, like a liturgy. Originality of any kind, even in praising the deity, was suspect.

Both the Japanese and the Soviet isolation eventually broke down. Permanent isolation may have made the system exceptionally vulnerable when its protective mechanism (isolation from the environment) disintegrated.

A General Organismic System Theory

From the foregoing, it is clear that the nature of identity-preserving mechanisms varies widely in systems of different types. Their function, however, that of preserving the system through maintaining certain constant features, is discernible in all of them. Investigations that seek to uncover analogies of this sort are subsumed under so-called general system theory. We have seen how mathematical isomorphisms provide the binding links of an analytic system theory. Corresponding links in organismic system theory are analogies based on the *structure, function,* and *evolution* of systems.

The structure of a system is its "architecture." It can be described by naming its parts, which themselves can be systems—the subsystems of the system described. Further, the organization of the structure is described by the relations among the parts. For example, the anatomy of an animal is its "architecture." Its organization is defined by the spatial relations between the organs and tissues. The structure of an institution may be described by its table of organization, showing the channels of communication and lines of authority and responsibility.

The functioning of a system is described by its responses to inputs from the outside and through its internal activities that serve to preserve the identity of the system. The homeostatic mechanisms described previously belong to the functioning aspect of a system. Overt behavior of organisms is also subsumed under function.

The evolution of a system comprises its history, usually described in terms of long-range, irreversible change.

In addition to these aspects, presumably common to all organismically described systems, general system theory singles out levels of organization of systems. In particular, a hierarchy of such levels can be discerned, as we examine so-called living systems. R. W. Gerard (1958) listed the principal levels of such a hierarchy.

On the lowest level of Gerard's hierarchy is the cell of a living system. Presumably one can descend to smaller "systems" within a cell, for example, its nucleus, if it has one, or the so-called "organelles." However, the hierarchy was described for purposes of illustration, rather than as a framework of a complete theory of living systems.

The cell can be said to have systemic properties, because it has a definite structure, engages in identity-preserving activities (takes in nourishment, secretes wastes), and goes through developmental phases.

Multitudes of cells constitute tissues or organs. These, too, have systemic properties. They have well-defined structures, react to inputs by producing outputs (muscles contract, glands secrete, neurons "fire"), and go through developmental phases.

Organs and tissues arranged in definite ways constitute an organism. Beyond the organism are still higher levels of organization. We can ascend to these levels either along the biological dimension, which will take us to species, aggregating in genera, families, classes, phyla, and the entire biosphere, or we can ascend along a social dimension, particularly in humans. Along this dimension we find small, organized groups of individuals, such as families, work teams, or clubs. Above these we find larger organizations, for example, firms or institutions, above these, states. A number of states together with interrelations among them constitute an international system.

Gerard's purpose in describing the hierarchy of system levels and the three aspects of systems was to present an overview of the biological and social sciences, stressing the analogies, in the light of which a unified view of science can be gained. The scheme is shown in table 3.

From the table we see that cytology, anatomy, and certain branches of sociology are concerned with structure on the level of the cell, the organism, and society respectively. We see that physiology, behavioral psychology, and some branches of political science are concerned with behavior on the level of the organ, the individual, and society respectively. Embryology, developmental psychology, and history are concerned with evolutionary processes on the level of the organ, the

TABLE 3. Gerard's Conception of a General Theory of Living Systems

Levels	Aspects		
	Structure	Function	Evolution
Society	Sociology	Political science	History
Organization			
Small group		Social psychology	
Individual	Anatomy	Behavioral psychology	Developmental psychology
Organ		Physiology	Embryology
Cell	Cytology		

individual, and society (or the international system) respectively. Recognition of such parallels, according to system theorists, should be conducive to cross-fertilization among the various disciplines.

The three aspects of systems singled out in organismic theory can also be identified in analytic theory. The structure of a system described by a mathematical model is reflected in the type of model. For example, the mathematical model describing a harmonic oscillator or, equivalently, the electrical system isomorphic to it is classified as a second-order linear differential equation. This type of equation will define the structure of all systems represented by it. The evolution of a system represented by a system of differential equations is represented by its trajectory. If by "functioning" of an organismic system we mean the actions that preserve its identity by maintaining some sort of steady state (recall the homeostatic mechanisms), then we must look for analogues in mathematically described systems. We find them in so-called steady states to which some such systems tend. Such steady states can be manifested in periodic behavior (cf. the behavior of the solar system), or by states in which the variables defining the state of the system fluctuate around constant values.

Examples of this sort of behavior are found in ecological systems. Consider a population consisting of two species and vegetation on which one of them, Prey, feeds. The other species, Predators, feeds on Prey. Suppose the rate of reproduction of Predators is such that this population increases. This leads to the depletion of Prey. As Prey becomes scarce, the reproduction rate of Predators decreases to the point that their numbers dwindle. This gives Prey the chance to increase its reproduction rate, so that this population grows. It can be shown mathematically that this system can tend toward a steady state, whereby the Predator and Prey populations are balanced. Slight deviations from this steady state are "corrected," as if each population exercised "control" over the other.

Of special interest is the stability of such steady states. They are stable if disturbances from the environment produce deviations that tend to be corrected when the disturbance is removed. The magnitude of the disturbance that can still be corrected is a measure of the degree of stability of the system. We have seen that the maintenance of steady states also characterizes the functioning of living systems. The concept of stability also applies to them because, when a disturbance exceeds a certain magnitude, restoration of the steady state may no longer be possible. An irreversible process sets in, for instance, death in the case of an individual or extinction in the case of a species.

Conditions of stability of a system can be derived from its mathematical model (if such a model can be constructed). Lewis F. Richardson, an early pioneer of peace research, derived conditions of stability for an arms race between two powers from a drastically simplified mathematical model based on a pair of differential equations (Richardson 1960). The model contained a pair of parameters of mutual stimulation and a pair of self-inhibition parameters. The mutual stimulation parameters reflected the tendency of each power to increase its level of armaments in response to an increase by the other power. The self-inhibition parameters expressed the tendency of each power to decrease its level of armament in response to its own level. To put it another way, the rate of increase of armament levels was assumed to be determined by a weighted difference of these levels, where the parameters were the weights assigned respectively to the adversary's and to one's own level of armaments.

It turned out that if the product of the self-inhibition parameters is larger than the product of the mutual stimulation parameters, the system tends toward a stable steady state, that is, the arms race could be stabilized. If the product of mutual stimulation parameters is greater than the product of the self-inhibition parameters, the system is unstable. Such an arms race would tend to accelerating escalation. However, depending on the initial conditions, the escalation could be positive or negative. In the latter case, a self-stimulating "disarmament race" would set in. This can be seen intuitively. If mutual stimulation is sufficiently strong, disarmament moves by one side can stimulate similar moves by the other to the extent of overcoming the action of the self-inhibition, which in this situation resists disarmament. Here we have another illustration of the duality of conflict and cooperation. Under certain conditions, one can suddenly turn into the other.

Concrete and Abstract Systems

In Gerard's scheme (see table 3), some levels of organization characterize concrete systems more or less identifiable as "objects" occupying circumscribed regions of space. Such are the cell, the organ, and the organism. Above this level of organization, systems generally do not occupy well-defined regions in space. A family, for example, could be imagined living in a house. However, spatial confinement is not a crucial characteristic of a system of this sort. Children may move away even before they begin families of their own. But whether they remain members of the family or not depends not on their location but on their feelings and the feelings of the other members. These cannot be established by some clear, objective criteria, such as the criterion of whether a leg belongs to a given body. Nor is the termination of a family as clearly established as, say, the death of one of its members. A family may have dissolved in the minds of some of its members but not in the minds of others.

If the notion of system is extended still further, as, for example, to institutions, the circumspection in space and time becomes still more problematic. By many criteria, the Roman Catholic Church can certainly be regarded as an institution, therefore, according to our conception, a system. In describing this system, its location is not of prime importance. Granted, it appears as if this institution is more firmly established in the southern countries of Europe than in the northern, and historical reasons for this localization can be discerned. However, the geographic property is surely not as important as, say, the confinement of an organism within its skin. Indeed, a fairly well-defined location of the Catholic Church can no longer be established. The same holds for the English language, for example. Systems of this sort are conceptual rather than physical.

The "habitat" of a conceptual system is generally in the noosphere. A language, a religion, an institution (defined as a set of practices) exists primarily in people's heads. They frequently "materialize" in concrete objects: a language in a book, a religion in a temple, an institution in its physical facilities. Conversely, conceptual systems serve as an environment for its concrete manifestations. As is generally the case with a system and its environment, a concrete system and the conceptual system in which it is embedded coevolve. This is particularly conspicuous in the case of institutions. Table 4 shows a list of conceptual institutions defined as a set of practices, rules, or ideas, and examples of their concrete manifestations.

War as an Evolving Institution

In subsequent chapters we will examine the evolution of war as an institution. Clearly, at any given time, war can be regarded as a set of practices—an organization of men and machines for carrying out conquests, destruction of enemy forces, and so forth. The organizations nurtured by the war system are specific armed forces—armies, fleets, general staffs, military academies, weapon-producing industrial plants, research institutions, and so on. Underlying the war system are ideational support systems. One such support system of war has been the system of conceptions and assumptions constituting so-called political realism, which pictures the global political system as a collection of sovereign states. Military potential appears in this ideational framework as an important component of the state's "security."

It would be a mistake, however, to suppose that because the conception of international relations inherent in the "realist" school of international relations has been congenial to the perpetuation of the war system, it has always been so. The institution of war is much older than the present international system. In fact, war has survived as an institution precisely because it readapted itself to a changing ideational environment, which, in turn, was modified by evolutionary changes in the war system. It should be clear that when we speak of war "adapting" to its ideational supportive system or to the society in which it is embedded, we mean adaptation in the Darwinian and not in the goal-directed, Lamarckian sense. There is no goal-directedness, let alone consciousness, in this adaptation. The contention that a system "adapts" in the Darwinian sense is a tautology: systems (whether species, artifacts, or institutions) that do not adapt to their environments cease to exist.

Opinions may differ about what particular institutions become maladapted. Some of these opinions may be severely mistaken. We have cited Amos's view that the war system is becoming rapidly maladapted and is therefore slated for extinction. This view was expressed in 1880. Since then, Europe was shaken by the cataclysm of 1914–18 and soon afterward by a war in which, contrary to Amos's prognosis of a steady

TABLE 4. Institutions as Components of a Culture and as Concrete Entities

Institution	As a Set of Practices	Constituent Organizations
Banking	Lending, holding money in trust, investing	A bank
An economy	Buying, selling, producing, consuming	A corporation A cartel A cooperative
Religion	Rituals, beliefs, moral obligations	A church A monastery
Education	Imparting information, training in skills, indoctrination, enlightenment	A university
Transport	Air transportation, traffic, navigation	A railroad network An airport
Political democracy	Elections, political campaigns, public discussion of issues	A political party A parliament
A penal system	Confinement of persons, executions, paroles	A prison
Organized crime	Robberies, smuggling, bribery of officials	A racket A drug ring

"humanization" of war, civilians were deliberately and routinely slaughtered.

In the wake of this recent history, the title of this book may appear as a repetition of Amos's foolhardy prognosis. However, it was not meant to be a prognosis. Rather, it was meant to be a stimulus to action. As we shall see, although the adaptability of the war system to its social environment has been most impressive, there may be a limit to this adaptability. If there is, the opportunity to take advantage of the mortality of the war system should not be missed, since coexistence of the institution of war and the human race seems no longer possible.

9

Adaptations of the War System to Its Social Environment

Primitive Genocidal Warfare

War as organized mass violence probably originated sometime during the Neolithic age when the domestication of plants and animals made a settled way of life possible. Agriculture provided more security against starvation than hunting or food gathering. The fruits of the soil were naturally appropriated by the people who cultivated it. Thus, cultivated land became their de facto property. Nomadic tribes looking for land to settle on found productive lands already occupied. The settlers were an obstacle. The most direct way of removing this obstacle was to kill the inhabitants. This appears to be a reasonable explanation of the genocidal wars to which much space is devoted in the Old Testament, which is, in part, a recorded history of the ancient Hebrews. Thus, genocide became an adaptation of war to the sort of function it served, namely, clearing the land to be settled. The adaptation was institutionalized, that is, the practice was actually prescribed. In Deuteronomy 20:16–18 we read:

> of the cities . . . that the Lord, thy God hath given thee for an inheritance, thou shalt save alive nothing that breatheth, but thou shalt utterly destroy them: the Hittites, and the Amorites, the Canaanites, and the Perizzites, the Hivites, and the Jebusites; as the Lord thy God hath commanded thee. That they teach you not to do after all their abominations, which they have done unto their gods and so ye sin against the Lord thy God.

The instructions are revealing. Note the rationalization of killing everyone and everything on the land to be occupied. This must be done to avoid corruption, incursions into the practices and taboos that bind the conquering tribe into a tightly knit fighting force.

The attribution of depravity to the prospective victims may have served still another function, namely, that of allaying the guilt feelings associated with killing one's own kind. Such aversion may well have been selected for in the course of evolution. We have seen that nonlethal fighting is usual in intraspecific combats. In some animals, the weapons used in such fighting were modified to make them less dangerous. In animals possessing dangerous weapons, modifications of fighting behavior have been observed. For instance, a wolf defeated in combat exposes his neck to the victor as if inviting him to kill him, whereupon the latter turns away, and the fight is over.[1] Similar inhibitions may have developed among humans. To facilitate the clearing of conquered land, these inhibitions had to be overcome. This was done by portraying the inhabitants as utterly evil. It is not only permissible to kill evil people, it is mandatory to kill them.

I do not pretend to have given an "explanation" of genocidal warfare—merely an interpretation of it, an attempted reconstruction of the state of mind of the people whose deeds are recorded in writings regarded as sacred. In consequence of the rationalization, war became institutionalized. Having changed the mental and emotional orientation of a people living in close contact with each other, that is, in a closely bound community (a survival mechanism), war created a new "environment" for itself and became adapted to it. The institution of war became an object of veneration together with its personification, the tribal deity, the Lord of Hosts.

A hymn to war attributed to Deborah, a female judge in premonarchical Israel, gives full expression to the veneration of war.

> I unto the Lord will sing. . . . When Thou didst march out of the fields of Edom the Earth trembled. . . . They quaked in the presence of the Lord . . . the Lord and God of Israel. (Judges 5:3–5)

Human Booty

Along with war, agriculture gave birth to slavery. Large-scale agriculture was a major factor in the institutionalization of slavery. It originated in

1. This gesture need not be interpreted anthropomorphically. The defeated wolf exposes his neck by turning away his muzzle. It is the sight of the muzzle (bared teeth) that stimulates aggression. When the stimulus is removed, aggression stops. In this connection recall E. O. Wilson's remark about the survival potential of "pacific maneuvering." A case can be made for unilateral disarmament as the removal of an aggression-triggering stimulus.

regions where rainfall was scant and had to be supplemented by irrigation. Thus "public works" became the mark of civilization. This sort of enterprise involves the coordination of mass labor, and this can be most easily accomplished by coercion. People are most easily coerced if they are removed from their habitat into strange surroundings among strangers. Thus arose the idea of capturing conquered people instead of killing them.

An important feature of institutionalized slavery was that the slave had to be an outsider. His resistance to coercion was broken as a consequence of his being uprooted. Over and above that, it is the uprooting that makes it possible to reduce the slave to a thing, something that can be owned. The necessary connection between "not belonging" and dehumanization was recognized in Roman classical law, which defined slavery as an institution "whereby someone is subject to the *dominium* of another contrary to nature." *Dominium* means "power." Besides, Roman law explicitly required that if a man is sold into slavery (e.g., as a punishment), he had to be sold abroad (Levy-Brühl [1931] 1960).

For these reasons, the most natural supply of slaves in large numbers was provided by warfare. Slave-owning societies more powerful than their neighbors raided with the express purpose of capturing slaves. Even between societies of comparable military power, the appetite for slaves was an important factor in the institutionalization of war. After the conquest of the New World by Europeans, slaves were imported from Africa in large numbers to work on plantations (commercialized agriculture). By then the whites had other uses for war. The capture of slaves was left to the Africans and so helped maintain the institution of war on that continent.

The Age of Empires

Although it was impossible to enslave people on their own soil, advances in the techniques of ruling and administration opened up possibilities for exploiting people's labor without reducing them to slavery. Conquest of territory became a principal war aim. The power of ruling elites could be extended far beyond the borders of the domains where they had risen to that status.

War of conquest necessitated armies, that is, organized masses of men who became proficient in the use of lethal weapons and did nothing else. Professionalization gave the impetus for the evolution of war technology, which, in turn, nurtured professionalization.

War technology was of two kinds: weapons and battle tactics. The development of both was another instance of coevolution. For example, the Macedonian phalanx, an infantry battle formation with which Alexander the Great conquered his empire, overwhelmed the enemy by shock of physical impact. Consequently, the infantry was heavily "armed," which in those days meant that the soldiers carried heavy shields. In contrast, the long bow, the weapon with which the English defeated the French in the battles of the Hundred Years' War, required no such protection, which would have been an encumbrance to the archers. In those battles, the infantry triumphed over the heavily armored cavalry and made a break in the conception of war, characteristic of the age of chivalry, namely, that war was the business of the nobility, not of the commoner.

In his extensive treatise, *A Study of War* ([1942] 1965), Wright lists eight great wars in the two millennia of Western civilization preceding what is commonly called the modern age (from the middle of the fifteenth century). Each of these wars brought about far-reaching cultural and political changes, which, in turn, had a profound effect on the further evolution of the institution of war.

With his phalanx, Alexander conquered an empire that was short-lived but rich in consequences. It prepared the soil for the Hellenization of the regions now comprising the Middle East.

The Romans conquered the Mediterranean world with their legions, whose power derived from superior discipline. After three centuries of warfare in Greece, Mesopotamia, Carthage, Spain, and Gaul, the Romans were able to establish an empire that maintained peace among 150 million people for about a century, during the reign of the Antonine Caesars. This century of peace was even given a name—Pax Romana—which became a synonym for peace established by conquest and the imposition of a uniform code of laws on a disarmed population. By analogy, Pax Britannica was the name given to British imperial rule during the nineteenth century.

The next large-scale war of conquest was the invasion of the Roman Empire by Attila and his mounted army of Huns and Germans. This conquest was not politically consolidated. On the contrary, it contributed to the subsequent disintegration of the Roman Empire through the deterioration of agriculture and through the necessity of relying on barbaric mercenaries for the defense of frontiers against further invasions.

Comparable in extent to the Roman Empire was the Islamic empire established by Muhammad and his successors in the seventh century. It stretched from India in the east to Spain in the west. An incursion was made into France, but further expansion was checked there by Charles Martel.

Charles the Great (Charlemagne), king of the Franks, established a short-lived empire in Germany, France, and Italy, a sort of shadowy restoration of the Roman Empire.

The Vikings invaded both northern and southern Europe (and even North America) and established lasting governments in Normandy, England, and Iceland.

The wars of European feudal princes against Islam were conceived as wars of conquest, but were unsuccessful in the sense of establishing lasting governments except for a short-lived kingdom in Palestine.

Finally, the last extended war of the premodern period was the Hundred Years' War between England and France, in which the initial victories of the English were reversed when the French rallied behind a female leader, Joan of Arc, and drove the English out of France.

Of these wars, the Arab conquests and the Hundred Years' War are of special interest because they introduced three new features into the etiology of war. One was ideological commitment manifested in war fueled by religious fervor, as in the Islamic conquests. Another was a war aim based on perceived legitimacy, which, in the time of the Hundred Years' War, was rooted in dynastic considerations. The third feature was national consciousness, which made the English perceive themselves as Englishmen and the French as Frenchmen during the Hundred Years' War. These features were still in incipient stages but were to play much more conspicuous roles in the wars of the modern period.

Holy War

The remarkably rapid and extensive conquests by the Arabs in the seventh century are, perhaps, the earliest and certainly the most conspicuous example of the so-called holy war (jihad). If we are intent on seeking the origins of these wars in more or less objectively verifiable conditions rather than in the state of mind of the conquerors, we can find them in the precarious situation of the Arabs at the time when Muhammad started preaching. The drying up of the climate and overpopulation had made living increasingly difficult. In addition, the Arabs were hard pressed by surrounding powerful states—Abyssinia and Yemen in the south, Persia in the east, and the Byzantine Empire in the west. Intertribal strife and blood feuds took a heavy toll. Such tensions frequently culminate in an explosion by providing a common channel for aggressions generated by frustrations.

Adroit use of light cavalry provided the Arabs with a substantial military advantage. As frequently happened in the time when news spread exclusively by word of mouth, fame preceding the invaders demoralized prospective victims, facilitating further successes. The decisive factor in paving the way of the conquerors may have been the policy of incorporating the vanquished in the expanding political realm instead of slaughtering or enslaving them. An invasion was preceded by a formal offer of peace on the condition that the population marked for conquest converted to Islam. If the offer was accepted, the converts became allies, swelling the armies of the conquerors. Refusal was *causus belli.* This policy must have provided a solid basis for high morale and fervor. Like the ancient Hebrews, the Arabs saw themselves as instruments of God and, at the same time, enhancing a self-image of merciful self-righteousness: the vanquished were conquered for their own good.

Many other wars seem to have been ideologically motivated but none so intensely as the original jihad, in which conversion was a sure way to escape the gruesome fate of the vanquished in a war of extermination.

The Crusades are sometimes also interpreted as holy wars. However, the invasion of the Holy Land (and, incidentally, the pillaging of the lands on the way there) had nothing in common with the Arab conquests except rhetoric. The Crusaders had none of the organizational skills of the Arabs, and their campaigns did not result in any political consolidation. We will allude to these campaigns as manifestations of the mentality that dominated the age of chivalry.

The Age of Chivalry

The Crusades were the most conspicuous wars in Europe from the end of the eleventh to the latter half of the thirteenth centuries. The objectively verifiable causes of the Crusades were cogently summarized by Ernest Barker in the fourteenth edition of the *Encyclopedia Britannica* (p. 273ff). The clergy had an interest in facilitating pilgrimages to the Holy Land and in diverting violence (rampant among the feudal lords) onto an external enemy. Norman princes were enthusiastic about the prospects of carving out fiefdoms in the new territory with only "infidels" protecting it. The commercially minded Italians saw opportunities to acquire the eastern markets cheaply. Since we are concerned here also with the way war was conceived by the participants, we must stress the primacy of the ideological factor. The Crusades were most characteristic of the age of chivalry, when war was regarded primarily as the occupation of men of noble birth. The religious motive in these wars served to emphasize the nobility of the warrior.

The nature of warfare in medieval Europe was shaped by the circumstance that the fighting men were predominantly of the nobility. This, in turn, can be traced to the social structure of the feudal system. With the dissolution of the Roman Empire, centralized authority dissolved and with it any security against pillage and murder. Survival depended on some sort of protection against roaming bands of marauders. This protection was provided by what amounted to a private "army" (actually just a band of armed men) who served a chieftain. This chieftain came to be called a lord or baron (cf. Russian *barin* as the peasants referred to the landlord whose serfs they were). The domicile of the lord was a fortified castle. In return for protection, the common folk (i.e., the peasantry) tilled the fields around the castle, which the lord owned by virtue of a grant from *his* lord.

The position of the peasants was not that of slaves in the sense that they were not chattel that could be bought and sold like cattle. The relation between the peasants and the lord was in effect, if not in form, a contractual one based on mutual obligations. The business of the peasants was to toil; that of the lord and his armed band (the knights) to fight.

Eventually, central authority emerged out of the anarchy of the Dark Ages in the form of monarchy. But the power of the monarch was in conflict with that of the Church. The latter was nurtured by the well-nigh universal belief that life in this world was no more than a short prelude to existence in eternity, and the latter, which would be either eternal bliss or eternal torment, depended on "salvation." The Church had the key to salvation. It provided the services required to attain it, such as baptism, organized prayer, and burial rituals. Thus, the power of the Church was based on what has come to be called the "spiritual needs" of the population. The power of the king, such as it was, was based on his position as the lords' lord. The grants of fiefdoms came from him. Supposedly he was a figure to whom the barons owed common loyalty, which attenuated, to some extent, the Hobbesian war of all against all. This power, however, was at first severely limited, for the king had no armed force of his own. He depended on the barons to provide fighting men when he fought against other kings.

Thus, rule in the Middle Ages was personal. Loyalty was to the person of a lord who held a fiefdom or to the king who granted the fiefdom, not to a country, as we take for granted today in the age of sovereign states. Personalized power and personalized obligations were the marks of the age of chivalry. The profession of arms was linked with the status of the nobleman. The nobleman was not only armed but also mounted. Indeed, the word *chivalry* (associated with nobility of character) is derived from the French word for horse, as is cavalry and cavalier. A man on a horse towers over the man on foot.

In war, a knight and his horse were regarded as inseparable. So were noble status and fighting. Barbara Tuchman (1978), in describing the knight's love of battle, quotes Garin li Loherains, the hero of a chanson de geste: "If I had one foot already in Paradise, I would withdraw it to go and fight." The troubadour Bertrand de Born wrote:

> My heart is filled with gladness when I see
> Strong castles besieged, stockades broken and overwhelmed,
> Many vassals struck down,
> Horses of the dead and wounded roving at random,
> And when battle is joined, let all men of good lineage
> Think of naught but the breaking of heads and arms,
> For it is better to die than be vanquished and live. . . .
> I tell you I have no such joy as when I hear the shout
> "On! On!" from both sides and the neighing of riderless steeds,
> And groans of "Help me! Help me!"
> And when I see both great and small
> Fall in the ditches and on the grass
> And see the dead transfixed by spear shafts!
> Lords, mortgage your domains, castles, cities,
> But never give up war!
> (Quoted in Tuchman 1978, 16)

The Institutionalization of War as a Political Instrument

Most of us think of the nation-state as the most natural form of social organization. Governments of nation-states have, on occasion, been accorded unswerving loyalty by their subjects or citizens, especially in times of war. Aside from the force of patriotic feelings that frequently provide the framework of strenuous cooperative effort, the state's monopoly on coercive power enhances conformity and obedience in most of its population—a mark of an organized society. A comparable extent and intensity of cooperation is not frequently observed among people belonging to different states.

The state did not always enjoy a monopoly of coercive power or have absolute claim on the loyalty of its subjects. It acquired its power and backed this claim as a consequence of consolidating its control over the instrument of coercion—the army. Today, armies are composed almost exclusively of the states' own citizens. This was not always so. Well into the nineteenth century, a substantial portion of European standing armes consisted of foreign mercenaries. Frederick the Great, for example, recruited his soldiers from all over the Holy Roman Empire. At the beginning of his reign, two-thirds of his soldiers were foreign mercenaries. From the end of the eighteenth century on, states imposed restrictions both on recruitment and the enlistment of their subjects in foreign armies.

Traditionally, the decline of mercenarism has been explained by economic reasons: the state's own subjects serving in its army received only nominal pay. As J. E. Thompson (1990) points out, however, the citizen soldier incurred other costs. Unlike the mercenary soldier who was bought or rented, the citizen had to be turned into a soldier. This took training. Moreover, the recruit had to satisfy certain minimal standards of physical and mental fitness. Thus, in order to have a pool of physically and mentally fit young men to draw upon as recruits, the state had to provide some health care and, at least in western Europe, some educational facilities. In 1917, two-thirds of the British young men called up for service were declared to be in less than satisfactory shape. E. J. Hobshawn points out that "for the first time public authorities and the state thought seriously about social improvement programmes" (Hobshawn 1969, 164–65).

Thus, according to Thompson, the economic explanation of the decline of mercenarism is insufficient. She offers an institutional analysis of the evolution of the state's authority claims. First, she raises the question of why, in the nineteenth century, states enacted legislation limiting military activities of their subjects. She argues that it was the appearance of the citizen, an individual possessing political and economic rights institutionalized in the state, that turned the state into a fully autonomous unit. At the same time, the citizen became a reliable tool in the state's coercive activities at home and abroad. In this way, states became what mainstream political theory depicts them as—Hobbesian actors in the international arena—as a consequence of consolidating their armies as coercive instruments.

In the Middle Ages, the power of the Church was greater than that of the state. It was dramatically illustrated by the conflict between Pope Gregory VII and Henry IV, Holy Roman Emperor. The pope had issued an edict prohibiting the investiture (i.e., appointment of bishops) by secular authority. Henry defied this order. The conflict escalated, culminating in Henry's declaring the pope deposed. The pope excommunicated Henry. Eventually, Henry capitulated and made the perilous journey across the Alps to Cassona, a castle in which Gregory had taken refuge, to plead for forgiveness. According to a story circulated at the time, Gregory had Henry standing barefoot in the snow for three days before he consented to see him. Although the story is probably apocryphal, it is known that Henry was refused admittance to the castle several times before the pope finally relented and forgave him.

The authority of the Church in western Europe probably reached its zenith in the thirteenth century. Thereafter it declined as technological progress, easier communication, and wider trade increased interest in things of this world. Awareness of the corruption of the clergy (an inevitable adjunct of unchallenged power) helped undermine the Church's authority until the final rupture of the Reformation.

The so-called wars of religion between Catholics and Protestants culminated in the Thirty Years' War. Most significant for the subsequent history of Europe was the provision of the Treaty of Westphalia (1648), which recognized the authority of princes in establishing the religion of their domains. Neither the Catholics nor the Protestants could claim "victory" in that devastating war. Instead, secular power emerged victorious. The period from 1648 to 1789 can be regarded as the era in which monarchical power was at its height. It was in that era that the system of sovereign states became the international system, which to this day is identified as such in textbooks on international relations. It ushered in the era of political war.

The wars of the eighteenth century are often referred to as "cabinet wars." The issues were legalistic, the sort of issues that, in a civilized society, are settled by recourse to the courts. A typical issue was the question of dynastic legitimacy as reflected in the so-called wars of succession. The eighteenth century witnessed the War of the Spanish Succession, the War of the Austrian Succession, the War of the Polish Succession, and the War of the Bavarian Succession. The means were as limited as the goals, usually professional standing armies supplemented by mercenaries. Great stress was put on the training of soldiers in the exercise of complex battle maneuvers and in conditioning them to automatonlike obedience. The length of service of a professional soldier was of the order of twenty-five years. These standing armies were expensive instruments, not lightly sacrificed. Consequently, the cabinet wars were not very sanguinary by modern standards. Battles were affairs of short duration, limited to circumscribed areas (often implicitly agreed upon). Patriotism and its attendant passions, glorification of war, fervent devotion to one's country, and hatred of the enemy, were not principal instigators of war. The common soldier seldom knew what he was fighting for; sometimes not even the identity of the enemy was known to him. The high command regarded themselves as highly competent specialists, not as conquerors or champions of an idea or defenders of "a way of life." It was regarded as perfectly proper in those days for a general to enter the service of another country, just as today it is normal for a corporation lawyer to leave one firm and join another or for one baseball player to leave one team and join another. Surrender was no disgrace. In fact, surrender ceremonies were sometimes subjects of grandiose paintings, just like parades and battle scenes. Sometimes court ladies and gentlemen came in their coaches to a site overlooking the battleground to see the event. In short, war was a gentlemanly occupation for the commanding personnel, a form of slavery for the soldiers of the standing armies, and a form of employment, or sometimes indentured servitude, for the mercenaries.

The style of eighteenth-century warfare may have been a reaction against the devastation and savagery of the Thirty Years' War, a transformation of war from a massive outburst of violence fueled by passions and marked by excesses to a "normal phase of international relations." In was an adaptation of the war system to a changed social environment—the secularization of states, the establishment of absolute monarchy as a predominant political system in Europe, and finally the interweaving of dynastic lines resulting in lasting family ties among the royal houses. Wars came to resemble family quarrels. Just as these seldom lead to murder, the aims of cabinet wars excluded the destruction of states or "overthrow of a form of government." The partition of Poland was an exception.[2] But then, Poland herself was an exception, "infected" with the ideas of the French Revolution, hence a disruptive agent in the established system. On the other hand, Prussia, decisively beaten by the coalition against her in the Seven Years' War (1756–63), was "rescued" at the last moment. This sudden reversal in the fortunes of that war is usually attributed to the death of Empress Elizabeth of Russia, Frederick II's most bitter enemy, and the accession of Peter III, a fervent admirer of Frederick. But another explanation seems at least equally plausible: the "system" had to be preserved, hence no major member could be eliminated for fear of disturbing the "balance of power," a concept that came to dominate international relations in Europe. Here we have evidence that the "international system" established in Europe by the Treaty of Westphalia was indeed a system in the organismic sense. The concept of "balance of power" was a sort of homeostatic mechanism that served to preserve its identity.[3] War at that time was regarded as a normal functioning of the system, a periodically recurring state like hunger or sexual activity in an animal.

The concept of war as a normal phase in relations between states is reflected in the meticulous observance of the "rules of war" in that era. In particular, formal declarations had to precede hostilities. Because of the difficulty of replacing highly trained armies, battles were only occasionally indulged in and were usually of short duration. Gruesome memories of the excesses of the Thirty Years' War led to hypertrophic emphasis on discipline as the primary virtue of an army. It was this era that best reflects Clausewitz's famous dictum, "War is the continuation of politics by other means."

Clausewitz, like Beethoven, straddled two centuries and, like Beethoven, he celebrated the transition from a "classical" to a "romantic" era in the history of warfare. The age of the cabinet wars deserves to be called classical because of its uniformity of style, its emphasis on

---

2. Poland was dismembered in three stages. In 1772, large territories were ceded to Russia, Austria, and Prussia. In 1773, additional regions were absorbed by Russia and Prussia. The final partition (again between Russia, Prussia, and Austria) removed Poland from the political map.

3. From the point of view of political realism, which ascribes to potentates the ability to make and implement rational decisions, the preservation of states in the eighteenth century was simply a consequence of limitations of military power. No state possessed sufficient military capability to destroy another major state. The systemic approach avoids voluntaristic explanations of large-scale political events if they can be derived from general principles of self-preserving systems.

craftsmanship and expertise, and because of the relative restraint of the emotional expression. The eighteenth century was appropriately called the Age of Reason.

Witness Tolstoy's description of General Pfuhl (Pfuel in German), the Prussian military expert in the service of Russia during the Napoleonic Wars. To Pfuhl, a relic of the eighteenth century, the highest military virtue was a thorough knowledge of military theory and its faithful application.

> Pfuhl . . . had a science—the theory of the oblique attack—which he had deduced from the wars of Frederick the Great; and everything he came across in more recent military history seemed to him imbecility, barbarism, crude struggle in which so many blunders were committed on both sides that those wars could not be called war at all. They had no place in his theory and could not be made a subject of science at all.
>
> In 1806 Pfuhl had been one of those responsible for the plan of campaign that ended in Jena and Auerstadt.[4] But in the failure of that war he did not see the slightest evidence of the weakness of his theory. On the contrary, the whole failure was to his thinking entirely due to the departures that had been made from his theory, and he used to say with characteristic gleeful sarcasm: "Didn't I always say the whole thing was going to the devil?" . . . He positively rejoiced in failure, for failure, being due to some departure in practice from the purity of the abstract theory, only convinced him of the correctness of his theory. (Tolstoy [1867–69] 1973, 692–93)

Clausewitz, who, incidentally, served on Pfuhl's staff, subjected this sort of pedantry to devastating criticism. The formalism, he felt, obscured the "true essence" of war, which was not in the intricacies of tactical maneuvers but in unswerving pursuit of a single goal, ". . . to compel our opponent to fulfill our will" (Clausewitz [1832] 1968, 101). Here it seems natural to ask "Whose will? Who is 'we'?" Clausewitz never raises this question, because the answer seems obvious. "We" are the State; our will is the State's will. International politics consists of interrelations

4. On the eve of that battle, in which Clausewitz was taken prisoner, he wrote to his fiancée that he looked forward to the engagement with the same joyous anticipation as to his wedding day (cf. Schwartz 1878, 226; the letter is quoted in Rapoport 1989, 180).

among states generated by the attempts of each to impose its will on others.

In the age of absolute monarchies, it seemed natural to identify the "will of the State" with the will of its monarch. However, the transition in the concept of war was an essential one. In 1795, Kant, in his essay *Perpetual Peace,* argued that a lasting peace (by which he meant a lasting peace in Europe) could be achieved only if the nations adopted a republican form of government (Kant [1795] 1903, 120ff.) For it seemed that, in the eighteenth century, ambitions of princes were the most important cause of wars. That this was a gross misconception had become apparent at the time Kant wrote his essay. For, just at that time, a sequence of wars began in Europe that dwarfed all the cabinet wars of the "classical" era in destructiveness. These wars were unleashed by the institution of the first republican form of government in a major European state. It seems that the institution of war made yet another adaptation to a changed social environment.

The Demise of "Classical" War

The eighteenth century is sometimes called the Enlightenment in Europe. The scientific view of the physical world was blossoming. Especially in France, the established social order based on absolute monarchy, on privileges of the aristocracy, and on the established Church was eloquently challenged by Voltaire, Rousseau, the Encyclopedists, and other intellectual professionals. In England, the century culminated in the Industrial Revolution, in North America in a declaration of human rights as the foundation of a legitimate government.

The recognition of war as an evil was not an innovation of the Enlightenment. Erasmus (1466–1536) had already condemned war as a crime against man and God. However, in the eighteenth century, the idea became widespread and independent of religious underpinnings. In condemning war, the focus of blame shifted from man's wickedness to the institution of monarchy.

One of the earliest works manifesting the "dream of perpetual peace" in the political rather than the religious mode was the *Memoirs* of M. de Bethune, Duke of Sully, published in 1634. In that work, Sully refers to a "grand Design," which he attributes to King Henry IV of France. The attribution seems to be fortuitous. It may have been made to deserve attention.

The "grand Design" is strikingly similar to the plan proposed of King George of Bohemia, including, as it does, an alliance against the Turks. It envisaged a Christian republic formed by a union of fifteen European powers on the principle of equality and given the mandate to "deliberate on questions that might arise, to occupy themselves with discussing different interests, to settle quarrels amicably, to throw light upon and arrange all the civil, political, and religious affairs of Europe whether internal or foreign" (cited in Smith 1903, 34).

Pertinent to this discussion is the skepticism with which the project was treated by eighteenth-century European thinkers. Voltaire dismissed the scheme in a sentence (Voltaire [1771] 1935, 351); Leibniz wrote,

> I have seen something of the plea for maintaining perpetual peace in Europe. It reminds me of an inscription outside of a church yard which ran "Pax Perpetua." For the dead, it is true, fight no more. But the living are of another kind, and the mightiest among them have little respect for tribunals. (Leibniz 1768, 5:65–66)

Of special significance to us is the circumstance that much of the scepticism that greeted the proposals for perpetual peace stemmed from the loss of confidence in the ability of sovereigns to establish a lasting peace among themselves. J. J. Rousseau ([1761] 1955), in particular, thought that sovereigns would never submit to any authority over them. Poet William Cowper, Rousseau's contemporary, voiced the idea that war was one of the pleasures of regal existence.

> Great princes have great playthings. Some have play'd
> At hewing mountains into men, and some
> At building human wonders mountains high
> . . . .
> Some seek diversion in the tented field,
> And make the sorrows of mankind their sport.
> But war's a game, which were their subjects wise,
> Kings should not play at. Nations would do well
> T'extort their truncheons from the puny hands
> Of heroes, whose infirm and baby minds
> Are gratified with mischief and the spoil.
>
> (Cowper 1856, 288–89)

Here, the idea of a revolution against the institution of war supported by monarchs comes over the intellectual horizon.

Immanuel Kant ([1795] 1903) refers to the rulers of states "unwearying in their love of war." He goes on to state the conditions of perpetual peace in six Preliminary Articles. They contain

1. A prohibition of secret reservation of material for a future war.
2. Inviolability of independence of states.
3. Abolition of standing armies.
4. Prohibition of contracting national debts to finance future wars.
5. Prohibition of interfering in the internal affairs of another state.
6. Prohibition of excesses in the conduct of war which "make mutual confidence impossible in a subsequent state of peace."

These are followed by three Definitive Articles. In the first, Kant explicitly reveals his view that the monarchical system is the root of war. The second Definitive Article describes the structure of the international system as a "federation of free states." The last mentions the rights of men as "citizens of the world."

When this was written, the "institution of monarchy" was already overthrown in France. The establishment of the First Republic was followed by the bloodiest wars since the Thirty Years' War. A century later, an even more destructive war wracked Europe, followed by the overthrow of the three most powerful monarchies on the continent, the Russian Empire, the German Empire, and the Austro-Hungarian Empire. Republican forms of government were established in their stead.

It would seem, then, that pointing to the institution of monarchy as the root of war by pacifist thinkers of the Enlightenment was profoundly mistaken. One way of reacting to their mistake is by looking for the "causes" of war elsewhere. There is no assurance, however, that another apparent "cause of war" will not turn out to be as ephemeral as the last. The difficulty of finding a satisfactory answer to such a question is that a vast variety of events and processes have been labeled by the same word—*war.* To be sure, all these events and processes have a common feature, namely, organized mass violence, but this common feature by no means implies common origins or common causes.

On the other hand, if we regard the war system as a firmly rooted institution of human societies, we can suppose that it shares the principal features of all systems, namely, preservation of an identity in spite of continual change, whereby most of its constituent parts have lost their original functions and have acquired quite different ones. In the same way, the olfactory organ of our ancestors evolved into our brain, whose principal function is to enable us to solve problems and foretell the future rather than to perceive the world as an avalanche of impinging smells.

The fundamental change in the nature of warfare in Europe at the end of the eighteenth century was brought about by the sudden appearance of a mass citizen army facing the standing armies of the monarchies. The citizen soldier differed in two vital respects from the rigidly trained professional soldier. First, he had something to fight for (or so he thought); second he was expendable: since he did not require meticulous and protracted training, he could be easily replaced. In fact, the entire male population of a state in the prime of life became a pool of military might. Napoleon lost almost his entire army of 600,000 men in the Russian campaign, but he was able to raise another one in less than a year.

Both the strong motivation and the expendability of the new soldier made possible innovations in battle tactics that proved to be decisive in the Revolutionary and Napoleonic Wars. The infantry no longer had to fight in closed formation to ensure rigid coordination. It could spread out in chains, leaving aiming and firing to the initiative of the individual soldier. Restraint in battle was no longer necessary. Engagements became slaughters, as Clausewitz, the apostle of massive extermination battles, noted and approved. As a matter of course, other states adopted the new mode of warfare. Eventually, Napoleon was defeated by the same factors that determined his initial brilliant successes: the arousal of patriotism as a principal ingredient in war and the escalating ferocity of battles.

It was this unleashing of fury, the anticipation of total war, that Clausewitz interpreted as the emergence of the "essence" of war. Yes, he still perceived war as the continuation of politics by other means. But now he perceived politics as not merely quarrels between princes but a clash of the will of states, now perceived as embodiments of the will of peoples. The era of nationalism was born.

The Era of Nationalism

Patriotism and nationalism were the principal components of what Lewis F. Richardson (1948) called "war moods" in nineteenth-century Europe. The extent to which these affects penetrated into the collective consciousness of populations varied. No doubt they were most widespread and strongest among the literate. The rapid spread of literacy in western Europe, a concomitant of industrialization and urbanization, stimulated the creation of the public press, which, in turn, became a vehicle for the spread of national consciousness and identification.

Until the last decades of the nineteenth century, nationalism was usually associated with liberal political ideas. For example, the short-lived 1848 revolution in Germany was a movement for the unification of Germany as a constitutional monarchy. The concurrent revolt in Hungary against Austria was also a nationalist movement. The wars that led to the eventual unification of Italy were also fueled by fervent nationalism.

It was only toward the end of the century that a rift appeared between the nationalist and the new, socialist ideology. At that time, the first groundwork was laid for transnational (as distinguished from international) cooperation. The first such organization was the International Workingmen's Association, founded by Karl Marx in 1864. Dissension led to its dissolution ten years later. The Second International, established in 1889, lasted longer. It was virtually crippled at the outbreak of World War I, when socialists (except for radical dissenters) supported their national governments. This event speaks for the formidable power of nationalist ideology at the time.

Even more impressive evidence for the intensity of nationalist feelings was provided by the scenes of jubilation in the European capitals at the outbreak of World War I. Strangers embraced each other on the street. Soldiers marched to the railroad stations between cheering mobs lining the thoroughfares. Never was the institution of war more in harmony with public sentiments. No other institution performed the function of "integrating" a society as thoroughly, except possibly the established church at the height of its power in Europe (in the thirteenth century). And no other institution (again except established church) defined so clearly the chasm between "us" and "them." No clearer example can be given of the "union of opposites," in this instance of love and hate, as by the nationalist hysteria that plunged Europe into World War I.

The Revival of Ideological War

The end of World War I was marked by widespread disillusionment. Mutinies in the armed forces had already occurred in 1917. In Russia, massive desertions leading to the virtual dissolution of the army followed the overthrow of the czarist government. The attempts of the provisional government to continue the war "to a victorious finish" led to its doom. The Bolsheviks skillfully exploited the antiwar groundswell to lead a revolution against the provisional government and to establish themselves as the rulers of Russia. The revolutions in Germany and Austria were instigated primarily by revulsion against the futile bloodletting that was blamed on the imperial governments.

However, the institution of war remained intact. Scarcely twenty years elapsed before another war surpassing World War I in ferocity and destructiveness broke out in Europe and became World War II. The distinguishing feature of that war was that bombastic pugnacity, the blowing up of nationalism into megalomania and frank glorification of conquest as a war aim, was all on one side, namely, the side of the Axis powers. The Germans raved about the destiny of the superior race, the Italian fascists about the revival of the Roman Empire, and the Japanese militarists about hegemony in Asia and the Pacific. The Allies presented themselves as democratic and peace loving, as forced into war by the imperative of self-defense. "A war to end war" was a phrase coined during World War I, as the rationale for the entry of the United States into that war. The failure of that war "to end war" inhibited the use of that phrase during World War II. But implicitly, the aim, as the Allies expressed it and perhaps sincerely believed in, was the same. Just as pacifists of the eighteenth century blamed the institution of monarchy as the instigator of wars, so the leaders of the democracies blamed "aggressor states" as the spoilers of global peace that, it seemed to some of them, was within reach if only the incubus of "aggression" could be rooted out of the international system.

In a way, therefore, ideology was revived as a rationale of war. The early declaration of human rights in the Atlantic Charter, when the end of the war was still by no means in sight, gave World War II an ideological aura, which World War I (except in the pronouncements of Woodrow Wilson) did not have. Also, the war aims of the Allies, which included refusal to accept anything short of "unconditional surrender" by the "aggressors," contained a promise of a serious attempt to establish a world order in which war would be regarded as a transgression, rather than as a "continuation of politics by other means."

The Era of "Technolatry"

The changing character of war throughout the ages can be regarded as a progressive "adaptation" to changing conditions. However, the implications of this interpretation suggested by evolutionary theory, namely, that if this adaptation had not taken place, war as an institution would have become extinct, are not entirely convincing. Throughout the ages, war, in spite of its rapidly changing character, could be said to perform some external function. That is, the goal to be achieved by a war could be expressed in terms other than the maintenance of the war system. To be sure, the goals could generally be identified as benefits to select groups—princes, privileged classes, or cliques. Thus, the goal of a dynastic war could hardly be justified as a benefit to anyone but the representatives of a dynasty. The war waged by the United States against Mexico in 1846–48 was, frankly, a war of conquest instigated by a drive to extend the territory where slave labor could be introduced. Victories in colonial wars benefited those who gained from exploiting the resources of the conquered territories, and so on. Still, the envisaged and often realized goals were *something for which* the wars were fought. Rightly or wrongly, some argument could be made that the benefits of victory would outweigh the costs, even if those "benefits" were as fatuous as "maintaining the status of a great power" (Austria's principal war aim in attacking Serbia in 1914), "to avenge an insult," and the like.

Hardly any other phenomenon can match war in the radical changes not only in its concrete manifestations but also in its conceptions. Compare the ecstatic paeans to war in ancient Israel with Erasmus of Rotterdam's contemptuous condemnation.

> If thou abhor theft, war doth teach it. . . . If thou esteem adultery, incest, and filthier things than those, . . . war is the master instigator of all these things. . . . (Erasmus [1517] 1946, 49)

Recall Treischke's glorification of war as the source of inspiration for our "boyhood and early manhood." But in his introduction to Treischke's *Politics,* Arthur James Balfour wrote:

> Political theories, from those of Aristotle downwards, have ever been related, either by harmony or contrast, to the political practice of their day; but of no theories is this more glaringly true than of those expounded in these volumes. They could not have been written before 1870. Nothing quite like them will be written after 1917. (Balfour 1916)

These remarks were published in the midst of World War I.

Treischke's ideas about the role of the state and about the nature of war did not die in 1917. They still energized the final spasms of German militarism a quarter of a century later. But they were never again clothed in intellectual respectability. Nevertheless, the defense of the war system couched in an entirely different language enjoys unprecedented respectability. Let us see how the institution of war found a new niche in the scheme of things.

With the advent of weapons of total destruction, no serious argument could be made for pursuing goals external to war itself on the grounds that the benefits would outweigh the costs, unless, of course, the costs are so defined that they appear justified, which makes the argument unassailable and therefore vacuous. As an example, consider the cost-benefit analysis based on the estimate of the number of U.S. casualties that could be deemed "acceptable" as a price for "standing up to the Russians." Kahn tells of consulting a number of colleagues on this question (1960). The numbers given after about fifteen minutes of discussion clustered around 60 million, which became the basis of a rough estimate of what could be meant by "acceptable" costs. Similarly, definitions have been offered of what one could mean by "winning" a nuclear war in terms of final "scores," such as the extent of destruction wreaked on each side, estimated time to "recover," and so forth.

If these persistent attempts to define the goals of war are discounted, nothing remains. Surely, no "economic gains" can be expected. The prospect of "victory" of one over the other "ideology" implies a belief that an ideology is what its rhetoric describes it to be, that is, something independent of a material and institutional infrastructure. Thus, the victory of an ideology is pictured in terms of reconstructing a totally ruined civilization in the image of the present with the adversary completely removed from the picture. To go on with conventional war aims, strategic advantages, for example, bases, staging areas from which to launch future wars, and the like, were frequently involved in recent wars, for example, in the attack of the USSR on Finland in 1939. But to speak of bases and staging areas in a post–nuclear war world is to assume that the present world order with its ideologies, power struggles, and structure of international relations would remain basically the same as today or, rather, the same as they were in the "classical" era of international relations that has already gone into an irretrievable past, though it still lingers in the minds of most political leaders.

In short, unless one is intent to infuse some meaning, be it economic, political, or ideological, into a possible external goal of a nuclear war at any cost, one must see that there can be no such meaningful goals. Here is where the institution of war succeeded in making an effective adaptation in the concrete sense of this term—a transformation that has so far saved it from extinction.

The justification of maintaining, nurturing, and expanding the war machine is completely embodied in one word: *defense*. Indeed, all ministries of war without exception have been renamed ministries of defense. In view of recent historical experience, prospects of lucrative conquests can no longer mobilize political support. Nationalism and its familiar trappings, trumpet blaring, flag waving, drum beating, and bond selling, is no longer a salable item, surely not in Europe, where a war between traditional enemies, for example, Denmark and Sweden, England and Holland, or France and Germany, is no longer thinkable. War still festers in areas where newly established regimes are following in the footsteps of European powers in the heydays of international power politics or where a white supremacy regime is attempting to stem the tide that threatens to overwhelm it. All these wars could easily be extinguished by the superpowers, if they could cooperate toward that end. As long as they could not, the war system remained intact on its impregnable support base—the supposed imperatives of defense.

The other adaptation of the war system to a changed social environment was the linkage of defense and its derived concepts, such as security or deterrence, to technological progress. It is a truism that war has become increasingly dependent on technology. World War I has been called the chemists' war (high explosives, poison gas); World War II, appropriately, the physicists' war (radar, the atomic bomb). World War III is pictured, in preparations for it, as the cyberneticists' and mathematicians' war. The following prognosis is revealing.

> On the battlefield of the future, enemy forces will be located and targeted almost instantaneously through the use of data banks, computerassisted intelligence evaluation, and automated fire control. With the first round kill probabilities approaching certainty, and with surveillance devices that can continuously track the enemy, the need for large forces to fix the opposition physically will be less important.
>
> Hundreds of years were required to achieve the mobility of the armoured division. A little over two decades later we have the airmobile division. With cooperative effort, no more than ten years

should separate us from the automated battlefield. (General William Westmoreland, quoted in Dickson 1971, 169)

The general was too sanguine. A quarter of a century after this prediction, the "automated battlefield" is still in the realm of pipe dreams. But while the specific predictions missed their mark, the spirit of the sort of progress that is manifested in war technology has been captured. It is the spirit of the Second Industrial Revolution, which superimposed information-processing technology upon energy-processing technology, the product of the First Industrial Revolution. It is in this sense that World War III can be conceived as the cyberneticists' and mathematicians' war.

The war machine is nurtured by the very frontiers of technology. The two coevolve. The gratification of participating in "progress" brings together competent and creative people who are given the opportunity to collaborate and to enjoy both the opportunities to put their expertise to work and the feeling of being near the centers of power. In technology, progress is an unambivalent, conspicuous, and irreversible process. It imbues life with a sense of direction and, thereby, makes it meaningful in a culture where success is regarded as the reward of virtue and technological devices are objects of veneration (technolatry).

Technological progress is propelled by the solution of problems that generate other problems. As an example, consider the weapon called the Trident, carried by a submarine. Its second "generation," called Trident II, was first conceived in the 1970s. It was equipped with more nuclear power than any previous U.S. submarine weapon, being five times more powerful than its immediate predecessor, Trident I. A submarine carrying 24 Trident II's will have destructive power equivalent to 7,200 Hiroshimas.

Let us see how Trident II became the culmination of an evolutionary process. "Efficiency" is one of the central concepts that dominates technological design. A device is more efficient than another if, by means of it, one can get more benefit for less cost. For example, the internal combustion engine is more efficient than the steam engine because it converts a larger proportion of the energy locked in fuel into work energy. The idea of efficiency became prominent after it was defined with quantitative precision, which made it possible to decide, on objective grounds, which of two devices is more efficient. In this way, a direction is defined in technological progress. In weapons, efficiency means more destructive power per unit cost, where cost may be represented by money or by the amount of material used or by the size of the device (using up valuable space, for example). The desirability of efficiency in weapons is eloquently represented by the slogan "bigger bang for the buck" or, converting the cost to Soviet currency, "more rubble for a ruble."

In the case of the Trident, the problem was to see how little plutonium or uranium could be converted into a bigger explosive force. Evidently, the problem was solved. This suggested the next problem, namely, how the size of the weapon could be reduced without sacrificing its explosive power. This was a problem in design; it was a matter of squeezing as many Trident II's into a submarine as possible. The idea of missiles with multiple warheads was already around. Thus, the next problem was to see how many warheads could be mounted on the Trident II missile. Finally, the problem of accuracy was tackled.

The problem of accuracy became increasingly central in the design of long-range missiles for two reasons. First, accuracy was obviously related to efficiency. If a missile could be counted on to destroy a target with an average probability of .20, five missiles per target slated for destruction would have to be spent. If this probability could be raised to .50, each target would "cost" only two missiles. There was, however, another basis of the appetite for efficiency. In the course of the cold war, U.S. nuclear strategy shifted away from "countervalue" to "counterforce." In accordance with countervalue strategy, intercontinental ballistic missiles were aimed at Soviet population centers. They were meant to "deter" an unprovoked strike on the United States by the Soviets. It was thought that the Soviets would hesitate to launch such a surprise attack, because a retaliatory strike would effectively destroy their country. In the 1960s, however, this strategy was replaced by the so-called counterforce strategy. Now the missiles were aimed at Soviet military installations, especially the sites where the land-based missiles were deployed. It was obviously more justifiable to "disarm" the enemy than to obliterate tens of millions of civilians in an act of revenge.

A counterforce strategy requires considerably more accurate missiles than a countervalue strategy. If one wants to kill all or most inhabitants of a large city, it does not matter much where the bombs fall as long as they fall on the city. Some will die from the blast, others from immediately fatal radiation damage, still others later from radiation sickness, still others from starvation, exposure, epidemic, or violence engendered by social disorganization. This is not the goal of counterforce strategy. Here the aim is to destroy heavily protected missile sites, and this can be done only by near-direct hits. It is imperative to destroy all or nearly all of them, for if some are left, they will be used in a retaliatory strike, and it will be the attacker's population that will be destroyed. For this reason accuracy becomes a prime concern if a counterforce strategy is adopted.

There is still another stimulus to the ascendancy of accuracy as a prime value in the design of missiles. The problem offers a greater challenge than the problem of getting "a bigger bang for the buck." For accuracy is not simply a matter of being "stronger." It is a matter of being more clever, more sophisticated, more elegant, if you will. There is every reason to believe that these esoteric considerations play a part in driving the arms race. These considerations nurture the morale and self-respect of the experts involved in the development of the technology.

In examining the adaptation of the war system to the post–World War II social environment, it is well to keep in mind the features of that institution that endangered its survival. One is militarism, which, in its bombastic form, never had much appeal to the North American public and lost its appeal in Europe after the bloodlettings of the two world wars. The other is militant nationalism, which, although by no means extinct, has been also on the wane.

In their heyday, the blatant symptoms of militarism were manifested in conspicuous dress and in a caste mentality of military personnel (see Vagts 1937). We no longer see the gaudy outfits of the hussars, the dragoons, the uhlans, or the lancers. Officers no longer fight duels to uphold the code of honor. The military has blended with the general population, so to speak. In fact, the borders of the military profession are no longer fixed, especially in the United States, where the well-known (and genuine) openness of that society has broken down the barriers that had traditionally isolated the military caste. This integration of the military and civilian personnel of the war system was vividly described by Colin Gray, himself a member of the so-called strategic community.

> . . . only in the United States is it possible for individuals with relative ease to have "mixed careers" involving occasional periods of official service, university teaching (or affiliation at least), "think tank" research, private consulting, possibly employment in the defense industry. (Gray 1982, 2)

The traditional martial virtues, physical strength, bravery, and fierceness, are no longer relevant. The warrior no longer has to tote heavy swords, shields, or spears. He no longer has to steel himself against fear in battle, since he need not see the enemy. He no longer has to overcome his aversion against killing his own kind, since he no longer sees his victims, nor even knows who they may be.

The war system is served by scientists, masters of linking esoteric science to technology; by engineers, masters of linking technology to the war machine; and by corporation executives, masters of organizing and coordinating collective endeavors on a huge scale. Cost-benefit analysis has become as much a part of preparing for a holocaust as strategic planning is part of an advertising campaign. The following is an example. The authors are concerned with the economics of deterrence. They take into account not merely getting "more bang for the buck" but also more refined indices of efficiency. Specifically, they are concerned with more destruction "of the right kind" achievable (N.B.) within a given budget.

> *a*). Number and weight of offensive weapons (for a given budget). Criteria of this general type are used in surprisingly large number of cases by military correspondents, columnists, and other "experts," who should know better. . . . Little thought is required to dismiss such crude devices. . . . A missile that can carry a small bomb and deliver it within 10 miles of the target presents nothing like the deterrence threat of a missile than can carry a large bomb and deliver it within 2 miles.
>
> *b*). The number and value of enemy targets that can be destroyed (for a given budget). This is a criterion that makes a little more sense. It takes into account not only the numbers of our offense bombers and missiles but also their operational effectiveness. . . . It still is, of course, an ambiguous criterion and requires more precise definition. For example, what target systems—population, industry, or military bases—should be used to keep score . . . ?
>
> *c*.) The number and value of enemy targets that can be destroyed (for a given budget) after an enemy first strike. This is much closer to what we want. It requires us, in allocating our given budget, to reduce the vulnerability of our force whenever money spent on reducing vulnerability . . . will increase our "strike second" capability more than the same money spent on additional bombers or missiles and the personnel to operate them. (Hitch and McKean 1965, 126)

Substitute "sales volume increment per dollar spent" for "value of enemy targets" and the presentation becomes indistinguishable from that of a corporation officer discussing the pros and cons of mass advertising versus promotion campaigns in pushing a product. Note also the allusion to sport, another activity with a positive image: ". . . what target systems . . . should we use to keep score?" In adopting the practices and language of business, the institution of war adapts itself to a society that a U.S. president characterized by a profound remark: "The business of America is business."

In decoupling war from militant, that is, hate-propelled nationalism, the institution has adapted itself to the cosmopolitan attitudes of the technocratic and scientific communities. A promising application of mathematics in the conduct of future wars (as these are envisaged by the "defense community") is in the development of sophisticated decision theory, particularly, the theory of games.

In this connection, some misunderstandings should be cleared up. In the popular conception, the subject matter of game theory is often identified with gamesmanship, that is, skill in outwitting or taking advantage of others by the use of clever ploys and stratagems. There is some substance to this conception inasmuch as a class of problems posed in the theory of games concerns the identification of optimal strategies in conflict situations. In fact, O'Neill (1989) has pointed out that game-theoretic ideas have been developed in three different areas, which he names proto–game theory, low game theory, and high game theory. The main task of proto–game theory is that of formulating decision problems involving two or more actors with generally diverse interests in a way that permits posing concrete questions concerning the value of different strategies to be undertaken in solving the problems. Proto–game theory is not concerned with solutions of such problems. It is low game theory that is concerned with techniques of "solving" decision problems in conflict situations. High game theory is concerned with "mathematical spin-offs" of problems arising in the theory of games.

High game theory need not concern us here. Its subject matter and methods are highly esoteric and are of interest almost exclusively to mathematicians, as can be gathered from the title of a sample paper: "Extension of the Aumann-Shapley Value Concept to Functions on Arbitrary Banach Spaces." Perhaps the content of problems of this sort can be made somewhat clearer by an example of a (fictitious) paper entitled "What would the universe be like if gravitational attraction were governed by the inverse fifth-power law and if space were seven-dimensional?"

One may well ask whether the "defense community" is seriously concerned about the development of game theory as an aid to constructing sophisticated mathematical tools for designing "rational" doctrines, strategies, or tactics. One would think that low game theory, being most directly involved in solving strategic or tactical problems, would be most likely to attract the attention of military planners. However, with the possible exception of one branch to be mentioned below, low game theory does not hold much promise for a mathematicized military science. Game-theoretic models of tactical or strategic problems are of necessity drastic simplifications confined to elementary textbook illustrations. They cannot possibly capture the intricacies and idiosyncratic features of real military situations and their irremovable uncertainties that cannot be reduced to neat probability distributions. Military professionals are justifiably skeptical about the application potential of low game theory. They are likely to share Clausewitz's judgment that war is an art rather than a science. As for proto–game theory and high game theory, their contents are conceptual rather than technical and so are not likely to appeal to the military professional. Nevertheless, the defense community has provided generous support for the development of all three branches of game theory, possibly in the (justified) expectation that mathematicians attracted by opportunities to pursue research in fields that interest them are likely to remain in the scientific infrastructure of the war establishment. In fact, the intellectualization of war has been another important adaptation of the war system to a climate in which the prestige of even abstract and abstruse science has been steadily rising.

The one branch of low (i.e., directly applicable) game theory that may be of relevance to military technology, especially in the age of high tech, is called *differential games.* One example of such a game will suffice to illustrate the nature of the problems attacked by the theory. Consider an antiballistic missile (ABM) designed to intercept an attacking intercontinental ballistic missile (ICBM). The designers want to build a "pursuit strategy" into the ABM, whereby its sensors take readings of the position, velocity, and acceleration of the ICBM, and its information-processing system translates these readings into command signals that chart a pursuit course. Similarly, an "evasion strategy" can be built into the ICBM that enables it to escape from the pursuing ABM (if possible).

The "interests" of the two devices are clearly diametrically opposed. The ICBM "endeavors" to come as near to the target as possible, the ABM to intercept the ICBM as far from the target as possible. Formally, therefore, the situation can be depicted as a game. Differential games are distinguished by the fact that the strategies available to the players are "dynamic," that is, are described as action directions continually changing in time. The "pursuit and evasion game" is clearly a game of this sort.

The difficulties of "solving" such games, that is, prescribing optimal strategies to both players, are formidable and hence present a tantalizing challenge to the creative mathematician. The generation of challenges of this sort represents yet another adaptation of the war system to a social climate in which war itself has acquired a bad name. Hardly anyone professes to love war. Although Lord Balfour was mistaken in predicting the demise of accolades of war by 1917, he was wrong only about the longevity of that style. The glorification of war survived 1917 but not 1945. However, the preparations of war under such Orwellian labels as "defense," "security," or "deterrence," are now depicted in equally glowing terms. The recollections of R. Isaacs, who is credited with the most important pioneering work on differential games, will serve as an example of the sort of mood that pervades the intellectual sector of the defense community in the United States.

As a young man, Isaacs worked for the Rand Corporation. The basic ideas of differential games occurred to him then, and he was free to work them out. However, he wanted the work to be undertaken on a larger scale, say by a team, and, for this, enthusiastic collaborators and administrative approval were required. His efforts did not succeed, and eventually his connection with Rand was terminated. He decided to make his ideas known in a monograph. Recalling those days, he wrote:

> During the galley proof stage, there was a national meeting on control theory. The experience was unique and bizarre. The speakers were largely grappling with one-player versions of differential games such as I had solved years before. I had the eerie feeling of a bird who could fly with two wings watching fledglings attempt it with one. . . . The eminent Pontriagin had come from Russia to present the featured address. Its title—"Differential Games"! How had this phrase, then published only in my Rand reports, reached the Soviet

> Union? His topic? A pursuit game, virtually the isotropic rocket, which he treated splendidly and plainly had just made a beginning. . . . Since then the subject bloomed. There have been national meetings exclusively on it and now an international one. It had even attained sufficient orthodoxy for the bestowal of research grants. Even the ears of the armed services, once so tenaciously sealed, are open a bit, for I have seen sponsored papers on the military use of differential games. (Isaacs 1975, 4–5)

Most striking in this account is the casual reference to the spread of the idea of differential games to the Soviet Union. Isaacs wonders how this could have happened, but he is not alarmed, say, by the thought that the Rand Corporation may have been infiltrated by Soviet spies. On the contrary, he is delighted that "the eminent Pontriagin," an outstanding Soviet mathematician, was, like himself, engrossed in differential games. Papers in pure mathematics were seldom classified, even in preglasnost Soviet Union. Thus, Isaacs and Pontriagin could read each other's papers and so engage in the most fruitful and extensive form of cooperation, namely, on the level of exchange of scientific ideas! The irony of the situation should escape no one. Such cooperation could result in making ever more sophisticated and ever more destabilizing weapons of total destruction possible. Recall that even the arms race between the Soviet Union and the United States has been called a form of international cooperation (see Wohlstetter 1974).

In sum, the sort of adaptation of the war system to contemporary social climates exemplified in Isaacs's story is an adaptation to "rationality." Science is recognized more widely than ever before as the flowering of the most powerful faculty of the human organism—reason. Science, besides being the soil that nurtures technology, the fountainhead of power, is also the epitome of the problem-solving mode of thought—the essence of rationality. Indeed, resistance to the baroque excesses of ubiquitous militarization of human societies is dismissed as a symptom of misguided "idealism" or naive sentimentality, to which mature, reality-oriented strategic thought is juxtaposed.

10

Conceptions of Peace

A chapter on the evolution of peace might be logical following the preceding chapter. However, such a chapter cannot yet be written, because, in contrast to war, peace is not yet an institution. There are, of course institutions (plural) that contribute to the development of activities conducive to peace, at times, to prevention of war. But there is no universal "peace machine" that so clearly possesses the characteristic of a system and reveals an evolutionary process characteristic of the global war machine.

We can, however, attempt to classify conceptions of peace. These cannot be systematically arranged on a time line as a developing system can. Except for the ancient utopian conception of peace in the Old Testament, all the conceptions we shall examine are prominent today. I will classify them on a spectrum on one end of which will be a conception wholly consistent with acceptance of the institution of war and at the other a conception implying an unconditional rejection of it.

The Utopian Vision

The earliest conception of perpetual peace must have been conjured up by people who found themselves on the receiving end of wars of conquest. Ironically, the most eloquent expression of the longing for peace is found in the writings of the ancient Hebrews, the descendants of the tribes that practiced genocidal wars some centuries previously. Thus, we read in Isaiah:

> And they shall beat their swords into ploughshares
> And their spears into pruning hooks;
> Nation shall not lift up sword against nation.
> Neither shall they learn war any more.
> (Isaiah 2:4)

It is noteworthy that the renunciation of violence was extended to nonhumans.

> And the wolf shall dwell with the lamb
> And the leopard shall lie down with the kid
> . . . .
> And the lion shall eat straw like the ox
> And the suckling child shall play on the hole of the asp.
> (Isaiah 11:6, 8)

It is equally noteworthy that in other circumstances, the same metaphor was used with the opposite sign.

> Proclaim yet this among the nations,
> Prepare war;
> . . . . .
> Beat your ploughshares into swords,
> And your pruning hooks into spears.
> (Joel 4:9, 10)

Dimensions in the Conceptions of Peace

Aside from these utopian visions, ideas of peace fit into patterns determined by a problem that was regarded to be of fundamental importance. The way such a problem was formulated suggested a conception of a solution. This solution, in turn, directed attention to persons possessing or claiming a particular expertise who could be expected to cope with the problem. There are other connotations associated with each formulation of a problem, its envisaged solution, and the principal actors expected to cope with it, namely, modalities of social control.

K. E. Boulding (1974) identified three such modalities, which he associated respectively with a threat system, a trade system, and an integrative system. A *threat system* of control emphasizes sanctions or punishments to be imposed on those who do what is prohibited or fail to do what is demanded. A *trade system* depends on promises of benefits or concessions in return for reciprocal benefits or concessions. In an *integrative system*, the interests of participants are fused into a common goal. Individuals identify with each other and with the collective, regarding comembers and the system as a whole as extensions of their Selves.

Further, each image induces a psychological state that harmonizes with the particular formulation of the central problem, the conception of a solution, characteristics assigned to the principal actors, and the modality of the associated social control.

Finally, associated with each conception of peace is an envisaged role of international cooperation in bringing peace about or in preserving it. As we shall see, this envisaged role varies from insignificant to decisive.

Peace through Strength

This conception of peace is encapsulated in the ancient Roman dictum, *Si vis pacem, para bellum* 'If you want peace, prepare for war'. It reflects a distinctly defensive posture and prevails among successful conquerors, who have put a higher priority on protecting their gains than on further expansion. Thus, the devotion of peace inherent in this conception is often genuine, provided peace is identified with an acceptance of existing conditions. No contradiction is seen, however, between this devotion and, at times, obsessive preoccupation with war. The self-image of a power so oriented is that of a peacekeeper, where peacekeeping is identified with the preservation of existing relations of dominance and submission. The terms *Pax Romana, Pax Britannica,* and the suggested *Pax Americana* reflect this conception. They implicitly identify the preservation of peace with the unchallengeable military might of an empire.

Bismarck's Germany (1871–90) is another prominent example of an attempt to preserve peace through strength. Having achieved the unification of the German states into an empire in the wake of successful wars against Denmark, Austria, and France, Bismarck turned his attention to the consolidation of the fruits of victory—the creation of a political and economic framework conducive to a rapid growth of national wealth and prestige. For the time being, all thoughts of further conquests were set aside. Foreign policy was centered on establishing friendly relations with Russia and an alliance with the erstwhile rival, Austria. France was still regarded as an enemy; but an "enemy" is an indispensable adjunct to peace through strength. Germany became the most militarized state in the late nineteenth-century Europe.

The critical problem singled out in the peace through strength paradigm is that of an external threat, usually from a specified source. In the case of imperial Germany it was France; in the case of the Soviet Union, a coalition of "capitalist states"; in the case of the United States, following victory in World War II it was the Soviet Union.

The solution of the problem of the external threat, as it appears to the holders of the peace through strength conception, is simple: military superiority. Consequently, the most prominent and influential actors on the political stage of the "strong" states have been military personages. The nineteenth-century monarchs of the strongest European states wore military uniforms as their everyday attire. In Germany, the general staff dictated the development of the railway network and the allocation of resources to industries. Increasingly, however, as the decisive role of technology in war became apparent, scientists, technocrats, and "captains of industry" matched and, in some cases, surpassed the men in uniform as people whose advice was sought and taken.

The modality of social control most congenial to the proponents of peace through strength is threat. Deterrence is regarded by them as by far the most important, at times the only effective, preventative of war. "Peace is our profession" is the slogan of the United States Air Force. The MX missile has been nicknamed the "peacekeeper." The nuclear arsenal is called an "umbrella."

The dominant psychological state induced by the peace through strength conception of peace is pugnacity and its obverse, fear; that is, pugnacity in the country's own population, fear, presumably induced in the leadership of the adversary but also implicit in the country's own leadership. Reliance on threat induces a feeling of being threatened. At times, however, a hegemonial power may seem so secure against challenge that the mood of its ruling elite reflects self-confidence, superiority, or paternalistic condescension toward dominated populations. At the zenith of their power, the ruling elites of the Roman and British empires might have felt this way.

It goes without saying that in this conception of peace, the role assigned to international cooperation in the establishment or the preservation of peace is negligible. The phrase "blood and iron" coined by Bismarck at the time when Germany was attempting to establish its hegemony in Europe referred to what, in Bismarck's opinion, was and ought to be the decisive factor in international relations, rather than diplomacy and treaties. Contempt for obligations under treaties has been repeatedly demonstrated by the "great powers"—violation of Belgian neutrality by Germany in 1914; attacks on or annexation of states with which a "great power" had signed nonaggression pacts as carried out by the Soviet Union in 1939 and 1940; subversion and overthrow of governments in Latin America by the United States in flagrant violation of the Organization of American States charter, and so on.

In sum, the peace through strength paradigm regards the ability and the readiness to resort to violence as the only reliable guarantee of peace.

Balance of Power

The problem singled out in the "balance of power" conception of peace is disequilibrium in the distribution of power among major states. Solution of the problem requires, according to this conception, a careful tuning of the opposing forces with the aim of reducing temptations to go to war in the hope of achieving a victory. A solution of this sort is likely to entail considerable complexities and, thus, sophisticated expertise—military for evaluating relative war potential of states, diplomatic for implementing the solutions. As in the case of the peace through strength paradigm, the solution is again entrusted to elites of one's own state.

Since, as in the case of the peace through strength paradigm, power ascribed to states is still a key concept in the balance of power paradigm, threat still plays a major role as the envisaged mechanism of control. However, emphasis now shifts to trade as the dominant modality of interaction, inasmuch as peace is no longer associated with hegemony. By definition, vying for power in the balance of power paradigm takes place among perceived equals. "Give and take" replaces arm twisting, blackmail, and chastisement of the recalcitrant, the usual means by which hegemony is established.

Balance of power policies are generally favored by the political right, though not usually by the extreme right. The idea dominated European international politics during the nineteenth century. In some ways, the balance of power conception envisages a degree of international cooperation, not necessarily directed against a specified state or bloc of states. However, the conservative tradition sought out another type of adversary—movements challenging the established social and political order. Recall that the so-called Concert of Europe, established at the close of the Napoleonic Wars, viewed the suppression of revolution as the main item on its agenda. The central idea of Metternich, the architect of the Grand Coalition against subversion of the reestablished order, reemerged in the political and diplomatic activities of Henry Kissinger. In *A World Restored,* Kissinger wrote:

> . . . it is of essence of revolutionary power that it preserves the courage of its convictions, that it is willing indeed eager to push the principles to their ultimate conclusion. Whatever else a revolution by power may achieve, therefore, it tends to erode, if not the legitimacy of the international order, at least the restraint with which such an order operates. (1973, 3)

On the other hand:

> Stability . . . has commonly resulted not from a quest for peace but from generally accepted legitimacy. Legitimacy as here used should not be confused with justice. It means no more than an international agreement about the nature of workable arrangements and about the permissible aims and methods of foreign policy. (1)

An assessment of the role of international cooperation embodied in the balance of power doctrine can be gleaned from the formulation of the so-called realist theory of international relations (Political Realism), of which Hans J. Morgenthau (1963) was a leading exponent.

First, Morgenthau argued, it is assumed that politics, like all forms of human activity, is governed by "laws." Laws in this context do not refer to rules of behavior designed and enforced by human authorities but rather to something akin to natural laws. The implication is that, just as in the natural sciences, knowledge of natural laws enables us at least to understand and often to predict observed events, so knowledge of laws that govern political behavior can help us understand and, perhaps, predict this form of behavior.

Second, political realism recognizes states as actors and ascribes to these actors "interests." It identifies the interest of a state with attaining, preserving, and/or increasing its power. Power, then, becomes the principal theme of politics, in particular of international relations, in the same way as wealth (its production, acquisition, distribution, and consumption) is the principal theme of economics.

Third, political realism pays due attention to changes in the content of power and its manifestations. Consequently, realist political theory is empirically oriented. It does not resemble a philosophical doctrine in the sense of free-wheeling speculations divorced from concrete observations of processes and events. It is this concern with observable realities that, in the opinion of political realists, justifies the term *political realism.*

Fourth, while recognizing the moral significance of political actions, political realism recognizes the "tension" between moral and political imperatives. This means, plainly speaking, that moral imperatives do not apply to political acts. This does not mean that the political sphere is devoid of values, only that its values are different from those in other spheres of human activity. According to Morgenthau, the principal virtue in politics is "prudence," a pragmatic principle that dictates weighing the consequences of alternative political actions and deliberately choosing the one that, as far as the political actor can see, is likely to lead to the most advantageous consequence.

Fifth, political realism categorically rejects all claims of nations to being instruments of Providence, executives of God's will, Chosen People, and the like. This rejection also constitutes a value. It implies a condemnation of all forms of crusades and holy wars, a dismissal of all romantic notions about war and the noble sentiments that it supposedly fosters as irrelevant to political imperatives.

Thus, political realists cannot be accused of denigrating values. They espouse very clearly stated values, which appear to be values inherent in science—objectivity and rationality. Morgenthau explicitly presents foreign policy based on the tenets of political realism as a "rational" foreign policy and regards a rational policy as a good policy because it minimizes risks and maximizes benefits "and hence complies both with the moral concept of prudence and the practical requirements of success" (Morgenthau 1963, 8).

In sum, the balance of power idea is most compatible with the philosophy of political realism, first because the identification of power as the supreme value in international politics finds its clearest expression in that philosophy, second because "prudence" and "rationality," the central political virtues in that philosophy, point to balance of power as a guarantee of stability and, presumably, of peace. A prudent and rational political leader will not readily engage in military adventures if he is aware of the risks involved in attempting to increase his own power at the expense of others who possess comparable power.

There is some room for international cooperation in this paradigm, since considerable political (as opposed to military) activity is expected to be involved in creating a credible balance of power in the international system. The qualification, "credible," is crucial, since it is not the "objective" power relations (whatever these may mean) but the perceived power relations that are supposed to determine the stability or instability of the international system. It follows that actors in the international arena must share modes of perception and assessment. They must get to know each other thoroughly, understanding each other's predilections and aspirations. Such understanding entails a certain level of cooperation.

In this mode of thinking, "cooperation" can be extended even to fighting a war. Kissinger, for example, in discussing the prospect of a "limited" nuclear war, wrote:

> . . . it is possible to conceive of a pattern of limited nuclear war with its own appropriate tactics and with limitations as to targets, areas, and the size of weapons used. Such a mode of conflict cannot be improvised in the confusion of battle, however. The limitation of war is established not only by our intentions but also by the manner in which the other side interprets them. It, therefore, becomes the task of our diplomacy to convey to our opponent what we understand by limited nuclear war, or at least what limitations we are willing to observe. . . . If the Soviet leadership is clear about our intentions . . . a framework of war limitation may be established by the operation of self-interest—by fear of all-out war and by the fact that new tactics make many of the targets of traditional warfare less profitable. (Kissinger 1957, 185)

If, as is implied in this passage, cooperation can be achieved even in fighting a nuclear war, it can presumably be made an important component in the nonlethal phases of international politics.

Collective Security

The "collective security" paradigm envisages every state potentially allied with every other. Thus, the image of an "obvious" or "natural" adversary disappears altogether. International cooperation replaces rivalry as the "normal" mode of interaction between states. Aggression is assumed to be clearly recognized by all and is regarded as an affront to everyone.

The main business of international relations becomes the initiation and development of cooperative projects. Conceptions of national security give way to conceptions of international security as military alliances of blocs of states are dissolved. Nevertheless, the military aspects of security are still prominent in the minds of political leaders. The conviction that force must be countered with force remains intact. The role of international cooperation in the preservation of peace is envisaged as the readiness and ability to resort to collective violence. Hence, armies, arsenals, and all the adjuncts of the military machine are presumed to remain indispensable for preserving peace.

The collective security paradigm achieved prominence when it was institutionalized in the League of Nations after World War I and, later, in the United Nations at the close of World War II. For the first time in the history of warfare, denunciation of war as an anomaly in international relations rather than a normal instrument of policy was routinely mentioned in public pronouncements by heads of state, diplomats, and other representatives of governments instead of by critics of the established order, as had been the case before the trauma of World War I produced significant shifts in public attitudes toward war.

Although the League of Nations was founded by the victors of World War I, in whose perceptions Germany appeared as "the aggressor," this image gradually faded. By 1925, the "rehabilitation" of Germany was implicitly established in the Treaty of Locarno binding England, France, Italy, Germany, Belgium, Czechoslovakia, and Poland into a "nonmilitary alliance" pledging to resort to arbitration in cases of dispute. The western boundaries of Germany were guaranteed as fixed by the Treaty of Versailles. Germany, for its part, agreed to demilitarize a strip of the Rhineland and was subsequently admitted into the League of Nations.

It seemed at the time that polarization of the international system (which was still identified with the complex of European states, just as it was at the close of the Napoleonic Wars) was finally dissolved. The Soviet Union still appeared as a pariah in the system, but even it was admitted to the League of Nations in 1933, albeit under circumstances that revealed the failure of the collective security paradigm of global peace.

The demise of the League of Nations as an instrument of preserving peace can be directly attributed to the failure to implement the cardinal principle of collective security, namely, the imposition of sanctions on whatever state commits aggression. There should not have been any difficulty in deciding whether aggression was committed by a given state.

Whatever may be the role of the nation-state in the preservation or breach of peace, it provides a clear criterion for an unambiguous definition of aggression. The most notable (though futile) definition was offered by Maxim Litvinov, foreign minister of the USSR at the London Economic Conference in 1933. The definition identified clearly recognizable acts by a state as acts of aggression, namely,

> (1) declaration of war on another State; (2) invasion by its armed forces, with or without a declaration of war, of the territory of another State; (3) attack by its land, naval, or air forces, with or without a declaration of war, on the territory, vessels, or aircraft of another State; (4) naval blockade of the coasts or ports of another State; (5) provision of support to armed bands formed in its territory which have invaded the territory of another State, or refusal, notwithstanding the request of the invaded State, to take in its own territory all the measures in its power to deprive those bands of all assistance or protection. (Schuman 1939, 37)

Afghanistan, Estonia, Latvia, Persia, Rumania, and Turkey signed a convention with the Soviet Union adopting among themselves the preceding definition of aggression. Other countries bordering on the USSR soon joined. The treaty sought to remove the basis of any justification of aggression as defined by stipulating "that no political, military, economic, or other considerations could serve as an excuse or justification for such acts of aggression" (Schuman 1939, 38).

It is interesting, though futile for lack of concrete evidence, to speculate on the reasons why this straightforward and unambiguous definition of aggression failed to attract all the parties to the collective security covenant that the League of Nations supposedly represented. One reason suggests itself: that definition and the treaty based on it was proposed by the representative of a state of which the members of the "established" international community were deeply suspicious. Just two years later, it was the same Litvinov who passionately urged the imposition of sanctions against Italy, whose role as "aggressor" on Ethiopia could not be disputed in the light of any meaningful definition of "aggression." Ironically, it was the Soviet Union that was subsequently expelled from the League of Nations (already moribund) for its equally flagrant aggression against Finland in December, 1939.

Although the League of Nations was a conspicuous failure as an instrument of preserving global peace, its historical significance as a reflection of "changed ways of thinking" ought not be underestimated. As I have said, for the first time, war was "universally" recognized, at least in rhetoric, as a calamity or a breakdown of the international order, at any rate as an anomaly rather than a normal activity of a state.

The idea of collective security did not die. It remained prominent in the founding of the United Nations. Unlike World War I, World War II was not followed by a few years of apparent freedom from immediate danger of a general war, as were the years before Japan, then Italy, then Germany embarked on frank programs of conquest. Following the Allied victory over the Axis, polarization again crystallized around the principal victors almost immediately. Consequently, the Security Council, the peacekeeping body of the United Nations, was crippled by the unanimity rule. Initially, the Soviet Union routinely vetoed all resolutions that it interpreted as directed against itself or against the Third World.

In the first twenty-eight years of the United Nations, the Soviet Union vetoed 104 Security Council Resolutions, while the United States vetoed none. In the next sixteen years, however, a very different picture emerged. The Soviet Union vetoed only 10 Security Council Resolutions, while the United States vetoed 42. All in all, superpower vetoes were by far the most frequent obstacle to collective security actions by the United Nations; 146 vetoes in forty years. By way of comparison, the United Kingdom used the veto 14 times during that period, France 19 times, and China 4 times (all by the representative of Taiwan) (Hovet 1986, 317).

Among the most flagrant violations of both the spirit and the letter of the United Nations Charter was the dismissal, by the United States, of the judgment of the World Court condemning acts of aggression by the United States against Nicaragua.

No more effective has been the collective security covenant of the Organization of American States (OAS). Article 15 of its charter reads:

> No State or group of States has the right to interfere directly or indirectly, for any reason whatsoever, in the internal affairs of any other State. The foregoing principle prohibits not only armed force but also any other form of interference or attempted threat against the personality of the State or against its political, economic and cultural elements.

Interference in the affairs of another member state, direct or indirect, can be convincingly attributed to most of the signatories of the OAS treaty. The most flagrant violations, too obvious to be enumerated, were perpetrated by the strongest member.

In sum, the collective security conception of peace has consistently failed to be realized in practice whenever any participant in a collective security pact felt that "national interest" was jeopardized. Violations were by no means always by the strongest states. States that could have been easily forced to comply with a provision of such a pact violated the treaties as frequently and as flagrantly. Collective sanctions against violators could not be applied because, rhetoric notwithstanding, the principle of solidarity, the imperative "all for one, one for all" was never internalized by leaders of sovereign states. The degree of international cooperation required to put the principle of collective security into effect was much too high for the accustomed commitments of the power elites of our era.

Nonetheless, the peacekeeping scores of collective security blocs are not vacuous. Some successes were scored, where the interests of major powers were not threatened or where the prospect of applying collective sanctions did not loom. Thus, the League of Nations settled the Swedish-Finnish dispute of the Aland Islands, held plebiscites to determine the status of Upper Silesia, and supervised population exchanges between Greece, Turkey, and Bulgaria. The United Nations was able to bring about several cease-fires, notably in the Middle East, in Kashmir, and, after two years of negotiations, in Korea. On the other hand, claims that the issues were domestic blocked UN intervention in conflicts in Algeria, Morocco, Tunisia, Cyprus, South Africa, and Hungary.

Peace through Law

In this conception, world peace is pictured as an extension, to global scale, of the internal peace that reflects a modern, civilized society. The term *civilized* in this context is semantically related to civil or civility. Internal peace is a consequence of a general respect for law as the arbiter of all conflicts and renunciation of violence as a means of imposing one's will on others or, to use a more polite phrase, "protecting one's interests." Renunciation of violence necessitates a degree of imposed self-control or affect control. Actually such control has become a feature of civilized life in consequence of widening, impersonal economic activity. Participating in this activity, that is, behaving in the modality of trade, affects the psychology of the participants. As impersonal economic activity becomes more important, so does the attendant affect control and vice versa. In this way, the system comprising not only economic but also political and social aspects of a human aggregate and the inner life of the individuals composing it coevolve.

The most conspicuous feature of a civilized society (in the sense used here) is internal disarmament. The concept of "peace through law" envisages the extension of civilization to the international arena. The abolition of state sovereignty or the creation of a "world government" is not necessarily envisaged any more than the surrender of individual autonomy is envisaged as a feature of civilized society. Only one aspect of sovereignty (albeit one usually regarded as the most important) is abolished—the right to make war. Commitment to nonviolent resolution of conflicts implies a commitment to complete disarmament of the sovereign states and the surrender of peacekeeping functions to a supranational agency.

The most explicit formulation of a plan designed to replace the present international anarchy by a global system based on peace through law was proposed by Clark and Sohn (1966). Essentially, the plan involves a restructuring of the United Nations aimed at creating an institution in accord with the image of peaceful society on a global scale.

Some of the proposed revisions, although important, are not particularly controversial today, although they were when the book was first written, when the issue of admitting the People's Republic of China into the United Nations was the subject of acerbic debates. Most controversial are the provisions that empower the new organization to enforce the disarmament process, for example, "imposing the final responsibility for the enforcement of the disarmament process and the maintenance of peace upon the General Assembly and giving the Assembly adequate power to this end" (Clark and Sohn 1966, xix).

The proposed plan contains a carefully constructed program for the elimination—not mere reduction or limitation—of all national armaments. A world police force is provided for—the only military force permitted anywhere in the world.

The organization, maintenance, recruitment, training, equipment, and disposition of such a force are functions described in minute detail. A similar, detailed description is given of the judicial and conciliation systems, indispensable to genuine peace in consequence of the abolition of national armaments. Of prime importance is the proposed World

Development Authority, through which global cooperative efforts aimed at improving human life on the planet are implemented.

From the foregoing it is clear that the central problem singled out by the peace through law paradigm is the persistence of international anarchy in a progressively more interdependent world. The solution of the problem is envisaged as the abolition of the right to make war and the implementation of this abrogation by general and complete disarmament, relegating peacekeeping to a supranational authority. The level of international cooperation required to implement this plan is obviously extremely high, since what is demanded is the transcendence of "national interests" as these are still conventionally understood, especially in international relations. The psychological state conducive to this transcendence is "civility," analogous to the orientation demanded of a "good citizen" in a civilized society. Less clear is the class of principal actors who could be expected to cope effectively with the problem and its solution. That Granville Clark, the author who wrote the Introduction to *World Peace through World Law,* is not unaware of this ambiguity is apparent from his discussion of the "practical aspects" of the plan.

Clark begins by listing the obstacles to the implementation of the disarmament process. These are the well-known vested interests. These need not be conceived as bases of malevolent conspiracies of financial wizards or the "merchants of death" often blamed for World War I. The more relevant vested interests, as Clark pictures them, are rooted in deeply ingrained thinking habits and self-images. Thus, the opposition to general disarmament on the part of the military profession need not stem from vested interests in the armament industry. Nor does it necessarily reflect a lack of humaneness or civility of the average professional soldier compared with an average civilian. The professional soldier resists the idea of general disarmament because he has been conditioned to take for granted that his profession is indispensable. His self-image, his self-respect, the meaningfulness of his existence are challenged by the idea that his profession needs to be abolished. In the same way, traditional diplomacy is threatened by the radical changes in the manner of thinking that the peace through law paradigm suggests.

The most important obstacles to the implementation of the disarmament process, according to Clark, are mutual fear and recriminations, which poison the relations between the superpowers. He expects, however, that the barrier must eventually disappear "under pressure of necessity."

On the bright side, Clark sees the imperative of survival that, in his opinion, must eventually overcome the barriers to general and complete disarmament. He mentions the unprecedented destructiveness of nuclear weapons, the oppressive burdens of defense budgets, the obvious superiority of complete compared with partial disarmament (because complete disarmament bypasses the fruitless haggling over "balancing" destructive potentials of weapons); finally the inevitable realization by the small, powerless, and nonaligned nations that a confrontation between the superpowers threatens their existence. He also mentions the strong motivation of the United Kingdom to strive persistently for total disarmament (written in 1960) and the tendency on the part of the Commonwealth nations to support the plan. On the whole, Clark finds the favorable prospects outweighing the obstacles and predicts the implementation of the plan within five years. (As this is written, thirty years have passed since Clark's prediction.)

Writing a postscript in 1966, Clark confesses to having been unduly optimistic and revises his prognosis, setting 1985 as the date that the proposed plan will have been ratified by all or nearly all nations, including the major powers. As this is written, five years have passed since the predicted date. However, a first step of genuine disarmament was taken in 1987 when the Big Two reached an agreement on removing intermediate range missiles from continental Europe.

From the way Clark describes the "pressures" that will presumably force the implementation of the general disarmament plan, one can infer that the expected major actors in this development would be "men of good will" from everywhere, jurists, experts, charismatic leaders, who will ensure the victory of common sense and enlightenment over encrusted dogmas, compulsive reactions, and crippling fears nurtured by outmoded thinking habits. The mode of control associated with the transition to peace through law is clearly integration.

Personal or Religious Pacifism

The personal or religious concept of peace identifies the autonomous individual as the principal actor. The problem is seen as the persistence of aggressiveness, hostility, and hatred in the human soul. Global peace is envisaged as a consequence of expurgating aggressiveness from individual human psyches. Thus, the solution of the problem depends on individuals' efforts to attain internal peace.

In its extreme form, personal pacifism eschews or, at any rate, views skeptically all organized action. Tolstoy and Thoreau were quite explicit in expressing this attitude. Tolstoy went so far as to preach nonresistance, not merely the nonviolent resistance advocated by political pacifists. Among the latter was Gandhi, who, while adhering to the pacifist imperative of attaining internal peace as a prerequisite for action, instigated intense political activity.

The state and, hence, international cooperation is not envisaged to play any significant role in the establishment of peace, which the personal pacifist regards as an extension of the sort of serenity that is attained by an individual who unconditionally rejects violence. A pronounced contempt for well-meaning attempts to establish peace by international cooperation shines through the following excerpt from a letter by Leo Tolstoy.

> The Conference . . . it is said, will aim, if not at disarmament then at checking the increase of armaments. It is supposed that at this Conference, the representatives of governments will agree to cease increasing their forces. If so, the question involuntarily presents itself: How will the governments of those countries act which at the time of the meeting happen to be weaker than their neighbours? Such governments will hardly agree to remain in that condition—weaker than their neighbours. Or, if they have such firm belief in the validity of the stipulations made by the Conference as to agree to remain weaker, why should they not be weaker still? Why spend money on an army at all? (Tolstoy 1968, 113–14).

Tolstoy was alluding to the Hague Conference of 1898, a forerunner of recurring arms control and disarmament conferences that eventually became institutionalized and, essentially, ritualized events. Tolstoy appears to have put his finger on the apparently insuperable obstacle to halting arms races by international cooperation—the undissolvable linkage in the minds of statesmen between "security" and military potential, the linkage that persists to the present day.

Indeed, Tolstoy implicitly accepts the political realist's identification of politics with the struggle for power, and since in Christian ethos (which Tolstoy insisted is internalized in the human psyche) wielding power over others (even with the best intentions) is condemned, Tolstoy dismissed all organized political action.

Thoreau's uncompromising individualism is expressed in a similar attitude.

> What is called politics is comparatively something so superficial and inhuman that practically I have never fairly recognized that it concerns me at all. The newspapers, I perceive, devote some of their columns specially to politics or governments without charge, and this, one would say, is all that saves it; but as I love literature and to some extent truth, I never read those columns at any rate. I do not wish to blunt my sense of right so much. (Thoreau [1863] 1937, 824)

Not all religious pacifists renounce organized political activity. On the contrary, A. J. Muste's long life as a pacifist activist bears witness to an affinity between religious fervor and charismatic leadership. Writing in 1941, while World War II raged in Europe, Muste anticipated a revolutionary situation in the wake of that war similar to one generated by war weariness at the close of World War I. He did not, however, expect the populations of the war-ruined countries to turn to the political left for leadership, as many did at the close of World War I. For, he argued, it was the political left that helped push the continent into the war—a war against fascism. He expected that leadership in the process of rebuilding European societies would pass to a movement "which renounces war and organized violence of all kinds and which had made it clear beforehand that this was its stand." He envisages this movement as "a profoundly religious movement. For men will no longer be able to believe in the too simple and mechanical notion that if you will only set up a new system, all our problems will be solved" (Muste [1936] 1967, 220).

That a "systemic" reform is insufficient for establishing a genuine and lasting peace is stated explicitly.

> Pacifism—life—is built upon a central truth and the experience of that truth, its apprehension not by the mind alone but by the entire being in an act of faith and surrender. That truth is: God is love, love is God. Love is the central thing in the universe. Mankind is one in an ultimate spiritual reality. . . .
>
> Such an affirmation one must accept and make, first in one's own soul. If it is not there, it exists only in formulas and abstractions.

> The individual must therefore be won and saved. But since it is precisely love, to the apprehension of our unity with mankind, to the kingdom of God, that we are won, must carry this dynamic and method into every relationship—into family life, into race relations, into work in the labor movement, political activity, international relations. (Muste [1936] 1967, 201)

Disillusioned with the revolutionary movements of that time (1936), Muste turned away from the political left. He became convinced that a form of struggle that does not presuppose overcoming aggressive impulses within each participant (following Jesus' example) cannot, in the final analysis, be a struggle for peace.

The achievement of "internal peace" did not stop A. J. Muste from deliberately breaking laws to make a point or, as he put it, as an attempt at communication. Once he climbed over the fence of a missile base. Another time he was arrested for refusing to participate in an air raid drill. Professor John Oliver Nelson of Yale University characterized A. J. Muste as one

> . . . who kept the peace movement in this country from becoming a clubwoman's organization. Moreover, he went further than pacifism. He has never believed that if there were no more war man would automatically become good. He feels the heart of man requires radical redemption and his institutions must, as a result, be changed accordingly. A. J. is a devastating reminder to young pacifists of what a real radical is. (Quoted in Hentoff 1967, xiv)

In sum, the problem, as the personal or religious pacifist sees it, is insufficient genuine commitment to peace on the part of every individual, where peace is a psychological state rather than the absence of war. The solution is the attainment of this psychological state by everyone. The important people in coping with the problem are all people. The mode of social control is love (integration). The psychological state associated with coping is steadfastness. Although Muste mentions international relations as an area to which the information of love is to spread, international cooperation, as it is usually understood, is practically irrelevant to this approach to peace.

Revolutionary Pacifism

In the revolutionary pacifist conception of peace, as in the personal and religious conceptions, states are not seen as the principal actors. For example, in Marxist social philosophy, the historically significant struggle for power involves social classes with opposed interests. The state, in this conception, is only an agency of coercion whose principal function is to keep the ruling class in power. Of course, states go to war against each other as well, since the interests of ruling classes of different states clash. However, this interstate war is only a by-product of the class system. If society were "classless," that is, without a ruling class exploiting a subjugated class (be they slaves, serfs, or proletarians), there would be no wars, because the interests of classless societies would not clash.

I will generalize the notion of revolution by subsuming under it not only insurrections, violent overthrow of governments, and the like, but also any fundamental change in the social, political, or economic order that governs people's lives. Ideas about how these changes can be brought about differ widely. What they have in common is an emphasis on the necessity of dismantling or delegitimizing certain institutions. In this respect, Kissinger (1973) captured very well the nature of a "revolutionary power." In the present context, however, revolutionary power is not seen as emanating from a "revolutionary state" (as Kissinger envisaged it, obviously referring to the Soviet Union). Rather, the solution of the problem is entrusted to the grass roots—envisaged as playing a part analogous to the proletariat in Marx's theory of social revolution. The revolutionary concept of peace differs from the Marxist concept of social revolution in that the analogue of class consciousness is expected to emerge not from perceptions of social relations generated by a particular "mode of production" but rather from a realization that dismantling the institution of war is essential for the survival of the human race.

Regarding war as an institution rather than a recurring event is an integral component of the revolutionary concept of peace. Numerous historical examples lead the proponents of this view to believe that the institution of war can become extinct, as other institutions became extinct when they could no longer adapt themselves to changed social conditions. The Holy Inquisition, absolute hereditary monarchy, and chattel slavery are conspicuous examples.

In sum, in the revolutionary concept of peace, the problem is seen as the continued existence of the institution of war with all its adjunct institutions. The goal is the abolition of this institution. The task is delegated to the world population organized for energetic political action.

As in the peace through law paradigm, the modality of social control associated with revolutionary pacifism is integrative. In contrast to the peace through law paradigm, which implies a very high degree of international cooperation, the revolutionary concept of peace does not emphasize cooperation between states as an important component of peacemaking. It places much greater emphasis on transnational cooperation, that is, cooperation between organizations essentially independent of governments. Such are worldwide professional and cultural organizations, federations of labor unions, churches, and the like. It is, of course, true that, in some countries, such organizations are only nominally independent of their governments and for this reason are severely restricted in the extent to which they can cooperate with their counterparts in other countries. However, the global political situation should not be regarded as frozen in its present pattern. As in every other respect, revolutionary pacifism advances the view that the global political climate is in a state of flux. The proponents of this view stand ready to take advantage of whatever changes make an extension of transnational cooperation in the pursuit of peace more effective.

The foregoing should not be understood to mean that the revolutionary pacifist denigrates the importance of international cooperation as an activity reinforcing the integrative process. Where international cooperation that is not directed against a common adversary is most effective as an integrating force is precisely in those areas where the national interests of the cooperating states have already been transcended, that is, decoupled from the classical interstate power struggle. The postal union, international health protecting agencies, and the International Airline Travel Association, among others, are such areas of productive international cooperation.

In other words, from the point of view of the revolutionary pacifist paradigm, international cooperation appears not so much a contributing factor to the establishment and preservation of peace as a *consequence* of decoupling certain activities of states from the struggle for power.

In this connection, a difference can be pointed out between conceptions of the state inherent in revolutionary pacifism and in other paradigms, for example, political realism or Marxism. In political realism, the state appears as an agency that wields power vis-à-vis other states with the view of preserving that power against encroachments and/or with the view of extending it. In the Marxist view, the state is the instrument by means of which the ruling class keeps the oppressed class in subjugation. No such fixed role is ascribed to the state by revolutionary pacifism. The state can be a party in a power struggle if it possesses the requisite power to participate in such struggles; or it may not if it has no such power. For example, the United States and the Soviet Union are states that have been clearly engaged in a power struggle. But Austria and Switzerland are also states and are not engaged in any comparable activity. Again, some states clearly appear as instruments of oppression, others do not. In short, revolutionary pacifism does not advance any particular "theory of the state" and is not concerned with its preservation or abolition. It simply bypasses the state as an effective actor in the imperative task with which humanity is presently confronted. This task is assigned to humanity itself. Of course, "humanity" can in no sense be presently regarded as an actor. But becoming an actor is part of the task.

Freeman Dyson begins his book, *Weapons and Hope* (1984), by distinguishing two "classes"—the Warriors and the Victims. Membership in the one or the other is ascribed not to individuals but to roles. Thus, an individual can belong to both, as Dyson himself says he does. As a matter of fact, if the Warriors ever fulfill the tasks assigned to them, the class of Victims will include everyone, including the Warriors.

Marx's theory of society pictured the class struggle as the prime mover of history. The key to fundamental social change was supposed to be the recognition by the oppressed of the mechanism by which they are kept in submission. Presumably, this awareness empowered the oppressed to emancipate themselves by revolutionary action. A somewhat similar scenario is envisaged by the proponents of revolutionary pacifism. The dichotomy of Warriors and Victims is analogous to the Marxist class dichotomy, but with the important difference that only roles, not persons, are identified as members. The Warrior roles include all activities that keep the institution of war alive and functioning. In our age, those activities extend far beyond the traditional activities of people in uniform. They include vast realms of production, research, development, planning, and education. Analogous to Marx's class consciousness is simply the Warriors' preoccupation with workaday tasks on the performance of which they depend for their livelihood, careers, prestige, or self-image. Only in isolated instances does awareness of this identification with the war system become apparent, as in the following passage, reflecting the self-assurance of the Warrior class. C. S. Gray writes about the future of strategic studies, a branch of modern military science developed in a large network of institutions.

> It is safe to predict that strategic studies will enjoy a long and healthy future. Those scholars who believe that, in all save rococo variations, nearly the last important word has been written on issues of interest to strategists, may confidently be proclaimed to be in error. (Gray 1982, 7)

The optimism reflected in this passage reminds me of the enthusiasm with which technological progress was celebrated by those who reaped immediate benefits from it in expanding enterprises and new career opportunities. This optimism was as much a part of the class consciousness of the nineteenth-century bourgeoisie as the ideological defense of private property or economic inequality.

The analogue of class consciousness on the other side of the dichotomy is a growing and spreading awareness of the mechanism by which the Warrior class is able to maintain its position, especially when the last rationale of its role—defense against a formidable, identifiable enemy—has dissipated. Until the foundations of the cold war collapsed, it was possible, at least, to find words with which to describe some war aim, some goal extrinsic to war itself, for which it would be justifiable to wage war. Of course, implicit in such a justification there was always some allusion to a cost-benefit analysis, ranging from sophisticated geopolitical scenarios to a crude slogan such as "better dead than red."

Weapons of total destruction have deprived war of all goals external to war itself. It is still possible to say that the goal to be achieved by a war is "victory," but victory is an internal, not an external goal. It is no longer possible to specify concrete "fruits" of victory that can make sense in the age when any war between the superpowers must inevitably become a war of total destruction. "Victory" itself, on the other hand, can always be defined in terms acceptable to the Warrior, for example, in terms of which side first sues for cessation of hostilities or in terms of which side still has some resources left while the other side is finished. In fact, if we accept Clausewitz's definition of the prime goal of war, namely, the destruction of the adversary, then it follows that a nuclear war can, after all, be "won," in fact by both sides simultaneously.

To fully appreciate the orientation of the military professional toward war and its goals, consider the concerns of an experienced and skillful chess player. He does not need to be concerned with the "fruits" of victory (e.g., prizes), which may or may not be in prospect. The devoted chess player is concerned with victory for its own sake. The question of why victory should be preferred to defeat makes no sense to him. Victory is the preferred outcome by definition.

In his effort to achieve victory, the chess master resorts to extremely sophisticated thinking involving solid theoretical knowledge, vivid imagination, and thoroughly internalized experience. This process, no less than victory, is a source of satisfaction to him. About these matters the chess master will willingly enter a discussion and will generally give evidence of rationality, objectivity, and an appreciation of controversial arguments. If shown wrong, he will readily admit it; if vindicated, he may offer to share his knowledge with his interlocutor, thereby helping him become a better player. He will manifest all these admirable qualities of rational thought and of collegiality as long as matters discussed are internal to chess. He will be at a loss, however, to answer the question of why a game should be played at all. He starts with the game as given. Nor will he be able to look at the situation from the point of view of the pieces, which, in this context, is a silly notion, of course. Here, however, the analogy between war and chess breaks down. The "pieces" in war are not made of wood. Besides, the time has come when everyone is a "piece."

For this reason, the revolutionary pacifist cannot appreciate Freeman Dyson's plea for a dialogue between the Warriors and the Victims in which each would recognize the legitimacy of the other's concerns: the Warrior's concern for security or preservation of sovereignty and the Victim's concern for preservation of life. The abolitionist believes and strives to get others to see that, in view of the disappearance of external goals of war, the abolitionist's aim is to abolish the institution and, with it, the Warrior's role. Therefore, a dialogue based on a recognition of the Warrior's legitimate concerns is pointless.

The content of this chapter is summarized in table 5.

Underlying Assumptions and Implications of the Various Concepts of Peace

Of the six conceptions of peace shown in table 5, the first three are compatible with the war system, the last three are not. The conceptions were arranged in the order of increasing importance of integration as a

TABLE 5. Conceptions of Peace and Their Concomitants

	Peace through Strength	Balance of Power	Collective Security	Peace through Law	Personal Pacifism	Revolutionary Pacifism
Problem	external threat	disequilibrium	aggressor states	international anarchy	human aggressiveness	the institution of war
Solution	military might	balance of power	collective sanctions	world law	self-perfection	abolition
Principal actors	military elites	military and diplomatic elites	statesmen	jurists, political scientists	individuals	grass roots movements
Modality of social control	threat	trade threat[a]	trade threat[a] integration[a]	integration	integration	integration
Induced attitudes	pugnacity, fear	prudence	solidarity, vigilance	civility	love, steadfastness	global awareness
Envisaged peacekeeping role of international cooperation	none	low to moderate	high	very high	none	low

[a]Factors regarded as secondary.

mode of social control. In the Hobbesian world envisaged by the advocates of peace through strength, integration does not cross national boundaries. In the balance of power paradigm, it may do so to the extent of welding military alliances. Collective security implies the extension of the integrative process to a world community that is nevertheless still conceived of as a military alliance. The difference between this military alliance and those defined as blocs of states is that a specifically designated enemy no longer figures in a collective security system. The enemy is now potentially any state that becomes an "aggressor."

In a collective security system, the war establishments of the member states could be expected to confine their war planning to defensive operations, since offensive ones must be planned against specific enemies, which would presumably not exist in a genuine collective security system. The fact that the League of Nations failed as a collective security system suggests that the purely defensive posture of war establishments is unstable. "Mutations" can occur: "defensive" potential can be easily converted to "offensive," and states opting out of the system can go on a rampage, as the Axis powers did in the 1930s. This foreplay of World War II is usually cited as evidence of the failure of appeasement. There is no way of telling, however, whether "deterrence" in the form of emphatic and clearly spelled out threats would have stopped the aggressors. A result at least as likely may have been an earlier start of World War II.

The League of Nations did not have a Security Council empowered to impose mandatory sanctions on aggressors. As we have suggested, deep distrust of the Soviet Union by the liberal democracies precluded any significant cooperation with it. The United Nations collective security system does provide for mandatory sanctions. However, the clout could not be applied as long as the superpowers invariably found themselves at odds on any important issue. When unanimity was finally achieved, and strong sanctions were actually imposed on Iraq for its aggression against Kuwait in 1990, another circumstance brought the world to the brink of war: the United States seemed determined to push the crisis over the brink. It did.

One might surmise two reasons for the insistence by the United States on the use of military force against Iraq instead of relying on the economic force of a protracted blockade. First, the retreat of the Soviet Union from Eastern Europe was interpreted as a capitulation in the cold war, leaving the United States as the sole superpower, essentially in the role of both the shaper and the enforcer of a "new world order." Second, by stepping into the vacated role of the designated enemy, Saddam Hussein provided the U.S. war establishment with ample means to continue to live in the style to which it had become accustomed.

The Persian Gulf crisis demonstrated the limitations of collective security as a peacekeeping system in two ways. First, there is no guarantee that deterrence (i.e., threat as a mode of control) will always work. When it fails, war becomes a near certainty. Second, it leaves intact the global war machine, which can continue its parasitic existence even without a permanently designated enemy. Its continued existence is an insurmountable obstacle to the global integration on which global peace depends.

The "world law" concept of peace is based on the idea that peacekeeping machinery can be designed in the way codes of laws or constitutions are designed. General disarmament and some analogue of a world government are usually incorporated into such designs. The underlying assumptions rest on a faith in human rationality and predilection for problem solving, even on the level of state policy. Such assumptions should not be dismissed out of hand as idealistic or utopian, because, on occasions, states have been observed to acknowledge the futility of engaging in a power struggle in the conventional sense of political realism.

Mueller believes that this process can accelerate. He calls it "Hollandization" (Mueller 1989) in honor of Holland, which deliberately gave up its status as a "great power" in 1713 and thereafter devoted its energies to business instead of war. Sweden followed suit in 1721, Switzerland, a major military power in 1500, gradually opted out of the war system but became a "great power" in the world of finance. Japan was deprived of its "great power" status as a consequence of defeat. But its "involuntary" turn away from war toward business is universally recognized as a dramatic success. Presently, all of Europe seems to have arrived at a threshold of emancipation from the war disease.

Mueller's thesis, expressed in the subtitle of his book, is "The Obsolescence of Major War." He distinguishes two levels of recognition of this phenomenon, the rational and the subrational. Rational recognition results from a cost-benefit analysis. The costs of a major war, both to victor and to vanquished, must exceed any possible benefits. Far more can be gained by trade and cooperation than by conquest and exploitation of the vanquished. The dissolution of the colonial system was spurred by the realization that colonies became a liability instead of an asset. On the subrational level, the war option is not "rejected," it simply is not considered. Mueller asks us to think of a person who is trying to decide whether to reach the street level from the fifth floor by walking downstairs or by jumping out of the window. He could conceivably choose the former method after having realized that the time saved by jumping would not be worth the risk of being crippled or killed. This would be the "rational" decision. However, we would not expect a normal human being to resort to this sort of calculation. The option of jumping out of the window would simply not occur to him. This would lead to a decision on the subrational level.

Mueller then calls attention to regions where absence of war must be ascribed to such subrational internalization rather than to cost-benefit analysis. Barring certain highly unlikely situations (e. g., use of Canadian territory for Soviet missile sites), the failure of the United States to invade Canada (or vice versa) is not a result of a decision based on rational analysis. This option simply does not exist. A warless world would be one in which the war option no longer occurs to any state. It would disappear, as the option of fighting duels to settle a quarrel has disappeared, as the option of binding girls' feet to make them attractive has disappeared, as gladiatorial combats have disappeared. This will happen when war is regarded as not just counterproductive but also pernicious, repugnant, and, above all, silly, something one "does not do." One would imagine that just as dueling may be still (superfluously) prohibited by law, so a "world law" would include a total prohibition of war or preparations for war—after the war option has been eliminated from the repertoire of seriously thinkable actions of states.

This prognosis resembles that of Amos (1880), who argued that wars would gradually become more "civilized" (i. e., more humane) and less ruthless and destructive until they would disappear altogether. Mueller, however, looks not to civilization but to the ever more severe shock treatment administered by modern wars. He attributes the virtual disappearance of major wars among the states of the affluent world to these shock treatments.

Evidence of this development is presented by Maoz and Abdolali (1989), who examined the levels of war activity (defined by a number of criteria) among democratic states with those among states that are not democratic. Democracy is also defined operationally by a number of criteria (e. g., nature of executive selection, independence of the executive, type of political competition or opposition, scope of government functions). Maoz and Abdolali then examine instances when a regime changed from a democratic to an authoritarian one or vice versa and compare the "war levels" before and after the change. The results are unambiguous. The changes in type of regime are associated with changes in levels of war activity in the direction hypothesized, that is, democratization is associated with a decline and authoritarianism with an increase of war activity.

A similar confirmation emerges in dyadic comparisons of interstate wars. Wars between democratic states are significantly rarer than wars between states at least one of which is not democratic.

The period examined by Maoz and Abdolali is 1816 to 1976. In support of the argument that democracies are essentially peace minded, attention is often called to the observation that, at least since 1945, there have been practically no wars between states generally regarded as democratic. When we take into account that these states are predominantly more affluent than nondemocratic states, we can surmise that affluence and a proneness to peace tend to reinforce each other. Finally, the observation that, at present, the trend among the states is toward democratization can be taken as support for the conjecture that war is on the way out as an institution. The ending of the cold war in Europe following the collapse of authoritarian regimes in Eastern Europe and dramatic political changes in the direction of democratization in the Soviet Union lend further support to this conjecture.[1]

An optimistic interpretation of this apparent trend toward peace would be to identify it with a progressive integration of political units. However, such an integration has an opposite, disturbing side. Political integration has been frequently associated with an intensification of conflicts on another level. Internal pacification of states went hand in hand with the institutionalization of war between states. Military alliances have been ordinarily associated with wars between blocs of states. In fact, the "peace regions" in North America and Western Europe and in the Soviet bloc could be seen as by-products of the East-West polarization that carried humanity to the brink of an irreversible catastrophe.

Thus, the skepticism with which some view the emergence of a

1. The outbreak of war in the Persian Gulf shows that a "trend" need not prevent a sudden reversal. But neither does a reversal necessarily presage the end of a trend.

united Europe, even if the erstwhile Soviet bloc is integrated with it, is understandable. The disappearance of war in the First World would not guarantee its disappearance from the Third World, where destitution, political instability, and chronic violence continue unabated. Those deplorable conditions would probably be attenuated if the progressive integration were extended to the Third World, but such an integration would entail the creation of a world order radically different from the present, one in which the continued exploitation of the impoverished world by the affluent world would be impossible. The dismantling of the war system would be a necessary (though not a sufficient) condition for the dismantling of neocolonialism, that is, exploitation of the undeveloped countries by means other than direct colonial rule. I will call attention to two links between the war system and neocolonialism.

One such link has already been mentioned, namely, the arms trade. In early contacts with "primitive people," Europeans initiated trade with them by exchanging trinkets (glass beads, mirrors, etc.) for valuable resources. The trade may have been fraudulent, but it was not lethal. Arms trade is both fraudulent and lethal. It is fraudulent because weapons do not constitute wealth in any commonsense meaning of the word; and they are obviously lethal whether used against external "enemies" or against the power elites' own populations.

Another link between the war system and the exploitation of the Third World is the continued existence of armies in Latin America, which has also become a "peace region" if one compares the present situation with that of the nineteenth and early twentieth centuries, when interstate warfare in Latin America was chronic. However, the military establishments of those countries have become rapidly adapted to the new environment by changing their function: they now serve to suppress attempts to democratize their own countries and to emancipate them from neocolonialism.

In sum, the dismantling of the institution of war and, with it, of the institutions spawned by it is a prerequisite to the establishment of peace through world law.

The two unequivocally antimilitaristic conceptions of peace differ in their priorities. Personal or religious pacifism emphasizes the purging of the human psyche of aggressive urges as a prerequisite of the abolition of war. In assigning priority to the commitment of individuals to peace, the personal pacifist is seldom concerned with problems of peace politics, that is, organized actions guided by considerations of their political effectiveness. For the revolutionary pacifist, the attainment of "inner peace" is less relevant. Rejection of violence is regarded as a political weapon rather than a result of personal conversion. If the institution of war is to be abolished, its main support—the institutionalization of violence—must be demolished. It is for this reason that violence must be rejected, and it can be rejected whether one has attained "inner peace" or not.

Another distinguishing feature of revolutionary pacifism is the comparatively weak role it assigns to international cooperation on the level of the state. As long as state sovereignty includes the right to maintain an independent military establishment and the right to make war (and therefore the obligation to prepare for it), cooperation between states in the establishment of peace must be hampered primarily by resistance to disarmament on the part of the military establishments. In contrast, great emphasis is placed on *transnational* cooperation (bypassing relations between states), which is rapidly gaining in visibility and importance. This development will be discussed in the next chapter.

11

Transcending the Limitations of International Cooperation

I have mentioned some limitations of the role of international cooperation in establishing and preserving peace: on the one hand, obstructions blocking the expansion of political, conceptual, and ethical horizons and, on the other hand, repeated successful adaptations of the institution of war to the societies in which it is embedded. All of these factors are rooted in the so far unbreakable bond between national sovereignty and the "right" of sovereign states to prepare for and wage war against other sovereign states.

This right is based on two opposite political roles of states: internal pacification and external violence. Most states came into being or attained their present form through violence culminating in the monopolization of force and destroying the ability of smaller groups (clans, local enclaves of war lords, etc.) to fight each other. The opposite side of this monopolization of violence by the state was the growth of its own potential and, hence, predilection for violence.

Extension of political horizons entails the extension of loyalty based on identification. Thus, "nation building" requires a shift of identification from clan, tribe, or ethnic group to a state. In general, such shifts, entailing identification with larger units, are concomitant with a decrease of internal violence, so that narrow or local distinctions between "us" and "them" become blurred. At the same time, the distinctions between "us" and "them" on a larger scale, where "they" are those outside the now salient political or ethnic boundaries, become sharper. This double effect was most pronounced in the age of intense nationalism in Europe. In our day, the formation of military blocs has carried the process beyond national boundaries (with a concomitant decline of nationalism). The old rivalries, antagonisms, and fears were replaced by new ones across the so-called iron curtain. Note that the reality behind the phrase (extreme self-isolation of the Soviet Union and forced isolation of its allies from the West) has long been dissipated, but the phrase remained in common usage in the West until the ruins of the Berlin Wall deprived it of the last vestiges of meaning. The inertia of language carries over into the inertia of conceptualization and reinforces the barriers to expanding political horizons.

The expansion of conceptual horizons is still hampered by the rigid fixation on the state as the autonomous actor in the international arena. Hence, the notion of national interest appears to be the embodiment of a natural law, explicitly mentioned by Morgenthau in his formulation of the basis of "political realism" (1963). Consequently, important decisions by governments tend to be egocentric, where national interest has assumed the role of "natural right," the basis of political realism. Rationality is defined as an ability and readiness to act in a way most likely to enhance self-interest. As has been said, Self need not be an individual. It can refer to a firm, an organization, or a state. But in every case, the environment of this Self is conceived either as a world governed by chance events (i.e., a world devoid of other goal-oriented Selves) or else a world peopled by autonomous Selves, each seeking its own interest—a Hobbesian world. The fact that blocs and alliances are formed among these Selves does not transcend the paradigm. The blocs have become the Selves of the new model, in which the dichotomy between Self and Other is still paramount.

Criticisms of selfishness are more often dismissed as misguided idealism or naive sentimentality. Yet, we have seen how rigorous analysis reveals the inadequacy of the zero-sum game mentality. Biologists have shown that submicroscopic genes, pursuing their utterly selfish interests, have created a world in which the practice of altruism is a viable evolutionary strategy. To see this, it is only necessary to recognize that, in situations more complex than the two-person, zero-sum game, the value of a strategy may depend crucially on how many are using it. The dependence relation can go both ways: the more participants in an interactive process use a given strategy, the more valuable it may become for everyone; or else (equally frequently) the more participants use a given strategy, the less advantageous it becomes for every one. In spite of a host of examples of both effects, the actors in the international arena continue to ignore the principle. National interest is nowhere dethroned as a fixed reference point of policy.

The expansion of ethical horizons entails a projection of Self to include others. The phenomenon is common enough. It is the basis of all altruism. We observe it in birds and in mammals (care of young) and in social insects (the dissolution of the Self in the collective Self). We have no access to the inner "psyches" of those creatures, but we have access to our own. Few of us have never experienced empathy, which is nothing but the extension of consciousness to include the consciousness of another, for example, the feeling of another's pain. Again, because of encrusted prejudice, it seems almost indecent to speak of these matters in the context of "serious business," which, in our culture, is predominantly professional expertise, competitive business enterprise, electoral politics, and war. But here, too, we can leave sentiment aside and look at the concept of empathy in the light of hard-headed analysis.

As we have seen, when the players of Prisoner's Dilemma both choose *C*, each does better than he would if both chose *D*. Nevertheless, it is "individually rational" to choose *D*. The dilemma is magnified many times in a multiply repeated game. Thus, the rationality of *D* (or of the all *D* strategy in an iterated game) must inevitably be questioned. There is something wrong with a definition of rational choice that leads to a worse outcome than the apparently irrational one.

The inability to question the rationality of the *D* choice stems from a basic assumption concerning the thought processes of the two players. Each assumes these processes to be independent of each other. Thus, in a single play, it seems inconceivable that my choice, made independently of the other's, can influence the other's choice. However, let us suppose for a moment that the two choices are not independent. This can easily be imagined if each player regards the other as a mirror image of himself. Then, the reasoning might go something like this. "He is a person like me. If I think that *C* is a rational choice, then he must also think this way. If I think that *D* is the rational choice, so must he. Therefore, the outcome of our choices will be either *CC* or *DD*. Of these, both of us prefer *CC*. Therefore, *C* is the rational choice."

Of course, the conclusion is vulnerable. One can entertain the thought "What can prevent the other from choosing *D*, thus taking advantage of my trust in his 'rationality'?" If one abandons the mirror image, this thought appears to reflect "reality," and one is forced to choose *D* in self-defense. But there is nothing to prevent the mirror image from reasserting itself. It now suggests that if Self is moved to resort to *D* "in self-defense," so must the Other be moved to the detriment of both. The rationality of *C* is thus reestablished. If we further suppose that the image we form of the world is the result of learning, then commitment to the mirror image paradigm will be reinforced. Members of a population committed to the mirror image paradigm will develop a psychology wherein the extension of Self to include the Other is normal. This population will prosper. In contrast, members of a population commited to the independent choice paradigm will learn to choose unconditional *D*. They will learn that distrust is less punishing than betrayed trust. They will be worse off than the population of believers in the mirror image paradigm. Comparing their own prosperity with the deprivation of the *D* players, the *C* players will, with some justification, regard themselves as "rational" and the others as "deluded."

The reason the mirror image paradigm is difficult to accept in the context of Prisoner's Dilemma is because the choice of *D* is *individually* rational, and individual rationality is difficult to discard in favor of collective rationality in our culture. The mirror image seems to do violence to the autonomy of the individual, regarded as a supreme value. There are, however, situations in which the reasonableness of the mirror image model is much easier to accept. As an illustration, consider the following game.

Each of two players is invited to name independently a whole positive number. The player naming the larger number wins $1,000,000 divided by the number named. In case of a tie, the prize is divided equally between the two. Clearly, no choice of $n>1$ is individually rational, since if there were such a choice, say n, then naming the next larger number would be better, since $\$1{,}000{,}000/(n+1)>\$1{,}000{,}000/2n$ for all $n>1$, a contradiction. The collectively rational choice is obvious: both should name "1," and each will collect $500,000.

From the point of view of self-interest, neither is motivated to choose a number greater than 1 in the expectation that the other will choose 1. For example, a choice of 2 coupled with the other's choice of 1 brings $500,000, no more than the choice of 1. The choice of a number larger than 2 brings even less coupled with the other's choice of 1, and nothing if the other chooses a still larger number. One would think, therefore, that the decision to choose 1 is stable in the sense that neither player stands to gain by choosing a larger number. In the terminology of game theory, an outcome of this sort is called an equilibrium. Some game theorists, notably Harsanyi, maintain that, in noncooperative games, that is, games in which the players are not in a position to make a binding agreement on their choice of strategy, an individually rational outcome must be an equilibrium (Harsany 1977). Since the choice of 1 by both is an equilibrium in this game, it is declared to be, ipso facto, individually rational.

This conclusion, however, is tenable only if one accepts the mirror image paradigm, ascribing the same sort of rationality to the other as to oneself. For if one has reason to suspect that the other, for whatever reason, is tempted to choose 2, then one must choose 2 "in self-defense." Can one think of a reason why the other would contemplate choosing 2? One can. If one suspects that the other suspects *self* of choosing 2 and therefore feels compelled to choose 2 "in self-defense," then this very suspicion confirms itself. Therefore, if one believes in the mirror image, one should not permit such a suspicion to cross one's mind.

The parable of the two scorpions in a bottle has essentially the same structure as the Largest Number Game. Neither scorpion is assumed to derive any benefit from stinging the other. But if scorpion A suspects that, for some reason, scorpion B intends to sting him, he feels compelled to "preempt" by stinging first. And that is not all. Even if scorpion A does *not* suspect that scorpion B intends to sting him but thinks that scorpion B suspects that he, scorpion A, intends to sting B, then B must come to the conclusion that he must preempt and, on the basis of that conclusion (deduced also by A), A feels compelled to sting. The outcome is that both sting each other and both die. Had these thoughts not entered their minds, they would both live. The similarity of this "logic" to the logic of the preemptive strike (a seriously considered alternative in planning nuclear war) is obvious.

The most elementary example of a justifiable mirror image assumption is a game in which each of two players is invited to call "heads" or "tails" on a toss of a coin. If both call the same, both win; if their calls are different, both lose. It has been shown experimentally that a large number of U.S. subjects call heads on the assumption that heads is favored over tails by a majority. Now this conclusion is warranted even if the majority favoring heads is ever so slight. Moreover, calling heads is warranted even if that assumption is false provided that each assumes that the other assumes that the assumption is true. Here, the acceptance of the mirror image paradigm manifests itself quite clearly. Outcomes of decisions based on this paradigm have been called "salient solutions" by Schelling (1960).

While the reasonableness of such "extensions of consciousness" is readily admitted in trivial situations, it is challenged on the level of international relations and other "serious" competitive contexts. The mirror image paradigm is rejected if it suggests decisions incompatible with conventional conceptions of rationality based on the pursuit of self-interest.

There is still another way in which the expansion of ethical horizons is impeded, especially in technically advanced societies where individuals are easily insulated from the results of their collective efforts. The insulation is related to what is called "alienation" in Marxist philosophy. Intent on imbuing this concept (developed earlier by Hegel) with a materialist meaning, Marx called attention to the expropriation of the product of a worker's labor by the employer, which he identified with alienation and its psychological consequences. In our day, alienation has acquired a more sinister meaning. The progressive fractionalization of all productive processes has removed the finished product from the horizon of awareness of the participants. Just as the two components of a binary poison gas are harmless by themselves but lethal in combination, so the myriad component jobs in the service of the global war machine seem innocuous taken in isolation. In combination, they amount to preparations for collective suicide. The realization that this is so is possible only if "consciousness" is extended beyond the limits set by the nation-state, its absolute claim to loyalty, and the unassailable concept of national interest.

The state claims loyalty by virtue of the monopolization of ultimate coercive power. It follows that transcendence of the loyalty to the state is possible only if the role of power as the ultimate arbiter is denied. This denial is the ideological basis of revolutionary pacifism, which banks on transnational (rather than international) cooperation as a way toward global peace.

The essential difference between international and transnational cooperation stems from the way the participants are identified. The actors in international cooperation are, by definition, states. Given the best intentions of states to pursue common goals, the very way these goals are formulated must have a bearing on national interests, even if a coincidence of these interests in a given context is recognized. Therefore, cooperation between states must remain ad hoc, that is, with reference to specific goals. The modality of this cooperation is trade, not integration. Integration could entail the dissolution of states as autonomous entities, a process tenaciously resisted by all who identify with the state.

Questions of autonomy do not arise in transnational cooperation. Autonomy is not threatened because integration is incompatible with coercive power. Conversely, common goals not related to power relations are best pursued by integration activities. Concrete instances of these are the regulation of global air traffic, global health measures, humanitarian enterprises, and activities based on commitment to common values in art, religion, sports, scholarship, or science.

To a certain extent, the growing prominence of cooperating nongovernmental organizations (NGOs) has contributed to laying the groundwork of transnational cooperation in this sense. This may essentially be true also of the various branches of the global peace movement. The present feebleness of this movement as a counterweight to the solidly institutionalized war system is too obvious to be overlooked. Partly this weakness reflects an insufficient awareness of participants in peace movements of what the abolition of war entails. The idea that the roots of war are in "human nature" (e.g., in the "aggressive instincts") is still, perhaps, the most widespread of all the ideas about the "causes of war." Almost as prevalent is the somewhat more sophisticated idea that wars are instigated by "breakdowns" of the international system or by the inability of statesmen (with the best intentions) to find "solutions" to conflicts arising between states. These ideas are manifested in thousands of "proposals" on how such problems could be "solved," ranging from conciliation procedures to designs of world constitutions.

That the war machine is an "organism" embedded in human societies with a life and defense mechanisms of its own is still regarded as a picturesque metaphor rather than a realistic description of contemporary global reality. Nevertheless, it is precisely the recognition of the stark reality behind the metaphor that could precipitate the fundamental change in our mode of thinking, which, according to Einstein, is our only defense against the impending irreversible calamity.

12

Concluding Remarks

War has been conceived as a means of survival (by marauding tribes), as a means of integrating political entities into larger ones (pacification), as the sport of kings, as an instrument of foreign policy, as a breakdown of the international system, as a calamity (analogous to earthquakes and floods), as a punishment meted out by God, as an outlet of aggressive urges, and as a crime. In this book, war is conceived as an institution.

All of the enumerated conceptions of war are compatible with each other. They reflect the many-sidedness of war and the very different perspectives of people who engage in it or who are affected by it. So there is no point in evaluating the "validity" of this or that conception. The view of war as an institution is no exception. However, conceptions are seldom products of contemplation alone. They are usually induced by attitudes or by actions and themselves induce actions and attitudes. Actions are properly evaluated not with reference to their validity but by reference to their effects. So preferences among concepts can be determined by attitudes toward actions that may have induced them or actions which they themselves induce.

A concept of war as a tool of survival or as a tool of foreign policy induces participants to design more effective means of conducting wars. A concept of war as a disaster or a crime induces questions about how war can be prevented or stopped. The concept of war as an outlet of aggressive instincts may induce questions of how such instincts can be diverted into other channels or suppressed. This concept may also induce a conviction that nothing can be done about war, because "you can't change human nature." The concept of war as an institution coupled with a strong aversion to war induces questions of how this institution can be abolished. This is the stance of the revolutionary pacifist or the abolitionist.

The course of history is strewn with extinct or moribund institutions. Thus, the mortality of institutions is not in doubt. The abolitionist is interested in what actions can be undertaken to undermine the institution of war so that it is no longer viable. The question of who is to undertake such action must also be faced. In fact, it is raised in connection with all the conceptions of peace discussed in chapter 10, and answers are suggested. If peace is to be preserved by strength, the principal actors are to be the personnel of military establishments and their entourage. If peace is to be preserved by collective security, statesmen would presumably bear primary responsibility; if by establishing a world law, perhaps jurists.

In pacifist conceptions, peace is everyone's business. There is a difference, however, between the way peace action can be induced in people from the religious point of view and from the abolitionist's point of view. Recall that the religious pacifist requires the peacekeepers to establish peace within themselves. In other words, the religious pacifist undertakes to convert people. In particular, if conversion is a prerequisite of acting to establish and preserve peace, then it seems that the decision makers, including those presently engaged in elaborate preparations for war, must be converted to pacifism. The prospect of such a development is not bright. Such conversions sometimes occur, but exceedingly rarely. For this reason, they attract much attention when they do occur.

The abolitionist does not bank on radical changes in people's deepest feelings. Moreover, he does not address himself to the powerful of this world. His is the traditional task of the revolutionary—to undermine and ultimately destroy the legitimacy of an institution, in this case one that is already feared and held responsible for misery and destruction by many and is seen by many as a threat to the survival of humanity. The abolitionist seeks to mobilize this rising resentment so as to channel it into political action.

Note how much easier it is to implement negative goals than positive ones, to demolish than to build. Usually, this greater facility people have of tearing down than of building up is decried. But there are instances where demolition is an indispensable prerequisite to construction. Here, the readiness of people to break things may be put to good use.

As an example, consider the radical changes in the Soviet Union since 1985. These changes are summarized in two terms that have become household words throughout the world and are incorporated into all languages: *glasnost* and *perestroika*.

Glasnost (from *glas*, the archaic form of *golos* 'voice') means openness. The promotion of glasnost in the Soviet Union amounted to lifting the severe restrictions on communication, including both the public expression of views not sanctioned by the authorities and access to reading matter where such views (or even historical events) suppressed by the authorities are found. Within months, no trace remained of these restrictions, and the entire climate of public expression in the Soviet Union became unrecognizable. Glasnost has been an unqualified success. Note that glasnost amounted to negative action, namely, the demolition of a system of suppression.

Perestroika means restructuring. The Soviet New Deal was supposed to launch far-reaching reforms of the entire economic system. The envisaged changes were so pervasive that there was no question of preparing a blueprint or a schedule. No one was in a position to tell which steps would be successful, in what order they should be undertaken, which would fail, which were available to fall back on, and what the effects would be. In implementing perestroika, it was not enough to demolish. In dismantling the apparatus of a centrally controlled economy, it was necessary to put something in its place. In the case of glasnost, it was enough to let people write, speak, or think as they pleased. In the context of perestroika it was impossible to say, "We are into free enterprise now; everyone is free to start his or her own business. Compete and prosper." Perestroika has so far faltered. At any rate, no one hails its successes.

And yet it seems that although glasnost was not a sufficient condition for curing the country of the ills it had been subject to during seven decades of stifling dictatorship, it was without doubt a necessary condition for recovery. Only in a free exchange of ideas, criticisms, suggestions, and expressions of both enthusiasm and despair can one hope that eventually something will turn up that will prove viable, something endowed with "reproductive success," something that can take off to provide a foundation for building a decent society.

The 1989 revolution in Eastern Europe presented the world with a similar picture. Within months, the totalitarian or near-totalitarian regimes of six countries toppled. Absolutely nothing remained of their authority, which was thought to be impregnable to the last moment. The agencies of repression, the secret police, the censorship boards, and so on were simply dismantled like the Berlin Wall and the barbed wire fences that separated the countries from the rest of Europe. Only then the enormity of the task ahead came into view. Exuberant self-assurance induced by the exhilarating feeling of power in the acts of destruction has given way to, at best, hope. But the demolition was certainly a prerequiste of kindling that hope.

It is commonplace to hear such criticisms of revolutionary pacifism as "it emphasizes negative peace"—a revolt against the war system—without giving much thought to "positive peace," the nature of the peaceful world to be established if and when war is abolished. The answer to this criticism is that we cannot know what sort of world a warless world will be. Moreover, it would be much more difficult to agree on the sort of world we want than to agree on the sort of world we do not want, a world dominated by the institution of war. Acts calculated to undermine the legitimacy of the war system can be organized *now.* Alternative plans can be evaluated on the basis of experience already accumulated or soon to be acquired. It is easier to destroy than to create, and, while in this context, as in every other, destruction is not sufficient, it is in this case clearly necessary.

Above all, as has already been said, the task of converting people to a religion, no matter how inspiring that religion may seem to its adherents, is much more difficult than the task of undermining the legitimacy of war. In particular, few people are able to love all people, including enemies. For most people, this kind of love is simply too much to ask for. No demands are made on the psyche of the revolutionary pacifist except steadfastness and discipline in organized action, qualities demanded in many different kinds of collective action including, incidentally, war. This state of mind is not uncommon in persons dedicated to a cause, hence by no means unattainable.

Perhaps there is something to be learned from military practice. In the days when artillery was the most powerful offensive weapon, it was generally agreed that, in an offensive operation, concentrating artillery fire on some narrow sector of the defending force was more effective than an attack on a wide front. The purpose of the concentrated attack was to effect a breach in the defense, through which the infantry could pour to envelop the enemy forces.

Similar tactics may serve in a "war against war." To see this, consider the conception of war as a recurring disaster or as a breakdown of the international system. Such concepts were usually the points of departure for "peace research," an activity that, since its inception, has frequently centered on investigations aimed at uncovering the "causes of war." Now causes are of two kinds: necessary and sufficient. Event A is said to be necessary as a cause of event B if B cannot occur unless A occurs. A is said to be a sufficient cause of B if B must occur whenever A occurs. Now the identification of sufficient causes of wars is most difficult, if only because causes that may have been sufficent at one time are no longer so, for example, dynastic considerations or religious differences. Not so with a necessary cause of war, if by war we mean the sort of conflict that now threatens the survival of the human race. Possession of weapons is indispensable for fighting such a war and can, therefore, be regarded as a necessary (thought admittedly not a sufficient) cause of war.

If knowledge about the causes of wars is to be put to work with the aim of abolishing war, then only knowledge about necessary causes should suffice. There is a parallel here between peace research and medical research. Knowledge most relevant to the task of eliminating, controlling, preventing, or curing diseases is knowledge about necessary causes rather than about sufficient causes. Sufficient causes of diseases are often formidably complex; necessary causes are often simple. Presence of tubercle bacilli is a necessary (though not a sufficient) cause of tuberculosis. Vitamin C deficiency is a necessary cause of scurvy. Discovery of a necessary cause is often the critical step on the way of eliminating, controlling, preventing, or curing a disease.

Unfortunately, this cannot be said of the knowledge of a necessary cause of war. Indeed, as has been said, a necessary cause is weapons. In a way, therefore, peace researchers seeking the causes of wars have been breaking through an open door. At this point, however, the parallel between medical research and peace research breaks down. The reason knowledge of necessary causes of diseases in some cases solves the problem of eliminating or preventing them is because this knowledge can be put to work immediately and effectively. Hospitals, public health agencies, and clinics, stand ready to apply such knowledge. No comparable instititutions exist that are ready to receive the available knowledge about the causes of wars (weapons) and put it to work in the task of preventing or eliminating wars. On the contrary, there is no dearth of institutions standing ready to receive more knowledge about how to make wars more destructive and empowered to put that knowledge to work in designing new generations of weapons of total destruction.

However, this very circumstance provides a focal point for the abolitionist's attack on war. The disarmament issue is clear and unambiguous. In organizing political action to exert pressure for disarmament, the abolitionist can acquire many allies from the entire political spectrum, even in government circles of many countries, including the superpowers.

Moreover, the struggle for disarmament is one where successes, if they occur, are highly visible. Of course, some so-called arms control measures are no more than dabs of cosmetics on the brutal image of the war system. But then, anything that happens in this area is grist for the mill of critical analysis, which cannot be readily dismissed as "misguided idealism" or a "nonissue."

Analysis of the current state and trends of the arms race can be couched in the militarist's own language, except that the underlying value system of the abolitionist's analysis carries the opposite sign. What is regarded as "progress" in military circles is branded as an advance toward catastrophe and what is decried as jeopardy of security in the war establishment should be shown to be a retreat from the abyss. As we will argue below, it is necessary, at times, to carry the struggle for peace into the "enemy's" own territory instead of giving him the opportunity to lend a respectful ear to the usual pleas for peace and to dismiss them with some condescending remark: "Yes, that's certainly something to think about, but after all we must face the world as it is, not how we would want it to be."

Pierre Trudeau, prime minister of Canada (1968–79; 1980–84), frankly spoke of "suffocating" the arms race. The metaphor is an apt one and may well be adopted by the abolitionist, for the ultimate aim—killing the quasi-organism identified with the institution of war—should be frankly avowed and kept in the public eye.

The organism metaphor serves two functions—an educational one and an energizing one. The term *metaphor* is used here not in its poetic but its system-theoretic sense. A poetic metaphor serves to call attention to some apparently common property or quality of two widely disparate things and thereby provides an esthetic experience of being suddenly and somewhat surprisingly made aware of "unity in diversity." A system-theoretic metaphor points to an actual structural or functional correspondence between apparently disparate phenomena that is "theoretically fertile." That is, on the basis of the discovered correspondence, a substantive theory can be constructed that leads to further insights about the nature of the phenomena observed. Thus, the metaphor in the statement "The engine eats fuel" is theoretically fertile because it calls attention to oxidation as a process that keeps a living organism alive (by transforming ingested food into energy) and the engine working by transforming fuel into work energy.

To call the war system an organism is to call attention to a convincing analogy between an institution and a parasite or a malignant growth. Like a parasite, the war system deflects the resources of a society to its own uses without giving anything in return, if the "defense" function turns out to be vacuous. A parasite saps the vigor of its host and frequently kills it, usually slowly in order to postpone its own demise. The military establishments of the superpowers appear to be doing just that.

The comparison of the war system with a malignant growth is even more apt. The host can frequently mobilize defenses against a parasite in the form of antibodies or leucocytes to destroy it. The effectiveness of the defense depends on the ability of the defending forces to recognize the invading cells as "alien." The difficulty in attacking the cells of a malignant growth is that they are often not recognized as "alien." They are, in fact, the body's own cells that have escaped the regulating mechanisms of the body. These features can be recognized in war establishments. They are not "alien" to the societies in which they are embedded. In fact, traditionally they actually protected their societies from invaders or else helped the societies expand, which temporarily enhanced their viability and robustness. These functions, as I have argued, have atrophied. Nonetheless, military establishments successfully simulate the defense function. Conceptual inertia induces a view of the world that no longer corresponds to reality. It helps preserve the fiction and so masks the parasitic role of the military establishment.

An escape from the regulating mechanisms of the body is another characteristic of malignant growths. The hypertrophy of the military establishments, in the first instance of the superpowers, reflects the same sort of escape. Thus, to speak of the institution of war as if it were an organism is not merely to resort to picturesque rhetoric. The aim is to induce an insight.

The organism metaphor may be of help in mobilizing for a "war against war." We have argued that one of the firmest foundations of cooperation is the perception of a common enemy. An unfortunate feature of this duality of conflict and cooperation is that in allaying one form of conflict, cooperation often exacerbates another form. We have seen how the progressive integration of human groups into ever-larger political units, while alleviating internal strife, provided avenues for ever more severe and destructive strife, such as interstate or interbloc warfare.

There is, thus, a price to pay for making allies out of erstwhile enemies. The alliances create new rivals or enemies. The integrating potential of perceiving a common enemy could be utilized without exacerbating conflicts among humans by identifying a nonhuman enemy. Even here, however, the conflict may be ultimately destructive. The "conquest of nature," for example, which in the heydays of technocratic optimism was pictured as a triumph of humanity over a "hostile" environment, now appears as a Pyrrhic victory. In "defeating" nature, we have been destroying our own life-support system.

No such danger lurks in "killing" the institution of war, at least none that can be reasonably imagined. The institution has no more redeeming features than a cancer. To be sure, some aspects of it may be salvageable, as I will indicate below. But its main function, that of preparing and conducting wars among human beings, has become pathological. Once this is recognized, the organization of a war against war (as the perceived common enemy of humanity) could well provide a firm point of leverage for the integration of humanity. If aggressive instincts still lurk in humans (to the extent that they have not been eliminated, having lost reproductive advantage), mobilizing against the institution of war may be one promising way of putting human aggressiveness to good use.

I cited Amos's forecast of the eventual demise of the institution of war, to be brought about by moral repugnance. Amos believed in steady "moral progress" as a concomitant of the general progress supposedly inherent in civilization. It has been repeatedly pointed out that there is no convincing evidence of "moral progress" in human history. The genocidal orgies of the twentieth century matched the depravity of any earlier age. I have, however, argued that institutions, like organisms, remain viable only as long as they can adapt to their environments. I went on to show that the institution of war became adapted to many different social environments in the course of its history. In light of the nonteleological theory of evolution, these adaptations are not to be taken as evidence of some sort of "ingenuity" exercised by the institution of war any more than the adaptation of any evolutionary line to its environment is evidence of any deliberate effort. The evolving lines that did not adapt are no longer among us. We see only those that did.

Next, I suggested that the latest adaptation of the war system was to a social environment where, although war is not glorified as such, technical progress is. And since war had already achieved a symbiotic relationship with technical progress (each nurturing the other and co-evolving with it), it was able to adapt to a technolatrous society.

If this is, indeed, the basis of the war system's adaptation to the industrially highly developed societies, then the parasitic nature of the war establishment can be convincingly demonstrated by showing that even the imaginary functions of that establishment no longer make any sense and that the only discernible raison d'être of the war system is to maintain itself. (Note that self-maintenance is a function that all systems have in common by their definition as a system.)

The standard justification of nurturing the war establishment in all countries is now "defense." Particularly interesting are the establishments of the superpowers, for the continued existence of the global war machine depends on the continued existence and robustness of those establishments. Next, because the latest adaptation of the war system to a society that never expressly honored war per se is most conspicous in the United States, we should examine the justification of maintaining the war establishment in that country.

If the word *defense* is not to be reduced to a meaningless sound, the threat against which the United States war establishment is supposed to defend the country must be identified. Throughout the cold war era four threats, emanating from a single source (namely, the Soviet Union), were constantly indicated. One was the threat of an unprovoked attack upon the United States by nuclear weapons, a sort of nuclear version of Pearl Harbor. Another was an invasion of Western Europe by Soviet armies. The third was the establishment of Communist regimes throughout Latin America, turning those countries into staging areas for an attack on the United States. Finally, the expansive drive of the Soviet Union was imagined to lead to the communization of the entire planet, leaving the United States the only bastion of democracy, helpless against economic strangulation.

Present-day rulers may believe that this last formulation is a caricature. At any rate, the image is no longer seriously evoked and the others have been toned down. But a perusal of the relevant literature and public statements produced (even quite recently) will convince anyone that all these scenarios were taken seriously throughout the entire cold war. And the cold war mentality is by no means defunct in the United States.

It is difficult to say to what extent these scenarios were ever taken seriously by the designers of U.S. foreign and defense policies. That they have been used to justify these policies is indisputable. For example, acts of war against Cuba and Nicaragua were pictured as measures of self-defense by invoking the staging area scenario. Much was made of the fact that Cuba is "only 90 miles from our shores," and even Nicaragua was pictured as practically a next-door neighbor "just two days' drive from the Texas border."

The "conquest of the world" scenario was taken directly from board games, successors of Monopoly, where the winner was now the player who, instead of "taking over" all the enterprises, "takes over" countries. On a more modest scale, the "take over" was pictured as an invasion of Western Europe spearheaded by Soviet tanks that (as was repeatedly emphasized) outnumbered those of NATO by some impressive factor.

Completely missing from the last two scenarios was any indication of the logistic requirements of the military operations. Just what would it take to concentrate a military force, say in Nicaragua, put it on trucks, drive to the border of Texas in forty-eight hours, and start an invasion of the United States?

The vision of a massive invasion force rolling across Western Europe is, perhaps, not quite so absurd, if one side-steps the question of what is supposed to happen after they have gone as far as they are supposed to go—France? Spain? Portugal? In particular, what would it take to create a more or less permanent administrative apparatus to exercise authoritarian rule over Germany, the Low Countries, France, and Italy?

The scenario of a devastating nuclear attack is the most realistic, in the sense that it is physically possible. In fact, both sides have been poised to launch just such an attack for decades and some signals passed from the right sources to the right destinations could have started it. Aside from purely logistic considerations, however, there is also the question of political motivation. Recall the often-quoted dictum of Clausewitz: "War is the continuation of politics by other means." Dedicated as Clausewitz was to war as the expression of the very essence of a state, he kept insisting on the inseparability of war from politics, whereby the latter is supposed to play the leading role. War, Clausewitz wrote, "is an act of violence intended to compel our opponent to fulfill our will" ([1832] 1968, 101). Therefore, behind a war there must be a "will" to bring about something. What was a war assumed launched by the Soviet Union against the United States supposed to bring about? Of course, to this question there was always a ready answer: the imposition of a Communist system. If so, then the dramatic events of 1989 that brought about utter collapse of the Communist system (under which domination of countries other than the Soviet Union was always understood) have completely demolished the political basis of a war started by the Soviet Union against the West. So what happens to the rationale of "defense against Communist aggression?"

The rationale is gone, but if war is conceived as an institution instead of an instrument, a rationale for the continued existence of the institution is not needed. An institution is a system and, by definition, its "business" is to continue (i.e., safeguard) its own existence. And this is precisely what we observe.

Emancipation from Superstition as an Irreversible Process

As we have seen, evolutionary processes are typically irreversible. Whether one sees an evolutionary process representing progress or regress depends on one's values. Growth of scientific knowledge, that is, the broadening and refinement of knowledge available to humankind and of methods of attaining it, is a conspicuous irreversible process. This process arouses ambivalent, sometimes outspokenly negative feelings, because of the uses to which scientific knowledge has been put, primarily in the service of the war establishment. However, the fruits of scientific knowledge are not confined to technology (lethal or benign). This knowledge also contributes to enlightenment, that is, emancipation from delusions or compulsions that have been endemic in prescientific thought.

We have seen how compulsive preoccupation with rituals and taboos closed off a valuable resource that had been the source of a prosperous livelihood for a tribe. In the business of exploiting resources, we usually think of industrially developed societies as immune to superstitions of this sort. Yet there is one such superstition that severely restricts political options of the people of the United States, namely, the belief that the perpetual war economy is a source of prosperity. Indeed, this superstition is the most serious obstacle to the sort of political awakening that could empower the U.S. people to cure their society of the war disease and thereby to contribute to the security of the human race.

By a war economy I mean one in which substantive material and human resources are allocated to preparations to wage war (whether war is waged or not). Now, it is generally agreed that a prosperous economy is one that provides a plenitude of goods and services to a population. By goods and services I mean implicitly usable goods and services. To be sure, the meaning of usable is broad. Food is usable in the literal sense, since it is consumed. Clothing and housing are obviously usable. So are machines that produce usable things. Some things that are not used in the usual sense can nevertheless be regarded as usable by virtue of providing, say, esthetic gratification, for example, works of art. Services are usable in the sense that they satisfy needs, for example, the services of a barber, a physician, a musician, a teacher, or a priest. Although the services they provide are not of equal value to all, nevertheless, there is general agreement that all of them contribute to a decent or prosperous existence.

With a stretch of imagination, the same could be said of weapons that may provide satisfaction to a sector of the population by inducing a sense of power or security. However, this sense of power or security depends on the feeling that, under some circumstances, the weapons could be put to use for some acceptable purpose. This "usability" of the weapons of total destruction, however, is frequently and emphatically denied, even by some prominent exponents of the military establishment. The core of the deterrence concept is that these weapons are produced and stockpiled in order that they will *not* be put to use. It follows that a war economy is characterized by the allocation of resources to production of goods and services that are, *at best*, never to be used, since if they are ever put to use, we stand in danger of extinction.

To believe that this sort of economy contributes to "prosperity" is to believe an absurdity. Of course the basis of this belief is evident. The war economy is said to contribute to prosperity by creating jobs. But a "prosperity" of this sort can be more simply created by printing lots of money and passing it out to the population in unlimited amounts. To be sure, this "prosperity" would be short-lived, but while it lasts, some people might believe that it is genuine. For a few days or weeks, businesses would boom as people went on buying sprees. Soon, however, the stores would be empty, while the motivation to work (to produce more goods) would be impaired. This motivation stems largely from the prospect of being paid. But this prospect is not attractive when one has money to burn and nothing to spend it on.

The delusion of prosperity attributed to the war economy differs from the delusion that being rich means having a lot of money only in the sense that the impending fiasco is better camouflaged. The delusion of prosperity produced by the money deluge can last only a few days or weeks. The illusory prosperity of a war economy can last considerably longer. Nevertheless, it must collapse if resources simply go down a bottomless pit.

Because the inevitable disaster attendant on a war economy (which, incidentally, has already occurred in the Soviet Union) is still beyond the horizon of awareness of most people in the United States, the superstition persists. Political support for the war economy, for the parasitic war machine, is very largely based on this superstition. In the early 1960s, F. J. Cook illustrated the power of this delusion.

> In Tacoma, Washington, the owner of a shoe store fitted three small children for shoes. The father gave him a twenty dollar bill, and when the proprietor handed back the change, the father presented a small card. It read: "You have just done business with a Mount Rainier Ordnance Depot employee. How much money will you lose when the $14 million payroll goes to Utah? Write your Congressman, Senator, Governor, if you want to protest this move." (Cook 1962, 192)

This man was evidently a civilian employee of the military. To him, the most important effect of the "move to Utah" was the loss of a job. Such losses would be immediate consequences of curtailing the war economy and would be acutely felt by millions of people. For most of them, protests against such curtailments would seem to be the most natural political response. Thus, a massive, grass roots movement could develop with aims diametrically opposed to the aims of a peace movement, adding to the already formidable political leverage of the war establishment and all its corporate, professional, and scientific adjuncts. It appears, therefore, that the vigorous defenses of "business as usual" in the war establishment, regardless of political climate, are rationalizations—a front protecting commitments to the war economy as a way of life. The comment of one of the respondents in the Oxford Research Group survey makes this chillingly clear:

> . . . we've got to try to make stable deterrence work for the rest of human history.[1]

1. This and similar comments were elicited in a survey conducted by the Oxford Research Group (22 Warnborough Road, Oxford OX26JA, U.K.) from a sample of British nuclear weapons decision makers. The replies to the questions were made on condition of anonymity.

What is being defended here is more important to the average individual than any ideology and more relevant than the global political climate, namely, a way of life. A satisfactory way of life is defended with utmost tenacity.

Review of Views and Advocacies

Some justification of the title of this book is in order. First, the title does not imply that peace is about to break out on our planet. Second, it does imply that, in the wake of the demise of the cold war, opportunities will be created for the superpowers to collaborate in the cause of global peace. To say that the time of an idea has come is to say that the time has come to put the idea to work. Third, the title is not so much a *description* of the present situation as a call for certain kinds of *action*, aimed at making the recent developments more promising than they presently are.

It goes without saying that the cold war and its attendant arms race were not the only incubators of a major war. Indeed, since 1945, there has been continual warfare, almost completely confined to the Third World. The sources of this endemic violence are apparent. The breakup of the colonial system based on political control spawned a multitude of new "sovereign states," each with a military establishment and a new power elite, mostly western educated, eagerly emulating their erstwhile masters. A major factor in this proliferation of the war system has been the rapidly growing arms race. The First World equips the Third World with killing machines and with specialists who instruct the newly created military personnel in their uses. As in all trade, the profit motive has always provided the driving force, but additional stimuli were provided by linking the nurturing of the war machine with establishing and maintaining spheres of influence. During the cold war, the military establishment of the First World still thought in terms of geopolitics and its associated strategic and logistic problems. Hence, the importance of getting and maintaining a foothold on the Horn of Africa or the Philippines or in the Arctic or in the Indian Ocean or wherever.

The demise of the cold war may make such geopolitical considerations less pressing. Here, however, we must be careful not to fixate on unidirectional causal relationships. There is not much conviction in the argument that, as the tensions between the superpowers attenuate, their decision makers will be less interested in securing traditional strategic advantages or that the arms race will have lost its allure. It is the feedback process that may produce these effects. That is to say, once *some* collaboration between the superpowers gets started, even on the symbolic level or as standard public relations ploys, this form of behavior may induce changes in attitudes. There is an escalation potential in cooperation as well as in conflict. And just as rivals caught in an escalating conflict aggravate the conflict by mutually stimulating hostile acts, cooperators can strengthen their bond by simply practicing cooperation.

Furthermore, the assumption that the superpowers may begin to cooperate in earnest already contains an important tacit assumption, namely, that (in all likelihood) genuine cooperation can develop only if the present leadership in the United States is replaced by another, one more attuned to human needs than to the imperatives of power. The question in jest, "When will perestroika start in the United States?" should be asked seriously and not only asked but acted upon.

There is no guarantee that the new thinking released first by the ideological revolution in the Soviet Union, then by the political revolutions in Eastern Europe, and now beginning to spread throughout Europe will also spread to the United States. But it may, and therefore there is reason to hope and consequently a compelling reason to act.

Assuming, then, that a sufficiently far-reaching political revolution occurs in the United States, the superpowers can become genuine allies and can consolidate their power to establish a new world order. It goes without saying that a peaceful and just world order cannot be established by coercion in the usual sense of power politics. But the superpowers, together with Europe, can help a new leadership emerge in the Third World and so pave the way for the evolution of a global society.

Conflicts and even wars may still go on in that society. War cannot be eliminated by treaties, resolutions, or decrees. Nor can it be eliminated by "changing human nature." We do not even know the nature of human nature, let alone have techniques for changing it. But war can be eliminated by cutting its lifelines.

Most of the endemic wars in the Third World can be traced to interventions by the superpowers, either direct, as in the thirty-year war in Southeast Asia or in the ten-year war in Afghanistan, or indirect, as by establishing client states or insurgent groups or, most important, by supplying both warring sides with weapons. The explosive situation in the Middle East can be directly traced to U.S. intervention. The formidable military might of Israel was, of course, created by U.S. aid.

Sympathy for the Jews intent on establishing and protecting a homeland can be safely discounted. The principal motivation has been that of maintaining a reliable military ally in the region. As long as the establishment of peace based on a modus vivendi and a recognition of the rights of others is blocked by hawkish Israeli governments, the explosive situation will continue.

A secular democratic government might have been established in Iran after World War II under the leadership of Mohammed Mossadegh. That government was overthrown by the United States in 1953 and replaced by a dictatorship. When the Shah was overthrown, another, even more repressive dictatorship replaced him. Iraq, originally a Soviet client state, became a military dictatorship, and the stage was set for its bloody eight-year war with Iran. Ethiopia became a Soviet client state after the overthrow of the monarchy. Ironically, the war waged by this dictatorship was supplied with materiel and advisers from Israel, the most faithful ally of the United States.

It goes without saying that if the First World (into which the Soviet Union and its erstwhile satellites are to be incorporated) begins cooperating to establish peace and a just world order, the first task is to stop feeding the endemic war disease of the Third World. As has been said, "negative" actions are much easier to organize than "positive" ones and should, therefore, have priority. Feeding wars should be stopped. The arms trade should be declared a crime against humanity and stopped, as once the slave trade was stopped, as the drug trade could be stopped through the concerted action of powerful states. These tasks are perhaps among the very few where military action (of course authorized by proper supranational authority) could be justified.

Once these "negative" tasks are accomplished, the more difficult tasks of rebuilding the planet on new beginnings can be undertaken. The important thing is to create a momentum for the necessary operations. Such momentum could be provided by the initial acts of cooperation against a common enemy—the war system.

From the abolitionist point of view, the assault against the institution of war ought to develop independently of cooperation between governments, that is, in the context of transnational instead of international cooperation. Support should, of course, be given to governments that energetically promote disarmament, peacekeeping, and peacemaking with due regard to the needs of the people and without regard for the imperatives of power politics. But the independence of nongovernmental organizations from whatever foreign policies their respective governments may be pursuing should be safeguarded at all times. Since the practice of cooperation enhances further cooperation, especially after successes (no matter how minor), continually sustained transnational cooperation could eventually provide an infrastructure for a consolidated global peace movement with considerable political clout.

The three tasks of a peace movement are peace research, peace education, and peace action. Peace research should provide material for peace education, and peace education should provide cadres for peace action. The immediate goals of peace action will naturally vary from time to time and from place to place. The tasks of peace education, however, have a well-defined, common goal, namely, the creation and support of global awareness, an analogue of the class consciousness of Marxist revolutionary theory.

We will not discuss the strengths and weaknesses of Marxist revolutionary theory here except to point out that the failure of revolutions supposed to have been inspired by that theory to establish humane, classless societies can be related to the central position of power struggles in the implementation of the theory. Lord Acton's famous maxim, "all power corrupts, and absolute power corrupts absolutely," was nowhere more dramatically vindicated than in the fate of revolutions carried out under the banner of Marxism-Leninism.

Global awareness, like class consciousness, is centered on struggle, but against an enemy that is not human. Freeman Dyson's demarcation of humankind into Warriors and Victims defines the battleline, but the class of Warriors is defined by roles, not by persons. As persons, the Warriors also belong to the class of Victims. Thus, the abolitionism struggle is conducted in the mode of integration, not polarization.

Global awareness should be inculcated by enlightenment, not by indoctrination. Therefore, peace education should be education in the literal sense of the word, the sort of education that could be readily incorporated into the curricula of modern universities, provided their administrations and faculties are not intimidated by agencies with vested interests in the war system. With some adjustments, peace education materials could also be incorporated in secondary school curricula and in continuing education programs. Much of this material is now standard knowledge. It needs only to be oriented toward the fundamental task of peace education. This has been attempted in the present volume.

Review of Supporting Conceptual Frameworks

The reader may be puzzled by the variety of themes treated in this book—theories of evolution, philosophy of knowledge, philosophy of language, decision theory, psychology, and sociobiology, among others. He or she may or may not have come to see the relevance of all these themes to the theme of this book. I will risk redundancy by pointing it out and apologize in advance to those who have already seen through my goal and need not be reminded. The goal was to contribute to enlightenment. Enlightenment is essentially emancipation from superstition.

A superstition is a belief in something that is not so, that has its roots in some unwarranted generalization or an unwarranted establishment of a cause-and-effect relationship between events. Someone at some time may have had an unfortunate experience after having walked under a ladder or seen the new moon over his left shoulder or broken a mirror or whatever. Linking these events to a misfortune gives birth to a superstition. A superstition spreads rapidly and widely, because people are reluctant to take chances. Not long ago, tomatoes were thought to be poisonous. It took considerable courage to eat a tomato in order to prove that they are not.

There is a widespread superstition in Western Europe and in North America to the effect that nuclear weapons kept in readiness to be activated have kept peace in Europe since 1945. The fact that there has been no war in Europe since 1945 is cited as evidence that this is so. But with equal justification, the absence of war in Europe since 1945 could be attributed to the activities of the peace movement or to the establishment of Communist regimes in Eastern Europe or, for that matter, to the talisman that someone carries around.

One way to refute the "theory" that the talisman is a preventative of war is to destroy it to show that nothing will happen. But its owner cannot be persuaded to get rid of it. He is convinced that getting rid of the talisman will precipitate a war. The refusal to eliminate nuclear weapons may well be based on a similar superstition.

The conviction that the security of a country is directly related to its military potential is a superstition, because there is no historical evidence to support this belief. Militarily strong states, or at least their populations, suffered from wars no less than weak ones and were as frequently defeated.

Along with superstitions, conventional wisdom expressed in time-honored adages frequently closed off paths to enlightenment. One of the widespread ones is the belief that the "causes of wars" lie primarily in human "aggressiveness." This belief, as we have seen, pervaded Freud's view of human nature. Human aggressiveness is thought by many religious pacifists to be the main obstacle to eliminating war. A defeatist view like Freud's weakens the will in the struggle against the institution of war. Pacifists who believe that the most important task of the peace movement is that of converting people to pacifism may be misdirecting their energy. There may be no connection between human aggressiveness (assuming it exists) and modern war.

First, let us examine the belief in the "aggressive drive." Observations of the cruelties that people perpetrate on each other surely fail to provide suffcient evidence for the existence of such a drive. Different people (and also the same people under different circumstances) also behave kindly, at times altruistically. These observations are no less relevant to the assessment of human nature.

Somewhat more convincing are references to the survival value of the "aggressive instinct" in many vertebrates. For example, in competition for females or for territory (which is often manifested in combat), the reproductive advantage of the stronger males contributes to the vigor of the species. Nevertheless, in order to use the argument to support the presence of an aggressive drive in man as an evolutionary adaptation, two things must be proved: (1) that aggressive tendencies are genetically determined; and (2) that aggressiveness confers reproductive advantage on human beings. The first is difficult enough to show; the second practically impossible. There is no evidence that, in competing for females, the stronger or fiercer or braver male has an advantage, and even if he does in a particular situation (i.e., in winning a particular female), this need not give him the opportunity to sire more progeny, unless he happens to be a bigamist or, as a consequence of his victories, collects a harem.

Lack of evidence or of a convincing rationale for the existence of an aggressive drive in humans by no means proves that an aggressive drive does *not* exist in humans. It may exist in the form of a vestige, a carryover from the deep past when the drive did confer reproductive advantage. Or, what is more likely, it may be present in the gene pool, that is, it may exist in some people, manifesting itself under appropriate circumstances. Because these circumstances are often dramatic, for example, rape or murder, manifestations of aggressiveness are far more conspicuous than peaceful, cooperative, or nurturing behavior, which may also be in our evolutionary heritage.

Wars, of course, appear as massive outbursts of violence, but these outbreaks do not by any means constitute definitive evidence that all participants (or even most participants) in these outbreaks are acting out their aggressions. Recall that soldiers in the standing armies of the eighteenth century were trained by the application of severe punishments for disobedience to perform certain prescribed actions. These actions could be performed mechanically, unaccompained by any feelings of aggression. Recall that the mass armies of the post-Napoleonic era were composed of conscripts. They, too, had to do exactly what they were told. Finally extensive investigations of the behavior of U.S. infantry soldiers in World War II revealed that aggressiveness was by no means a major factor in their motivation to fight. It seems that the instinct of self-preservation was stronger than the aggressive drive in most soldiers (Stouffer et al. 1949, vol. 2, chap. 3).

The most serious objection to the assumption that it takes aggressive individuals to make war is the obvious circumstance that modern war makes aggressiveness irrelevant in the business of organizing and conducting vast and complex military operations. Few soldiers see their enemies in a modern battle, and even the battlefield appears to be on the way out. Moreover, the most important factor contributing to the destructiveness of war is the systematic development of ever more lethal weapons systems and of strategies and tactics related to their use. It is no longer necessary to hate anyone in order to kill everyone. The laboratory of a scientist working on a more deadly nerve gas appears no differently from that of a scientist working on a new life-saving drug. The offices of the Pentagon look no different from the offices of any large business center. Dyson's Warrior does not wear a horned helmet, carries no spear, has probably never killed anyone, and will probably never kill anyone.

It is to drive these points home that I made an excursion into system theory. A favorite slogan of system theorists of the holistic (organismic) persuasion is "the whole is greater than the sum of its parts." This way of putting it is not very enlightening. A better way of putting it is "a system need not have any of the properties that characterize its components." In chemistry, this is obvious. The properties that characterize water have little resemblance to those of oxygen and hydrogen, of which water is composed. A mob can behave in ways that no member of it can. Consider a person committing suicide. None of the cells of which he is composed are "committing suicide." They are behaving normally. As the suicide writes the farewell note, puts the revolver into his mouth, and pulls the trigger, his nerve cells are all "doing their job," that is, directing the proper muscles to contract in the proper order. They are unaware of what is happening. It is the coordinated sum total of all their actions that kills the system that they comprise and, of course, all of them as well. In the same way, it may appear to an outside observer, say an extraterrestrial being, who sees humankind as we see an anthill or a beehive—a sort of superorganism—that this "organism" is preparing to commit suicide. The weapon (war machine) is ready. It needs only to be activated. From the inside, we do not see the "psychological state" of the organism as a whole. We see only a conglomerate of policies, rationales, rhetoric, and so forth. But the outside observer sees the "psychological state" of humanity as a whole and interprets it as an intent to commit suicide. The "cells" in the meantime (i.e., all of us) go about their business, having apparently nothing to do with suicide. Yet all of these "normal" activities add up to collective suicide.

I have just invoked an analogy suggested by organismic system theory. Indeed, the entire method of general system theory is based on explorations of analogies. The ability to distinguish profound and theoretically fruitful analogies from superficial ones is acquired in the process of enlightenment. Here some acquaintance with modern scientific theories can be of help. It helps to understand how superficial or spurious analogies become incorporated into a belief system and are encrusted in superstitions and prejudices. The excursion into general semantics was an attempt to acquaint the reader with the role of language in shaping human affairs.

Recall the description of language as a screen between human beings and reality. That is, human beings do not see reality directly but only through the medium of language. We believe about reality what others (and we ourselves) say about it. Thus, all categories, generalizations, or causal relations are perceived as combinations of words. Language becomes a sort of map of a territory (reality). Moreover, maps of maps can be constructed and so on to higher order maps. In this process, connections between the maps and the underlying reality can be severed. Thus, we can be guided to our beliefs and actions by maps of nonexisting territories.

As far as we know, no other animal perceives reality (its environment) in this way. We humans owe everything we have and everything we are to the ability to construct verbal maps of our environment, both external and internal (what we say about our thoughts, feelings, etc.). This ability is our principal survival mechanism. And it can also lead us to quick extinction. Realization and appreciation of this dual role of human language is also part of enlightenment.

The noosphere is part of the environment of our species and only of our species. We coevolve with this environment, and our continued survival or our extinction depends on the direction taken by this coevolution. The noosphere (the sum total of human knowledge, beliefs, ideologies, etc.) is no less "real" than the geosphere, the atmosphere, or the biosphere. To be sure, its "level" of reality is on a different plane. But the planes of the inanimate spheres and of the biosphere are also different, since their evolution processes are determined by different laws. In light of the systemic approach, "materiality" is not a necessary aspect of reality. We can assert this without recourse to any mystic notions. A language, for example, is no less real than a population that speaks it. Its structure, function, and evolution can be studied by the methods of "hard science." A language is concrete, but not material. The same can be said of the whole noosphere.

The evolution of the noosphere is of fundamental relevance to the theme of this book. Like all evolutionary processes, the evolution of the noosphere is an irreversible process. This does not mean that nothing is ever lost from the store of accumulated knowledge. Languages can be "forgotten" just as species become extinct in biological evolution. On the whole, however, the noosphere evolves in one direction: it keeps getting richer.

The irreversibility of the process is especially marked in the sphere of scientific knowledge. Typically, scientific theories become generalizations of old ones, so that the old ones remain contained in the new ones as special cases. Associated with the increasing generalization of scientific cognition is its increasing abstraction. This can be most vividly illustrated in the evolution of mathematics. At first, numbers had to be linked with "things"—baskets, sheep, fingers. Measurement was more abstract. It was associated with distances, later with time periods. Still later numbers could be represented simply as points on a line, then, in the case of complex numbers, as points on a plane. Finally, visual representation disappeared altogether. Only the logic of deduction and operations remained. If this enrichment of mental processes represents a value, the development of mathematics can be cited as an instance of genuine progress.

The same applies to the growth of science, as a whole. If science is conceived as a mode of understanding the world we live in, and if this sort of understanding is valued, then the growth of science represents progress. Moreover, this growth, broadening, and enrichment are irreversible. Once something is understood in the scientific mode, it remains understood in that mode. There is no going back to prescientific modes of thinking about the phenomenon in question. Once thunderstorms are explained in terms of discharges of static electricity, one can no longer think that thunder is the rumbling of prophet Elijah's chariot across the sky. Once the connection between certain diseases and specific microorganisms is established, it becomes very difficult to take seriously the effects of an "evil eye" or the theory of humors that dominated eighteenth-century medicine.

Enlightenment is the dissipation of superstitions. The thesis developed in this book is that all rationales supporting the continued existence of war as an institution can now be exposed as superstitions. The discrediting of a superstition is an irreversible process. This is what is meant by the statement that peace is an idea whose time has come.

References

In the case of older works, the date of the edition consulted is preceded by the date of original publication, if known, e. g., Darwin [1859] 1964.

Amos. S. 1880. *Political and Legal Remedies for War.* London: Cassell, Porter, Galpin and Co.

Auerbach, N. M. 1968. "Edmund Burke." In *International Encyclopedia of the Social Sciences,* ed. D. L. Sills. New York: Macmillan and Free Press.

Axelrod, R. 1984. *The Evolution of Cooperation.* New York: Basic Books.

Balfour, A. J. 1916. "Introduction." In *Politics,* H. von Treischke. New York: Macmillan.

Barash, D. P. 1982. *Sociobiology and Behaviour.* New York: Elsevier.

Bellamy, E. [1888] 1960. *Looking Backward.* New York: New American Library.

Bergson, H. L. 1937. *Creative Evolution.* New York: H. Holt.

Bernhardi, F. von. 1914. *Germany and the Next War.* New York: Longmans, Green.

Boulding, K. E. 1974. "The Relation of Economic, Political, and Social Systems." In *Collected Papers,* ed. L. D. Singall, vol. 4. Boulder, Colo.: Associated University Press.

Broad, W. J. 1985. *Star Warriors.* New York: Simon and Shuster.

Buchanan, J., and Tullock, G. 1962. *The Calculus of Consent.* Ann Arbor: University of Michigan Press.

Bunge, M. 1981. *Scientific Materialism.* Dordrecht: Reidel.

Clark, G., and Sohn, L. B. 1966. *World Peace through World Law.* Cambridge, Mass.: Harvard University Press.

Clausewitz, C. von [1832] 1968. *On War.* Harmondsworth: Penguin Books.

Comte, A. [1830–32] 1877. *Cours de philosophie positive.* Vol. 4–5, *Philosophie sociale.* Paris: Bailliere.

Cook, F. J. 1962. *The Warfare State.* New York: Colliers Books.

Cowper, W. 1856. "The Winter's Morning Walk." In *The Poetical Works of William Cowper.* Edinburgh: James Nichol.

Czechoslovak Academy of Sciences. 1964. *The Universal Peace Organization of King George of Bohemia: A Fifteenth Century Plan for World Peace.* Prague: Czechslovak Academy of Sciences.

Darwin, C. [1859] 1964. *On the Origin of Species.* Cambridge, Mass.: Harvard University Press.

Dawkins, R. 1976. *The Selfish Gene.* Oxford: Oxford University Press.

Dickson, P. 1971. *Think Tanks.* New York: Atheneum.

Dyson, F. 1984. *Weapons and Hope.* New York: Harper and Row.

Emerson, A. E. 1939. "Social Coordination and the Superorganism." *American Midland Naturalist* 21:182–209.

Erasmus, D. [1517] 1946. *The Complaint of Peace.* New York: Scholars' Facsimiles and Reprints.

Fisher, R., and Ury, W. 1981. *Getting to Yes.* Boston: Houghton Mifflin.

Gerard, R. W. 1958. "Concepts and Principles of Biology." *Behavioral Science* 3: 95–102.

Gray, C. S. 1982. *Strategic Studies and Public Policy.* Lexington, Ky: University of Kentucky Press.

Harsanyi, J. C. 1977. *Rational Behavior and Bargaining Equilibrium in Games and Social Situations.* Cambridge: Cambridge University Press.

Henthoff, N. 1967. "Introduction." In *The Essays of A. J. Muste,* ed. N. Henthoff. Indianapolis: Bobbs-Merrill.

Hitch, C. J., and McKean, R. N. 1965. "The Criterion Problem." In *American National Security,* ed. M. Berkowitz and P. G. Bock. New York: Free Press.

Hobshawn, E. J. 1969. *Industry and Empire.* Harmondsworth: Penguin Books.

Hovet, T. 1986. *A Chronology and Fact Book of the United Nations* 1941–1985. Dobbs Ferry, N. Y.: Oceana Publications.

Huxley, A. [1932] 1964. *Brave New World.* Harmondsworth: Penguin Books.

Isaacs, R. 1975. "The Past and a Bit of the Future." In *The Theory and Applications of Differential Games,* ed. J. D. Grote. Dordrecht: Reidel.

Kahn, H. 1960. *On Thermonuclear War.* Princeton: Princeton University Press.

Kant, I. [1795] 1903. *Perpetual Peace: A Philosophical Essay.* London: Swan Sonnenschein.

Kennedy, R. 1968. *Thirteen Days.* New York: Norton.

Kissinger, H. A. 1957. *Nuclear Weapons and Foreign Policy.* New York: Harper and Row.

Kissinger, H. A. 1973. *A World Restored.* Gloucester, Mass.: Peter Smith.

Korzybski, A. 1921. *Manhood of Humanity.* New York: E. P. Dutton.

Korzybski, A. 1933. *Science and Sanity.* Lancaster, Pa.: Science Press.

Lamarck, J. B. [1809] 1963. *Zoological Philosophy: An Exposition with Regard to the Natural History of Animals.* New York: Hafner Publishing.

Leibniz, G. W. 1968. *Opera Omnia.* Geneva: L. Dutton.

Lenin, V. I. [1909] 1964. *Materialism and Empiriocriticism.* Moscow: Progress Publishers.

Levy-Brühl, H. [1931] 1960. "Theorie de l'esclavage." In *Slavery in Classical Antiquity: Views and Controversies,* ed. M. I. Findley. Cambridge, Mass.: Heffer.

Lorenz, K. 1966. *On Aggression.* New York: Harcourt, Brace and World.

Maimonides, M. 1919. *The Guide for the Perplexed.* London: Routledge.

Malthus, T. R. [1798] 1966. *An Essay on the Principle of Population.* New York: St. Martin's Press.

Maoz, Z., and Abdolali, N. 1989. "Regime Types and International Conflict, 1816–1976." *Journal of Conflict Resolution* 33:1–35.

Maynard Smith, J., and Price, C. R. 1973. "The Logic of Animal Conflict." *Nature* 246 (November 2): 15–18.

Meggitt, M. 1977. *Blood Is Their Argument: Warfare among the Mae Enge.* Palo Alto, Calif.: Mayfield Publishing.

Morgenthau, H. 1963. *Politics among Nations.* New York: Knopf.

Muste, A. J. [1936] 1967. *The Essays of A. J. Muste,* ed. N. Henthoff. Indianapolis: Bobbs-Merrill.

Mueller, J. 1989. *Retreat from Doomsday.* New York: Basic Books.

O'Neill, B. 1989. "Game Theory and the Study of the Deterrence of War." In *Perspectives on Deterrence,* ed. P. Stern, R. Axelrod, R. Jervis, and R. Radner. New York: Oxford University Press.

Orwell, G. 1949. *Nineteen Eighty-Four.* London: Secker and Warburg.

Piaget, J. 1928. *Judgment and Reasoning in the Child.* London: Routledge and Kegan Paul.

Popper, K. 1982. *The Open Universe.* Totowa, N. J.: Rowan and Littlefield.

Popper, K. R., and Eccles, J. C. 1977. *The Self and Its Brain.* New York: Springer International.

Rapoport, A. 1989. *The Origins of Violence.* New York: Paragon House.

Richardson, L. F. 1948. "War Moods." *Psychometrika* 13:147–74, 197–232.

Richardson, L. F. 1960. *Arms and Insecurity.* Chicago: Quadrangle Books.

Riechert, S. E. 1978. "Games Spiders Play: Behavioral Variability in Territorial Disputes." *Behavioral Ecology and Sociobiology* 3:135–63.

Rousseau, J. J. [1761] 1955. *A Lasting Peace through the Federation of Europe and the State of War.* New Haven: Whitlock's.

Rushton, J. P. 1988. "Race Differences in Behavior: A Review and Evolutionary Analysis." *Personality and Individual Differences* 9:1009–24.

Schelling, T. C. 1960. *The Strategy of Conflict.* Cambridge, Mass.: Harvard University Press.

Schuman, F. L. 1939. *Europe on the Eve: The Crises of Diplomacy* 1933–1939. New York: Knopf.

Schwartz, K. 1878. *Das Leben des Generals Carl von Clausewitz und der Frau Maria von Clausewitz.* Berlin: Dümmlers Verlag.

Sherif, M., Harvey, O. J., White, B. J., Hood, W. R., and Sherif, C. W. 1961. *Intergroup Conflict and Cooperation: The Robber's Cave Experiment.* Norman, Okla.: University of Oklahoma Press.

Simpson, G. G. 1950. *The Meaning of Evolution.* New Haven: Yale University Press.

Smith, A. [1776] 1910. *The Wealth of Nations.* New York: E. P. Dutton.

Smith, M. C. 1903. Translator's Introduction to *Perpetual Peace: A Philosophical Essay,* by I. Kant. London: Swan Sonnenschein.

Stouffer, S. A. et al. 1949. *The American Soldier.* Princeton: Princeton University Press.

Sumner, W. G. [1883] 1952. *What Social Classes Owe to Each Other.* Caldwell, Ohio: Caxton.

Tait, C. W. 1965. "What Happened to the State Department?" *Nation,* September 13, 138.

Thompson, J. E. 1990. "State Practices, International Norms, and the Decline of Mercenarism." *International Studies Quarterly* 34:29–47.

Thoreau, H. D. [1863] 1937. *The Writings of Thoreau*, ed. H. S. Canby. Boston: Houghton Mifflin.

Tolstoy, L. 1968. "Letter to the Peace Conference." In *Tolstoy's Writings on Civil Disobedience*. New York: New American Library.

Tolstoy, L. [1867–69] 1973. *War and Peace*. London: William Heinemann.

Treischke, H. von [1897–98] 1916. *Politics*. New York: Macmillan.

Tuchman, B. W. 1978. *A Distant Mirror*. New York: Ballantine Books.

Vagts, A. 1937. *A History of Militarism*. New York: Norton.

Voltaire. [1771] 1935. *Dictionnaire Philosophique*. Paris: Libraire Garnier Freres.

Wicksteed, P. H. 1933. *The Common Sense of Political Economy*. London: Routledge.

Wilson, D. S. 1989. "Levels of Selection: An Alternative to Individualism in Biology and the Human Sciences." *Social Networks* 11:257–72.

Wilson, E. O. 1975. *Sociobiology: The New Synthesis*. Cambridge, Mass.: Belknap Press.

Wohlstetter, A. 1974. "Is There a Strategic Arms Race?" *Foreign Policy* 15:3–20; 16:48–81.

Wright, Q. [1942] 1965. *A Study of War*. Chicago: University of Chicago Press.

Name Index

Subject Index